Make History with this fantastic CGP book...

OK, so the new Edexcel GCSE History exams are pretty tricky... but with this brilliant CGP Revision Guide, you'll be ready to go into battle!

It's packed with everything you need to get your head around the subject, including crystal-clear notes, maps, diagrams and photos for each topic.

We've also included exam-style practice questions throughout the book, plus plenty of advice on how to pick up top marks. After all that, you'll be like an heir to the throne — destined to succeed.

CGP — still the best! ☺

Our sole aim here at CGP is to produce the highest quality books — carefully written, immaculately presented and dangerously close to being funny.

Then we work our socks off to get them out to you — at the cheapest possible prices.

Contents

How History Works

Exam Skills for the Thematic Study

Medicine in Britain, c.1250-present

The British Sector of the Western Front, 1914-1918

Exam Skills for the Historical Environment

Exam Skills for the Period Study

The American West, c.1835-c.1895

Superpower Relations and the Cold War, 1941-1991

The Origins of the Cold War, 1941-58

Cold War Crises, 1958-70

The End of the Cold War, 1970-91

Exam Skills for the Depth Studies

Early Elizabethan England, 1558-88

Queen, Government and Religion, 1558-1569

Challenges at Home and Abroad, 1569-1588

Elizabethan Society in the Age of Exploration, 1558-88

Weimar and Nazi Germany, 1918-39

The Weimar Republic, 1918-29

Hitler's Rise to Power, 1919-33

Nazi Control and Dictatorship, 1933-39

Life in Nazi Germany, 1933-39

Published by CGP

Editors:
Chloe Anderson, Emma Bonney, Izzy Bowen, Emma Cleasby, Alex Fairer,
Catherine Heygate, Andy Park, Jack Perry, Rebecca Tate and Louise Taylor.

Contributors:
Peter Callaghan, Rene Cochlin, Rachel Ellis-Lomas, John Etty, Paddy Gannon, Robert Gibson and John Pritchard.

With thanks to John Broadbent, Dan Heaney, Catherine Heygate, Anthony Muller
and Rebecca Tate for the proofreading.
With thanks to Ana Pungartnik and Holly Poynton for the copyright research.

Acknowledgements:
With thanks to The Art Archive / Palazzo Barberini Rome / Collection Dagli Orti for permission to use the image on page 1.
With thanks to iStock.com for permission to use the images on page 5, 16, 19 and 110.
With thanks to Photo Researchers / Mary Evans Picture Library for permission to use the images on pages 6, 25 and 64.
With thanks to Mary Evans Picture Library for permission to use the images on pages 9, 15, 17, 21, 26, 96, 98, 115 and 128.
With thanks to INTERFOTO / Bildarchiv Hansmann / Mary E for permission to use the image on page 11.
With thanks to Mary Evans / Everett Collection for permission to use the images on pages 13, 62, 68 and 127.
With thanks to Illustrated London News Ltd/Mary Evans for permission to use the images on pages 29 and 113.
Trench diagram on page 34. Contains public sector information licensed under the Open Government Licence v3.0
Extract from D.M. Ormond's War Diary on page 37. From 'War Diary of the 10th Canadian Battalion', April 1915, ref. WO 95/3770, National Archives, Kew, Surrey, England.
Trench map of Hill 60 in April 1917 on page 34. Reproduced by permission of the National Library of Scotland.
Extract from Sir Anthony Bowlby's 1916 lecture on page 37. Bowlby A. 'The Bradshaw Lecture on Wounds in War' British Medical Journal. 1915; 2(2869): 913-921.
Extract on page 41, Source: http://chestofbooks.com/
With thanks to Mary Evans/Interfoto for permission to use the image on page 46.
With thanks to Mary Evans/Classic Stock/C.P. Cushing for permission to use the image on page 51.
With thanks to The Art Archive / Granger Collection for permission to use the images on pages 52, 53, 57, 58 and 60.
With thanks to Mary Evans Picture Library/Imagno for permission to use the images on pages 74 and 81.
With thanks to Mary Evans / Iberfoto for permission to use the images on pages 78 and 91.
With thanks to Mary Evans / Seuddeutsche Zeitung Photo for permission to use the images on pages 83, 126 and 128.
First extract from history textbook on page 88. Layton, G. (2000). Access to History: Germany the Third Reich 1933-1945 2ED. London: Hodder Education. © Geoff Layton 2005. Reproduced by permission of Hodder Education.
Second extract from history textbook on page 88. © Ian Kershaw, 2015, The Nazi Dictatorship, Bloomsbury Academic, an imprint of Bloomsbury Publishing Plc.
With thanks to Mary Evans Picture Library/WEIMAR ARCHIVE for permission to use the image on page 88.
Coat of arms image on page 94. This image is licensed under the Creative Commons Attribution-Share Alike 3.0 Unported, 2.5 Generic, 2.0 Generic and 1.0 Generic license - http://creativecommons.org/licenses/by-sa/3.0/
With thanks to Mary Evans / INTERFOTO / Bildarchiv Hansmann for permission to use the photo on page 100.
With thanks to Antiquarian Images/Mary Evans for permission to use the image on page 103.
With thanks to Mary Evans Picture Library/DOUGLAS MCCARTHY for permission to use the image on page 106
With thanks to Mary Evans / SZ Photo / Scherl for permission to use the image on page 131.
Extract on page 132. From School for Barbarians: Education Under the Nazis (Dover Books on History, Political and Social Science). Dover Publications Inc.; Reprint edition (28 Mar. 2014)

ISBN: 978 1 78294 605 2
Printed by Elanders Ltd, Newcastle upon Tyne.
Clipart from Corel®

Based on the classic CGP style created by Richard Parsons.

Sources: the Building Blocks of History

Historians have such an easy life. They read old documents and rewrite them... right? Actually, they do a bit more than that. For GCSE History, you have to become a historian, so you'd best be sure what they really do.

Historians use Sources to Find Out about the Past

1) Sources are things that historians use to find out about and make sense of the past.
2) They can be written (e.g. newspapers, government reports) or visual (e.g. photographs, maps, films).
3) Sources can be categorised as either primary or secondary:

Primary sources — evidence from the period you're studying

For example, a newspaper report on the First World War from 4th September 1914, or a picture of Henry VIII that was painted during his reign.

Secondary sources — evidence about (but not from) the period you're studying

For example, a 1989 book called 'Origins of the First World War', or a website providing information about all the portraits ever painted of Henry VIII.

Historians have to Interrogate and Interpret every source

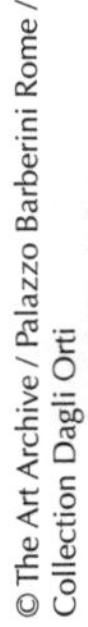

King Henry VIII, 1540

1) Historians have to be very careful with sources. To make sure they're using sources accurately, historians interrogate every source they use. This means they ask themselves a series of questions about the source's background.

- **What** is this source?
  E.g. It is a painting of King Henry VIII.
- **Who** made this source?
  E.g. It was produced by the King's official painter, Hans Holbein.
- **Why** did they make the source?
  E.g. He was asked to paint it by the King.
- **Where** and **when** was it made?
  E.g. It was made in the Palace of Whitehall in 1540.

2) Historians use their answers to work out how useful and how reliable a source is. For example:
   - This is a professional painting made during Henry's reign (meaning the painter could have met Henry). So this should be a useful source for finding out what Henry looked like.
   - BUT perhaps the painter would have been punished if he didn't show Henry looking good, so it may not be entirely reliable.

A source that presents a one-sided view is biased.

3) After they've interrogated a source, historians need to interpret it.

This means deciding what it tells them about the topic they're studying.

4) For example, Henry was probably quite a large man with fair hair and a beard. But the painter may have been told to make the picture to Henry's liking — so based on just this picture, you can't really say for sure how big he really was.

Henry was the king — people would have done what he told them to.

5) Historians look at lots of sources, and compare them against each other. If sources contradict one another, they'll try to work out why, and what this tells them about the past.

For example, another painting might show Henry as very unattractive. But a historian might interpret it differently, depending on whether Henry had seen and approved of the painting, or whether it had been made by one of Henry's enemies and was perhaps biased against him.

And if you're really good at history — they'll let you on the telly...

When you're studying GCSE History, you need to interrogate and interpret every source you see. Don't always assume what you see or read is an exact description of life way back when.

Building a Picture of the Past

Historians can use the information in various sources to get a better understanding of a particular period. This involves linking events together, and working out why things happened the way they did.

Historians study Change and Continuity

1) One way to get an idea of what happened in the past is to look at changes and continuities over time.
2) Change is when something happens to make things different.
   - Changes can be quick — e.g. a law making secondary education free.
   - Or they can be slow — e.g. a gradual change in a society's literacy levels.
3) Continuity is the opposite of change — it's when things stay the same — e.g. people believed for hundreds of years that disease was God's punishment for sin.
4) These ideas are opposites — think of continuity as a flat line going along until there is a sudden change and the line becomes a zigzag:

The most important changes in history are called turning points. After a turning point, life might never be the same again.

5) Change and continuity can happen at the same time in different parts of society.
   - For example, when the Normans conquered England in 1066, many of the richest people in English society lost their jobs and status (= change).
   - But life didn't actually change very much for peasant farmers (= continuity).
6) There are all sorts of things that a historian might look at for change or continuity. Some things might be obvious (e.g. a new king or queen would be an obvious change). But historians are also very interested in whether more everyday aspects of society are showing change or continuity — e.g. attitudes, lifestyles, beliefs, fashions, diets... the list is endless.

Historians think about Causes and Consequences

1) Cause means the reason something happened — e.g. the causes of the First World War.
2) Consequence means what happened because of an action — it's the result of an event, e.g. a consequence of the First World War was that a lot of young men were killed.
3) Causes and consequences can be either short-term or long-term.

Any time you have an event in history, think about what caused it and the effect it had — it's a really good way to show the examiner how different historical events are linked to each other.

Short-term cause: protest march on Washington

Long-term cause: growing resistance to discrimination against African Americans

EVENT: The introduction of new civil rights laws in America

Short-term consequence: an increase in the number of black voters

Long-term consequence: some people start to challenge discrimination against other groups (e.g. women).

4) Historians also think about how different causes and consequences interact. For example, there might be a chain of causes that lead to an event, or one consequence of an event might be more important than all the rest.

You can think of these as the Four Cs of history...

As you use this book, make sure you think about 'the Four Cs' on each page. When you identify causes, consequences, changes and continuities, add them to your revision notes and learn them.

Exam Skills for the Thematic Study

These two pages are all about how to tackle the thematic study section of your exam.

The Thematic Study covers a Long Period of time

For more general advice on how to answer exam questions, see p.135.

1) The thematic study covers up to 1000 years of history, right up to the present day. It's divided into four different time periods — but you'll need to think about the topic as a whole for the exam and make links between certain aspects of the different periods.
2) The study focuses on what changed (and what didn't change) over time and why.
3) You'll be expected to know the main factors of society in different periods — things like religion, government, science, technology and people's attitudes. You also need to know how these features affected the area of your thematic study — e.g. how improvements in science helped prevent disease.
4) Here are some things to bear in mind when you're revising for the thematic study part of your exam:

- What created a need for change, or enabled it to happen? Did anything hinder change?
- Important turning points — what were the most significant developments?
- The extent of change — how much progress was made? What remained unchanged?
- The impact of change — did some changes spark further developments?

There are Three basic types of exam question

1) You'll need to compare two different time periods. You'll be asked about a similarity or difference between these two periods, and will need to explain your answer.

   Explain one way that beliefs about the spread of disease in the fourteenth century were similar to those in the seventeenth century. [4 marks]

2) The next question will ask you to explain something about a change — e.g. why something changed over a certain time, or why changes were slow / quick to happen. Make sure you analyse each point fully, including plenty of detail.

   Explain why access to healthcare improved rapidly in the nineteenth century. [12 marks]

3) The final task will cover at least 200 years of history. You'll get a choice of two questions — answer the one you're most comfortable with. Each one will give a statement and you'll be asked how far you agree with it.

   'The discovery of anaesthetics was an important development in surgery between c.1700 and c.1900.' Explain how far you agree. [16 marks]

   - Decide your opinion before you start writing, and state it clearly at the beginning and end of your answer.
   - Include evidence for both sides of the debate, and explain which factors are more important — these more important factors should be the ones backing up the opinion you've given.

There are also 4 marks available for spelling, punctuation and grammar in this question (see p.136-137), so it's worth 20 marks in total.

In question types 2) and 3), you'll be given some 'stimulus points' — hints about things you could include in your answer. You don't have to include details about these stimulus points, so don't panic if you can't remember much about them. Even if you do write about the stimulus points, you must add other information too — if you don't, you can't get full marks.

Remember these things for All the questions

1) Always back up your points with specific evidence — this means that having a good knowledge of the facts is important. The evidence you use should be relevant to the question, and you should explain how it illustrates your point.
2) Your answer should be well organised and structured — each of your points should lead clearly to your conclusion.

Make sure you get your dates right — remember that the seventeenth century refers to the 1600s, the eighteenth century refers to the 1700s, and so on.

Exam Skills for the Thematic Study

Here are some sample answers to questions in the thematic study section of the exam.

Have a look at this Sample Answer

This sample answer will give you an idea of how to compare two historical periods. It's worth spending time thinking about how the answer has been structured — the comments will help you with this.

Explain one way that beliefs about the spread of disease in the fourteenth century were similar to those in the seventeenth century. [4 marks]

One thing that was similar about people's beliefs about the spread of disease in both centuries was their belief in the 'miasma' theory. People believed that diseases were caught by breathing in 'bad air'. They thought that diseases came from things that weren't hygienic and had a bad smell, like abattoirs or dead bodies, and that the air transferred the disease. When the Great Plague hit London in 1665, people tried to stop it spreading by carrying around herbs and flowers to 'purify' the air around them.

The first sentence directly addresses the question.

This gives more specific information.

This is an important feature of both periods.

The answer shows a good level of knowledge by giving an example of how people's actions were influenced by their beliefs.

Here's another Sample Answer to help you

This sample answer will give you an idea of how to respond to the 'how far do you agree' question. Look at the points that have been made and how they have been supported with evidence.

'The discovery of anaesthetics was an important development in surgery between c.1700 and c.1900.' Explain how far you agree. [16 marks]

I agree that the discovery of anaesthetics was an important development. Before anaesthetics were discovered, many patients died from the trauma of pain in surgery. Anaesthetics such as chloroform, whose effects were discovered by James Simpson in 1847, improved surgery by removing pain. They also allowed surgeons to carry out longer and more complicated procedures.

However, the importance of anaesthetics was limited at first because they also caused a rise in death rates in the short term. The period between 1846 and 1870 is known as the 'Black Period' of surgery, because surgeons used anaesthetics to perform more complicated operations, which caused greater bleeding and infection. While anaesthetics saved some lives, they also caused more deaths because of the way they were used by surgeons, meaning their impact was limited at first.

Overall, I agree that the discovery of anaesthetics was an important development in surgery because they meant patients were in a lot less pain and made it easier for surgeons to operate. Although they contributed to more deaths in the short term, anaesthetics (combined with the use of antiseptics) had greatly improved surgery by 1900.

This gives a basic answer to the question straight away.

It's important to give counter-arguments to show you've considered all the evidence.

It's good to end by clearly stating your overall opinion in the conclusion.

This explains how things used to be, to show that the development of anaesthetics was significant.

The answer gives examples of how anaesthetics improved surgery.

This is a shortened example — in the exam, you'll need to make several more points for both sides of the argument.

As painful as exams might be, anaesthetics won't help you...

Thematic studies are a long old haul, but don't worry — you'll probably know the last bits already because they'll have happened in your lifetime. That's sixteen-ish years in the bag. Just 984 years to go, then...

Timeline of Important Dates

Here's a timeline showing the order of key events in the history of British medicine since around 1250.

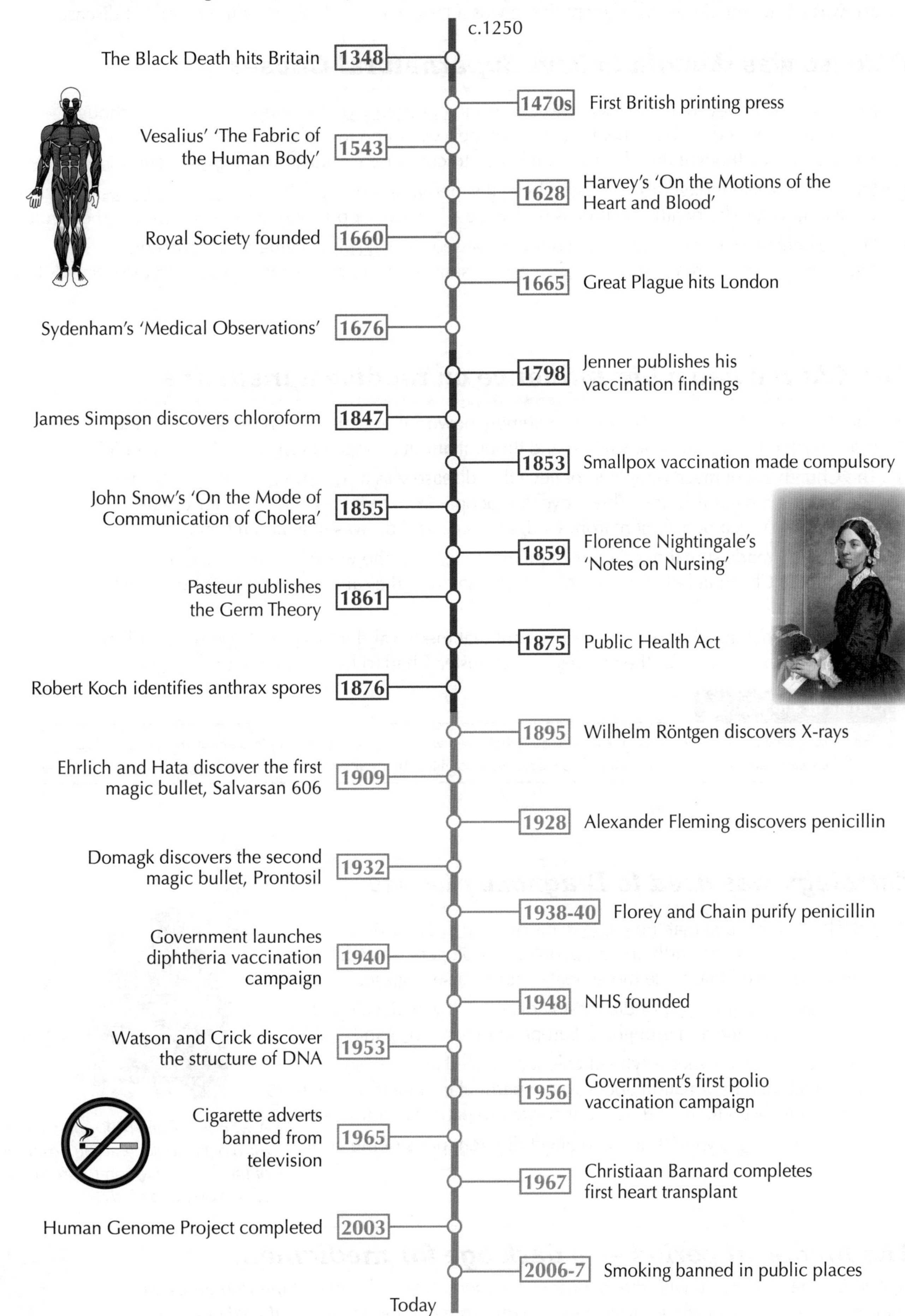

Disease and the Supernatural

In medieval England (and for the purposes of this section we're talking roughly 1250 to 1500), treatment of disease was a bit... medieval. The key problem was a lack of understanding of the causes of disease.

Disease was thought to have Supernatural Causes

1) Many people believed that disease was a punishment from God for people's sins. They thought that disease existed to show them the error of their ways and to make them become better people. Therefore, they thought that this meant the way to cure disease was through prayer and repentance.
2) Disease was also thought to be caused by evil supernatural beings, like demons or witches. Witches were believed to be behind outbreaks of disease — many people were tried as witches and executed.
3) People believed that some diseases could be caused by evil spirits living inside someone. Members of the Church performed exorcisms, using chants to remove the spirit from the person's body.

The Church had a big Influence on medieval medicine

1) The Roman Catholic Church was an extremely powerful organisation in medieval Europe. It dominated the way people studied and thought about a range of topics, including medicine.
2) The Church encouraged people to believe that disease was a punishment from God, rather than having a natural cause. This prevented people from trying to find cures for disease — if disease was a punishment from God, all you could do was pray and repent.
3) The Church made sure that scholars of medicine learned the works of Galen (see p.7) as his ideas fit the Christian belief that God created human bodies and made them to be perfect. Because Galen's work was so central to medical teaching, it was difficult to disagree with him.
4) The Church outlawed dissection. This meant that medieval doctors couldn't discover ideas about human anatomy for themselves — they instead had to learn Galen's incorrect ideas.

Comment and Analysis

The Church's influence over medieval medicine meant that there was very little change in ideas about the cause of disease until the Renaissance — the Church and its messages were so influential that people were unable to question them.

Astrology was used to Diagnose disease

1) Astrology is the idea that the movements of the planets and stars have an effect on the Earth and on people. Astrologers in medieval England believed that these movements could cause disease.
2) Astrology was a new way of diagnosing disease. It was developed in Arabic medicine and brought to Europe between 1100 and 1300.
3) Medieval doctors owned a type of calendar (called an almanac) which included information about where particular planets and stars were at any given time, and how this related to patients' illnesses.
4) Different star signs were thought to affect different parts of the body.

A woodcut from 1490 showing two astrologers looking at the positions of the Sun and Moon to predict the effects on people's lives.

The medieval period — a dark age for medicine...

Explain how far you agree with the following statement: 'The influence of the Roman Catholic Church was the main reason for the lack of change in medicine in medieval England.' [16]

Rational Explanations

Some treatments in medieval England were based less on religious faith and more on rational theories and observation of the physical world. But a reason-based theory can still be wrong.

Medicine was dominated by the Four Humours Theory

Many medieval doctors based their diagnosis and treatments on the Theory of the Four Humours.

1) The Theory of the Four Humours was created by the Ancient Greek doctor Hippocrates (c.460-c.377 BC). Hippocrates believed that the body was made up of four fluids (or humours) — blood, phlegm, yellow bile and black bile. These were linked to the four seasons and the four elements. They needed to be in balance for good health.

E.g. in winter we get colds. So Hippocrates thought that in winter the body created an excess of phlegm. Sadly, Hippocrates failed to see that a bunged-up nose, fevers and suchlike are symptoms of the disease — he thought they were the cause.

2) The Theory of the Four Humours was developed further by another Greek doctor, Galen, who was born in AD 129 and worked for much of his career in Rome.
3) Galen believed that diseases could be treated using opposites. He thought that different foods, drinks, herbs and spices had a humour, which could balance the excessive humour that was causing the disease.

E.g. someone with a cold (too much cold, wet phlegm) could be given chicken, pepper or wine (all considered hot and dry) to correct the imbalance.

The Miasma Theory blamed Bad Air for causing disease

1) The miasma theory is the idea that bad air (or miasma) causes disease when someone breathes it in. This bad air may come from human refuse, abattoirs or dead bodies — anything that creates a bad smell.
2) The miasma theory originated in Ancient Greece and Rome, and was incorporated by Galen into the Theory of the Four Humours. The idea became extremely popular in medieval England.
3) The miasma theory was so influential that it lasted until the 1860s, when it was replaced by the Germ Theory (see p.18). Miasma often prompted people to do hygienic things, like cleaning the streets, which sometimes helped to stop the spread of disease (but for the wrong reasons).

Comment and Analysis

The Four Humours and miasma were both incorrect theories. But they were rational — they assumed disease had a natural cause, rather than a supernatural one. This was important, as it suggested that people weren't powerless against disease — they could investigate and take action against it.

Hippocrates and Galen were very Influential

The work of Hippocrates and Galen was extremely influential in medical diagnosis and treatment (see p.8).

1) Hippocrates and Galen wrote down their beliefs about medicine. These were translated into Latin books, which were considered important texts by the Roman Catholic Church. Like the Bible, Hippocrates' and Galen's ideas were considered the absolute truth.
2) Many of their ideas were taught for centuries after their deaths, including the incorrect ones. E.g. Galen only ever dissected animals — animal and human bodies are very different, so some of his ideas about anatomy were wrong. Medieval doctors were not allowed to perform their own dissections, so they continued to learn Galen's incorrect ideas.
3) Some of Hippocrates' and Galen's ideas were so influential that they continue to be used today. The Hippocratic Oath is the promise made by doctors to obey rules of behaviour in their professional lives — a version of it is still in use today. Hippocrates and Galen also believed that doctors should observe their patients as they treat them.

The Four Humours — it's totally hilarious...

Split your page in two. On one side, list all of the supernatural causes of disease believed by people in medieval England. On the other side, do the same for the rational causes.

Treating Disease

As the Middle Ages went on, medical treatments continued to be based on ideas we'd nowadays consider very unscientific. Treatments were ambitious though, and theories quite sophisticated in their own ways.

Prayer and Repentance were major treatments

1) Disease was believed to be a punishment from God, so sick people were encouraged to pray. The sick often prayed to saints, in the hope they would intervene and stop the illness. Medieval people also believed that pilgrimages to holy shrines (e.g. sites containing the remains of saints) could cure illnesses.
2) Others took their repentance one step further. Flagellants were people who whipped themselves in public in order to show God that they were sorry for their past actions. They were particularly common at times of epidemics, such as the Black Death (see p.10).
3) Many doctors had superstitious beliefs — e.g. some doctors used astrology to diagnose and treat illness (see p.6). Others believed that saying certain words when administering treatment could make that treatment more effective.

Bloodletting and Purging aimed to make the Humours balanced

1) Bloodletting and purging were popular treatments because they fitted in with the Four Humours Theory.
2) If someone apparently had too much blood inside them, the doctor would take some blood out of their body through bloodletting — they might make a small cut to remove the blood or use blood-sucking leeches.
3) Some people were accidentally killed because too much blood was taken.
4) Purging is the act of getting rid of other fluids from the body by excreting — doctors gave their patients laxatives to help the purging process.

Comment and Analysis

Bloodletting caused more deaths than it prevented, but it remained a popular treatment. This shows the strength of medieval people's beliefs in the face of observational evidence.

Purifying the Air was thought to Prevent Disease

1) The miasma theory (see p.7) led people to believe in the power of purifying or cleaning the air to prevent sickness and improve health.
2) Physicians carried posies or oranges around with them when visiting patients to protect themselves from catching a disease.
3) During the Black Death (see p.10) juniper, myrrh and incense were burned so that the smoke and scent would fill the room and prevent bad air from bringing disease inside.

Purifying the air was also seen as important for helping with other health conditions. In the case of fainting, people burned feathers and made the patient breathe in their smoke.

Remedies were Early Natural Medicines

1) Remedies bought from an apothecary, local wise woman or made at home were all popular in medieval England and contained herbs, spices, animal parts and minerals.
2) These remedies were either passed down or written in books explaining how to mix them together. Some of these books were called 'Herbals'.
3) Other remedies were based on superstition, like lucky charms containing 'powdered unicorn's horn'.

Get the terminology right — no funny spellings...

Some of your marks in the exam are for using specialist terminology. Make sure you know how to spell any tricky words or names (like miasma), so you can happily use them in your answer.

Treating Disease

If you were ill in the Middle Ages, you couldn't just go to your local GP. But as there were various kinds of medical healers, there could still be an element of 'patient choice'...

Physicians had little Practical Experience

1) Physicians were male doctors who had trained at university for at least seven years. They read ancient texts as well as writings from the Islamic world, but their training involved little practical experience.
2) Physicians used handbooks (vademecums) and clinical observation to check patients' conditions.
3) In 1300, there were less than 100 physicians in England. Seeing a physician was very expensive — only the rich could afford it.

Most sick people went to see an Apothecary

This medieval print shows a doctor and an apothecary. The plants in the middle show the importance of herbal remedies.

1) Apothecaries prepared and sold remedies (see p.8) — and sometimes gave advice on how best to use them.
2) Apothecaries were trained through apprenticeships. Most apothecaries were men, but there were also many so-called 'wise women', who sold herbal remedies.
3) Apothecaries were the most common form of treatment in medieval England as they were the most accessible for those who could not afford a physician.

Quacks were people without any medical knowledge who sold medical treatments. They'd sell their wares at fairs and markets, and they often did more harm than good.

Surgery — work for Barbers, not doctors

1) Medieval surgery was very dangerous — there was no way to prevent blood loss, infection or pain. It was therefore only attempted rarely and for very minor procedures, e.g. treating hernias, pulling teeth or treating cataracts.
2) Although there were a few university-trained, highly paid surgeons, surgery as a whole was not a respected profession in medieval times — most operations were carried out by barber-surgeons (who also cut hair).

Comment and Analysis

Barber-surgeons weren't doctors, so they had little medical training or insight. This meant they had neither the ability nor the desire to experiment with new treatments.

There were Few Public Hospitals

1) There were relatively few hospitals in medieval Britain, so most sick people were treated at home by members of their family, mainly the women of the house.
2) Most hospitals were set up and run by monasteries. They were very popular and highly regarded.
3) The main purpose of hospitals was not to treat disease, but to care for the sick and elderly. They hospital provided its patients with food, water and a warm place to stay.
4) Hospitals also provided some basic medical treatments — Monks also had access to books on healing and they knew how to grow herbs and make herbal remedies.

Monastic hospitals were good for patients' health because they were more hygienic than elsewhere. Monasteries separated clean and dirty water. They had one water supply for cooking and drinking and one for drainage and washing, so people didn't have to drink dirty water. They also had good systems for getting rid of sewage.

Medieval medical treatment was varied and diverse...

Write out a list of all the different types of healers and treatments in medieval times. Then note down the pros and cons of each option for a person needing medical attention.

Case Study: The Black Death

The Black Death struck in the 14th century in Europe, and had a devastating effect. People tried to explain why it had happened, but there was little that could be done to stop the disease.

The Black Death was a devastating Epidemic

1) The Black Death was a series of plagues that first swept Europe in the mid 14th century. Two illnesses were involved:

   - Bubonic plague, spread by the bites of fleas from rats carried on ships. This caused headaches and a high temperature, followed by pus-filled swellings on the skin.
   - Pneumonic plague, which was airborne — it was spread by coughs and sneezes. It attacked the lungs, making it painful to breathe and causing victims to cough up blood.

2) The disease first arrived in Britain in 1348. Some historians think at least a third of the British population died as a result of the Black Death in 1348-50.

People Didn't Know what Caused the Black Death

No-one at the time knew what had caused the plague.

1) Some people believed that the Black Death was a judgement from God. They thought the cause of the disease was sin, so they tried to prevent the spread of the disease through prayer and fasting.
2) Some blamed humour imbalances, so tried to get rid of the Black Death through bloodletting and purging.
3) Those who thought that the disease was caused by miasma (see p.7) carried strong smelling herbs or lit fires to purify the air. In 1349, Edward III sent an order to the Lord Mayor of London to remove filth from the city streets, in the hope of removing bad smells.
4) Believers in astrology carried diamonds and rubies, which they believed could protect against the Black Death. People also carried charms or used 'magic' potions containing arsenic.

Comment and Analysis

The high death toll of the Black Death was in large part because people didn't know what caused the disease. People tried to use existing ideas about the cause of disease to come up with ways to prevent or cure the plague. But because their ideas about the cause of disease were wrong, their attempts at prevention and treatment were mostly ineffective.

Local Governments tried to Prevent the spread of the disease

1) Some people in Winchester thought that you could catch the plague from being close to the bodies of dead victims. When the town's cemetery became too full to take any more plague victims, the townspeople refused to let the bishop extend the cemetery in the town centre. Instead, they insisted that new cemeteries be built outside of the town, away from the houses.
2) The town of Gloucester tried to shut itself off from the outside world after hearing the Black Death had reached Bristol. This suggests that they thought the plague was spread by human contact. Their attempt at prevention was unsuccessful — many people in the town died of the Black Death.
3) By November 1348, the Black Death had reached London. In January 1349, King Edward III took the decision to close Parliament.

'Deadly pestilence had suddenly broken out in the said place and neighbourhood, and had daily increased in severity, so that grave fears were entertained for the safety of those coming here at the time.'
King Edward III on his decision to close Parliament.

Think about how far things changed or stayed the same...

'There was little progress in medicine in Britain during the medieval period.' Explain how far you agree with this statement. [16]

The Renaissance

The Renaissance was a time of new ideas and fresh thinking. People began to challenge old beliefs, and there were many new developments in doctors' knowledge and skills.

The Renaissance was a time of Continuity and Change

1) In the Renaissance there was a rediscovery of knowledge from classical Greek and Roman times. Western doctors gained access to the original writings of Hippocrates, Galen and Avicenna (a Persian physician who lived between 980 and 1037 AD). These hadn't been available in the medieval period. They led to greater interest in the Four Humours Theory and treatment by opposites (see p.7).
2) But the Renaissance also saw the emergence of science as we know it from the magic and mysticism of medieval medicine. People thought about how the human body worked based on direct observation and experimentation.
3) This was partly because many of the new books that had been found said that anatomy and dissections were very important. This encouraged people to examine the body themselves, and to come to their own conclusions about the causes of disease.
4) People began to question Galen's thinking and that of other ancient doctors. However, his writings continued to be studied.

Protestant Christianity spread across Europe during the Reformation, reducing the influence of the Catholic Church. Although religion was still important, the Church no longer had so much control over medical teaching.

This woodcut shows physicians debating over a medicine book.

The Medical Knowledge of doctors Improved

1) Many doctors in the Renaissance trained at the College of Physicians, which had been set up in 1518. Here they read books by Galen, but also studied recent medical developments. Dissections — showing how the body actually worked — also became a key part of medical training.
2) The College of Physicians encouraged the licensing of doctors to stop the influence of quacks, who sold fake medicines (see p.9). Some of the college's physicians (such as Harvey — see p.13) made important discoveries about disease and the human body.
3) New weapons like cannons and guns were being used in war. This meant that doctors and surgeons had to treat injuries they hadn't seen before, forcing them to quickly find new treatments.
4) Explorations abroad brought new ingredients for drugs back to Britain, including guaiacum — believed to cure syphilis — and quinine, a drug for malaria from the bark of the Cinchona tree.

There were some technological developments too. Peter Chamberlen invented the forceps (probably at some point in the 1600s), which are still used today to help with childbirth.

5) In the 1530s, Henry VIII closed down most of Britain's monasteries (this was called the 'dissolution of the monasteries'). Since most hospitals had been set up and run by monasteries (see p.9), this also led to the closure of a large number of hospitals. The sudden loss of so many hospitals was bad for people's health.
6) The monastic hospitals were gradually replaced by some free hospitals, which were paid for by charitable donations. Unlike the monastic hospitals, which had been run by monks, these new hospitals were run by trained physicians, who focused more on getting better from illness.

Use relevant facts to support your answer...

It really helps to add some important facts — a useful date, for example. But make sure it's relevant to what you're trying to say — the details should be used to support your argument.

Vesalius and Sydenham

Vesalius and Sydenham believed that direct observation was the best way to learn about the body. They encouraged people to gain practical experience, and to use dissection to understand anatomy.

Vesalius wrote Anatomy books with Accurate Diagrams

1) Vesalius was born in 1514 and was a medical professor in Padua, Italy. He believed that successful surgery would only be possible if doctors had a proper understanding of the anatomy.
2) Vesalius was able to perform dissections on criminals who had been executed. This let him study the human anatomy more closely.
3) He wrote books based on his observations using accurate diagrams to illustrate his work. The most important were 'Six Anatomical Pictures' (1538) and 'The Fabric of the Human Body' (1543).
4) His works were printed and copied (see the printing press, p.14), allowing lots of people to read about his ideas.

> Vesalius' work helped point out some of Galen's mistakes. For example, in the second edition of 'The Fabric', Vesalius showed that there were no holes in the septum of the heart.

5) Vesalius's findings encouraged others to question Galen. Doctors also realised there was more to discover about the body because of Vesalius' questioning attitude.
6) Vesalius showed that dissecting bodies was important, to find out exactly how the human body was structured. Dissection was used more and more in medical training for this reason (see p.11).

Comment and Analysis

The work of Vesalius didn't have an immediate impact on the diagnosis or treatment of disease. However, by producing a realistic description of the human anatomy and encouraging dissection, Vesalius provided an essential first step to improving them.

Thomas Sydenham used Practical Experience

1) Thomas Sydenham (1624-1689) was a Renaissance physician who worked in London. He was the son of a country squire, and fought in the English Civil War before becoming a doctor. He has been called the 'English Hippocrates' because of the big impact of his medical achievements.
2) Sydenham didn't believe in the value of theoretical knowledge. Instead he thought that it was more important to gain practical experience in treating patients. As a doctor, he made detailed observations of his patients and kept accurate records of their symptoms.
3) Sydenham thought that diseases could be classified like animals or plants — the different types of disease could be discovered using patients' symptoms.
4) Sydenham is known for showing that scarlet fever was different to measles, and for introducing laudanum to relieve pain. He was also one of the first doctors to use iron to treat anaemia, and quinine for malaria (see p.11).
5) Sydenham wrote a book called 'Medical Observations' (published in 1676), which was used as a textbook by doctors for 200 years. His descriptions of medical conditions like gout helped other doctors to diagnose their patients more easily.

Comment and Analysis

Sydenham's work on classifying diseases helped make diagnosis a more important part of doctors' work. Before, the emphasis had been on prognosis — predicting what the disease would do next.

Sydenham and Vesalius believed in direct observation...

Scribble down the main achievements of both Sydenham and Vesalius. Then note down the impact of their ideas — did they change things? Think about short-term and long-term effects.

Case Study: William Harvey

William Harvey is a key person in the history of Renaissance medicine.
He made hugely important discoveries about how blood circulates around the body.

Harvey discovered the Circulation of the Blood

1) William Harvey was born in 1578 and worked in London at the Royal College of Physicians, before becoming Royal Physician to James I and Charles I.
2) Harvey studied both animals and humans for his work. He realised that he could observe living animal hearts in action, and that his findings would also apply to humans.
3) Before Harvey, people thought that there were two kinds of blood, and that they flowed through two completely separate systems of blood vessels. It was thought that:
   - Purple 'nutrition-carrying' blood was produced in the liver and then flowed through veins to the rest of the body, where it was consumed (used up).
   - Bright red 'life-giving' blood was produced in the lungs and flowed through arteries to the body, where it was also consumed.
   - This may show the continuing influence of Galen, who had suggested this kind of system about 1400 years earlier.
4) Harvey realised this theory was wrong. From experiments, he knew that too much blood was being pumped out of the heart for it to be continually formed and consumed. Instead he thought that blood must circulate — it must go round and round the body.

Comment and Analysis

A new type of water pump was invented at around the time of Harvey's birth. This new technology gave Harvey a comparison and inspiration for how the heart worked.

Harvey's research was a Major Breakthrough in Anatomy...

A diagram from Harvey's 'On the Motions of the Heart and Blood' (1628), showing blood circulation in the arm.

1) Harvey's ideas changed how people understood anatomy. His discoveries gave doctors a new map showing how the body worked. Without this map, blood transfusions or complex surgery couldn't be attempted.
2) Harvey also showed that Vesalius had been right about how important dissection was.

...but it had a Limited Impact on Diagnosis and Treatment

Not everyone believed Harvey's theories — it took a long time before doctors used them in their treatments.

1) When people did attempt blood transfusions, they were rarely successful — because of blood loss, shock, and because the wrong blood types were used.
2) Bloodletting, which was supposed to keep the Four Humours in balance (see p.8), also continued to be performed, even though Harvey had shown the reasoning behind it to be wrong.

Although people knew more about the body's anatomy because of Harvey, medical treatments and surgical techniques were still very basic.

The circulation of the blood goes round and round...

'Harvey's discoveries were a major breakthrough in the development of medicine during the Renaissance period.' To what extent do you agree? Explain your answer. [16]

Transmission of Ideas

Greater scientific and medical progress in the Renaissance wasn't just the result of improved understanding of the anatomy. New technology allowed ideas to be circulated more easily, making change even quicker.

The Printing Press allowed New Ideas to be Spread

1) The first British printing press was set up in the 1470s. The invention of printing accelerated the rate of progress in medicine (and everything else).
   - Making a single copy of a book by hand could take many months or even years. Books were therefore very rare and precious.
   - New ideas would have to be widely accepted before anyone would go to the bother of copying them by hand.
   - The invention of printing allowed books to be copied much more easily.
2) Students in universities could have their own textbooks for the first time, letting them study in detail.
3) New ideas could be spread and debated more easily. Ambroise Paré (1510-1590) was a French army surgeon whose ideas about surgery were translated into different languages and reprinted. His works influenced several other books about surgery from this time.
4) The printing press also meant people could question existing ideas. At least 600 different editions of Galen's books were printed between 1473 and 1599. This meant that lots of people knew his theories. However, with so many different versions around, it was unclear what Galen had originally written — this made his writings seem less reliable.

Comment and Analysis

The printing press had a huge impact on the communication of ideas. Think about the impact the Internet has had in the last two decades — that should give you an idea of how important it was.

The Royal Society changed Perceptions of Medicine

1) The Royal Society was a prestigious scientific body founded in 1660.
2) It was supported by King Charles II, which gave it high status. It's still the highest authority on scientific matters in Britain today.
3) The society was important in spreading new scientific theories and getting people to trust new techonology.
4) Its motto was 'Nullius in verba', which means 'take no-one's word for it' — the society wanted to encourage people to be sceptical and to question scientific ideas.
5) Through its scientific journal 'Philosophical Transactions', more people could read about new inventions and discoveries.
6) It also published Robert Hooke's 1665 'Micrographia', which showed the first drawings of a flea made using a microscope.

Comment and Analysis

Huge progress was made in the Renaissance — and the printing press and the Royal Society helped spread the new ideas. But because most people couldn't read or write, these things could only have an impact on a small part of society. Most people in the Renaissance were using the same cures and treatments as people in the Middle Ages (see p.8).

Different factors affect change and continuity...

Individuals can have an impact on the rate of change. But so can institutions, society's attitudes, and developments in science and technology — like the printing press. Don't forget any of these.

Medical Treatment: Continuity

Despite the rapid pace of change in the Renaissance, there was continuity in many aspects of medical care. For most ordinary people, medical treatment was very similar to how it had been in medieval times.

Some Doctors still followed Old Ideas

Many doctors were reluctant to accept that Galen was wrong. This meant that they continued to use similar treatments to the Middle Ages, like bloodletting and purging (see p.8). Doctors tended to focus more on reading books than on treating patients.

People continued to use Other Healers

A woodcut from c.1670 showing a quack selling his 'miraculous' cures.

1) Doctors were also still very expensive. As a result, most people used other healers, like in the medieval period (see p.9):
   - Apothecaries sold medicines and drugs from their shops.
   - Barber-surgeons were used for small operations.
   - Some people turned to quack doctors, who sold medicines and treatments in the streets. Many of these drugs were fake — although some might have worked.
2) Superstition and religion were still important. People thought the King's touch could cure scrofula (a skin disease known as the 'King's Evil'). Thousands of people with scrofula are thought to have visited King Charles I (1600-1649) in the hope of being cured.

People sought care in the Community and at Home

1) Wise women, who were skilled in herbal remedies, continued to provide medical attention within the community. This role was sometimes taken by wealthy ladies, who would care for local families.
2) People would also keep their own medical or recipe books, passed down in the family.

Lady Grace Mildmay (1552-1620) was a wise woman who was highly educated and read lots of medical books. She used her knowledge to help patients. She also kept detailed records of her treatments.

Hospitals were still Fairly Basic

1) Most Renaissance hospitals were for the sick and the 'deserving' poor — those who led hardworking, respectable lives. People might have to work in hospital, not just be treated. Those with incurable or infectious diseases like smallpox were often not allowed in.
2) St Mary of Bethlehem's hospital (or 'Bedlam') was Britain's first 'lunatic' institution. Many of its inmates actually had learning disabilities or epilepsy, or were just poor. People even visited the hospital to watch the patients for entertainment.
3) Other hospitals like St Bartholemew's in London became centres of innovation and new research.

Comment and Analysis

Hospital care was still in its early stages in the Renaissance. Many hospitals mainly focused on moral or spiritual education. But health and sickness were becoming more of a priority.

Those Renaissance doctors — stuck in the past...

Make two lists of the key features of medieval and Renaissance medicine — how much had changed? Think about the experience of the average person, as well as new scientific discoveries.

Case Study: The Great Plague

The continuity of treatments was most felt when the Great Plague struck London in 1665. From prayers to bloodletting, the responses to the plague were eerily similar to the reaction to the Black Death (see p.10).

The Great Plague hit London in 1665

1) In 1665, London was struck by the Great Plague. This was a rare but deadly recurrence of the medieval Black Death.
2) London's death toll was about 100,000 — this was around 20% of the city's population.
3) Many people fled the city, but only richer people had this option.
4) Doctors and priests were often most affected because the sick went to them for help.

Like the Black Death, the Great Plague was spread by the bites of fleas from rats. The people at the time didn't know this, though.

Superstition still dominated Treatment

Just like responses to the Black Death 300 years before (see p.10), most treatments for the Great Plague were based on magic, religion and superstition.

1) This included wearing lucky charms or amulets, saying prayers and fasting.
2) Special remedies were made using ingredients like dried toad.
3) Bloodletting was still used, even though this probably made the plague worse — it created wounds which could become infected.
4) Other people thought that miasma caused the disease (see p.7). They carried around posies of herbs or flowers to improve the air.
5) Perhaps the most extreme treatment was strapping a live chicken to the swellings — people thought the disease could be transferred from the plague victim to the chicken.

Comment and Analysis

Living conditions were very poor in Renaissance England, so it isn't a surprise that the plague came back. Death records show that the poorest, most crowded areas of London were worst hit.

People tried to Prevent the plague from Spreading

Local councils took measures to try to stop the spread of the plague. They were largely ineffective because they didn't know the cause of the disease.

1) Councils tried to quarantine plague victims to prevent them passing on the disease to others. The victim's house was locked and a red cross was painted on their door, along with the words "Lord have mercy upon us."
2) Areas where people crowded together such as theatres were closed.
3) People tried not to touch other people. E.g. if someone had to give money in a shop, the coins might be placed in a jar of vinegar.
4) The dead bodies of plague victims were buried in mass graves away from houses. Carts organised by the authorities roamed the city to the infamous cry of "bring out your dead!", collecting corpses for burial.
5) Local councils paid for lots of cats and dogs to be killed, because they thought they carried the plague.

Comment and Analysis

The responses to the plague came from local councils — they did more to try to combat the Great Plague than they had done for the Black Death 300 years previously. But there were no national government attempts at prevention.

The plague gradually began to disappear. Many people think the Great Fire of London in 1666 helped wipe it out, by effectively sterilising large parts of London — it burned down the old, crowded houses, killing the plague bacteria.

Another deadly attack of the plague...

Explain one difference between people's reactions to the Great Plague in the 17th century and the Black Death in the 14th century. [4]

EXAM QUESTION

Case Study: Vaccination

Until the 1700s, people had few effective ways to prevent the spread of disease. Edward Jenner's discovery of the smallpox vaccine was a landmark in the development of preventive medicine.

Before Jenner the only way to prevent Smallpox was Inoculation

1) In the 1700s, smallpox was one of the most deadly diseases — in 1751, over 3500 people died of smallpox in London alone.
2) At the time, the only way to prevent smallpox was through inoculation. This was introduced into Britain from Turkey by Lady Mary Wortley Montagu in 1718.
3) Inoculation involved making a cut in a patient's arm and soaking it in pus taken from the swelling of somebody who already had a mild form of smallpox.

Inoculation was successful in preventing the disease, but it meant patients had to experience smallpox before they could become immune — some died as a result.

Jenner discovered a link between Smallpox and Cowpox

1) Edward Jenner (born in 1749) was a country doctor in Gloucestershire. He heard that milkmaids didn't get smallpox, but they did catch the much milder cowpox.
2) Using careful scientific methods Jenner investigated and discovered that it was true that people who had had cowpox didn't get smallpox.
3) In 1796 Jenner tested his theory. He injected a small boy, James Phipps, with pus from the sores of Sarah Nelmes, a milkmaid with cowpox. Jenner then infected him with smallpox. James didn't catch the disease.
4) Jenner published his findings in 1798. He coined the term vaccination using the Latin word for cow, vacca.

Comment and Analysis

Jenner was important because he used an experiment to test his theory. Although experiments had been used during the Renaissance, it was still unusual for doctors to test their theories.

Jenner's vaccination was Successful despite Opposition

1) Some people resisted vaccination. Some doctors who gave the older type of inoculation saw it as a threat to their livelihood, and many people were worried about giving themselves a disease from cows.
2) But Jenner's discovery soon got the approval of Parliament, which gave Jenner £10,000 in 1802 to open a vaccination clinic. It gave Jenner a further £20,000 a few years later.
3) In 1840 vaccination against smallpox was made free for infants. In 1853 it was made compulsory.
4) The vaccine was a success — it contributed to a big fall in the number of smallpox cases in Britain.

A cartoon from 1802 by James Gillray, with cows bursting out of vaccinated patients' sores. Vaccination was met with a lot of opposition — some groups in Britain published pamphlets against vaccination.

Comment and Analysis

The government's attempts to get people vaccinated against smallpox were surprising given attitudes at the time. People believed in a laissez-faire style of government — they thought that government shouldn't get involved in people's lives. The vaccination policy went against this general attitude.

Jenner didn't know why his vaccine worked. This lack of understanding meant Jenner couldn't develop any other vaccines. This was only possible after the Germ Theory was published (see p.18), when Pasteur and others worked to discover vaccines against other diseases, like chicken cholera and anthrax.

Jenner's vaccine got things mooving on disease prevention...

EXAM QUESTION

'The smallpox vaccination was the most important medical discovery in Britain between the years 1700 and 1900.' To what extent do you agree? Explain your answer. [16]

The Germ Theory

Although people's understanding of anatomy had improved greatly during the Renaissance, there was still plenty to learn. The causes of disease was an area that still needed proper explanation.

People knew about Germs but hadn't linked them to Disease

1) Germs and other micro-organisms were discovered as early as the 17th century. Scientists thought that these microbes were created by decaying matter, like rotting food or human waste — this theory was known as spontaneous generation. It led people to believe that disease caused germs.
2) People still thought miasma (see p.7) was the main cause of disease. The cholera outbreak of 1831-32 (see p.22) saw the government regulate the burial of the dead bodies to stop them creating bad air.

Pasteur was the first to suggest that Germs cause disease

1) The French chemist Louis Pasteur was employed in 1857 to find the explanation for the souring of sugar beet used in fermenting industrial alcohol. His answer was to blame germs.
2) Pasteur proved there were germs in the air — he showed that sterilised water in a closed flask stayed sterile, while sterilised water in an open flask bred germs.
3) In 1861, Pasteur published his Germ Theory. In it he argued that microbes in the air caused decay, not the other way round. He also suggested that some germs caused disease.

Pasteur's discovery was partly due to Antonie van Leeuwenhoek's invention of the microscope in the 17th century. More advanced microscopes were developed during the 1800s. They allowed scientists to see much clearer images with a lot less light distortion.

It took Time for the Germ Theory to have an Impact

1) The Germ Theory was first met with scepticism — people couldn't believe tiny microbes caused disease. It didn't help that the germ responsible for each disease had to be identified individually, as this meant it was several years before the theory became useful.

'I am afraid that the experiments you quote, M. Pasteur, will turn against you. The world into which you wish to take us is really too fantastic.'
La Presse, a French Newspaper, 1860.

2) The Germ Theory soon gained popularity in Britain.
   - The theory inspired Joseph Lister to develop antiseptics (p.21).
   - It proved John Snow's findings about cholera (p.22).
   - It linked disease to poor living conditions (like squalor and contaminated water). This put pressure on the government to pass the 1875 Public Health Act (see p.23).

'Thanks for having, by your brilliant researches, proved to me the truth of the germ theory. You furnished me with the principle upon which alone the antiseptic system can be carried out.'
The founder of antiseptic surgery, Joseph Lister, in a letter to Louis Pasteur, 1874.

Robert Koch used dyes to identify microbes

1) The German scientist Robert Koch built on Pasteur's work by linking specific diseases to the particular microbe that caused them. Koch identified anthrax spores (1876) and the bacteria that cause septicaemia (1878), tuberculosis (1882) and cholera (1883).
2) Koch used revolutionary scientific methods:
   - He used agar jelly to create solid cultures, allowing him to breed lots of bacteria.
   - He used dyes to stain the bacteria so they were more visible under the microscope.
   - He employed the newly-invented photography to record his findings.

Pasteur's theory — more than the germ of an idea...

Split your page into three sections, with the headings: individuals, technology and changing attitudes. Under each heading, list the ways in which that factor contributed to the Germ Theory.

Developments in Nursing

Before the 1800s, hospitals were often dirty places that people associated with death and infection. Florence Nightingale helped change that — by improving hospital hygiene and raising nursing standards.

Florence Nightingale improved army hospitals

1) Florence Nightingale (1820-1910) brought a new discipline and professionalism to a job that had a very bad reputation at the time. Despite opposition from her family, she studied to become a nurse in 1849.
2) When the Crimean War broke out in 1853-54, horror stories emerged about the Barrack Hospital in Scutari, where the British wounded were treated.
3) Sidney Herbert, who was both the Secretary of War and a friend of her family, asked for Nightingale to go to Scutari and sort out the hospital's nursing care.
4) The military opposed women nurses, as they were considered a distraction and inferior to male nurses. Nightingale went anyway, with 38 hand-picked nurses.
5) Using methods she had learned from her training in Europe, Nightingale made sure that all the wards were clean and hygienic, that water supplies were adequate and that patients were fed properly.
6) Nightingale improved the hospital a lot. Before she arrived, the death rate in the hospital stood at 42%. Two years later it had fallen to just 2%.

Mary Seacole (1805-1881) also nursed in the Crimea.

1) She learnt nursing from her mother, who ran a boarding house for soldiers in Jamaica.
2) In 1854, Seacole came to England to volunteer as a nurse in the Crimean War. She was rejected (possibly on racist grounds) but went anyway, paying for her own passage.
3) Financing herself by selling goods to the soldiers and travellers, she nursed soldiers on the battlefields and built the British Hotel — a small group of makeshift buildings that served as a hospital, shop and canteen for the soldiers.
4) Seacole couldn't find work as a nurse in England after the war and went bankrupt — though she did receive support due to the press interest in her story.

Nightingale used her fame to Change Nursing

1) In 1859, Nightingale published a book, 'Notes on Nursing'. This explained her methods — it emphasised the need for hygiene and a professional attitude. It was the standard textbook for generations of nurses.
2) The public raised £44,000 to help her train nurses, and she set up the Nightingale School of Nursing in St. Thomas' Hospital, London. Nurses were given three years of training before they could qualify. Discipline and attention to detail were important.
3) By 1900 there were 64,000 trained nurses in Britain from colleges across the country.
4) In 1919 (after Nightingale's death) the Nurses Registration Act was passed. This made training compulsory for all nurses.

As well as improving hospital care, Florence Nightingale is credited with helping turn nursing into a respectable profession, particularly for women. This was formalised in 1916, when The Royal College of Nursing was founded. It began to admit men in 1960.

The 1800s also saw a massive increase in hospital building. Hospitals became cleaner and more specialist, catering for rich patients as well as the poor.

Comment and Analysis

The Germ Theory wasn't published until 1861, so initially Florence Nightingale didn't know what the cause of disease was — she believed in the miasma theory. But her teachings suggested that good hygiene could prevent the spread of disease.

Like it or lamp it, you've got to learn it...

REVISION TASK

Write a list of all of Florence Nightingale's achievements. At the end of your list, write a sentence explaining what you think was her most important achievement.

Anaesthetics

Improving the hygiene and sanitation of hospitals helped to prevent many unnecessary deaths. But the two problems of pain and infection were yet to be solved. The answer to the first of those was anaesthetics.

Anaesthetics solved the problem of Pain

Pain was a problem for surgeons, especially because their patients could die from the trauma of extreme pain. Natural drugs like alcohol, opium and mandrake had long been used, but effective anaesthetics that didn't make the patient very ill were more difficult to produce.

- Nitrous oxide (laughing gas) was identified as a possible anaesthetic by British chemist Humphry Davy in 1799 — but he was ignored by surgeons at the time.
- The gas had been dismissed as a fairground novelty before American dentist Horace Wells suggested its use in his area of work. He did a public demonstration in 1845, but had the bad luck to pick a patient unaffected by nitrous oxide — it was again ignored.

- In 1842, American doctor Crawford Long discovered the anaesthetic qualities of ether, but didn't publish his work. The first public demonstration of ether as an anaesthetic was carried out in 1846 by American dental surgeon William Morton.
- Ether is an irritant and is also fairly explosive, so using it in this way was risky.

- James Simpson was a Professor of Midwifery at Edinburgh University. Looking for a safe alternative to ether that women could take during childbirth, he began to experiment on himself. In 1847, he discovered the effects of chloroform.
- After Queen Victoria gave birth to her eighth child while using chloroform in 1853, it became widely used in operating theatres and to reduce pain during childbirth.
- Chloroform sometimes affected the heart, causing patients to die suddenly.

General anaesthesia (complete unconsciousness) is risky, so local anaesthesia (numbing of the part being treated) is better for many operations. In 1884, William Halsted investigated the use of cocaine as a local anaesthetic. His self-experimentation led to a severe cocaine addiction.

Early Anaesthetics actually led to a Rise in death rates

1) Anaesthetics led to longer and more complex operations. This was because surgeons found that unconscious patients were easier to operate on, meaning they could take longer over their work.
2) Longer operating times led to higher death rates from infection, because surgeons didn't know that poor hygiene spread disease. Surgeons used very unhygienic methods.

- Surgeons didn't know that having clean clothes could save lives. Often they wore the same coats for years, which were covered in dried blood and pus from previous operations.
- Operations were often carried out in unhygienic conditions, including at the patient's house.
- Operating instruments also caused infections because they were usually unwashed and dirty.

Comment and Analysis

Anaesthetics helped solve the problem of pain, but patients were still dying from infection. This meant the attempts at more complicated surgery actually led to increased death rates amongst patients. The period between 1846 and 1870 is sometimes known as the 'Black Period' of surgery for this reason.

Anaesthetics revision — don't let it put you to sleep...

In the exam remember to be specific about the information you use. For example, rather than writing about anaesthetics in general terms, try to use specific types to explain your answer.

Antiseptics

Anaesthetics had solved the problem of pain, but surgeons were still faced with a high death rate from operations due to the amount of infection. Antiseptics and later asepsis helped prevent this by killing germs.

Antisepsis and Asepsis reduce infection

There are two main approaches to reducing infection during an operation:

- Antiseptic methods are used to kill germs that get near surgical wounds.
- Aseptic surgical methods aim to stop any germs getting near the wound.

Joseph Lister pioneered the use of Antiseptics

1) Ignaz Semmelweis showed that doctors could reduce the spread of infection by washing their hands with chloride of lime solution between patients. However, it was very unpleasant, so wasn't widely used.
2) Joseph Lister had seen carbolic acid sprays used in sewage works to keep down the smell. He tried this in the operating theatre in the early 1860s and saw reduced infection rates.
3) Lister heard about the Germ Theory in 1865 — he realised that germs could be in the air, on surgical instruments and on people's hands. He started using carbolic acid on instruments and bandages.
4) The use of antiseptics immediately reduced death rates from as high as 50% in 1864-66 to around 15% in 1867-70.
5) Antiseptics allowed surgeons to operate with less fear of patients dying from infection. The number of operations increased tenfold between 1867 and 1912 as a result.

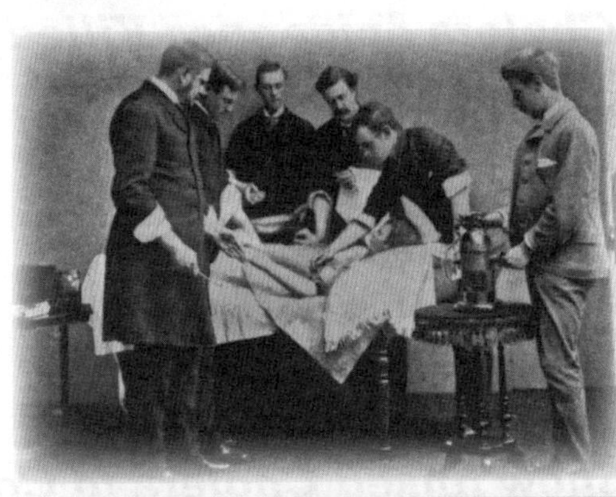

A photograph of a surgical operation taken in the late 1800s. You can see Lister's carbolic spray on the table on the right. The operating theatre isn't aseptic though — the surgeons aren't wearing sterile gowns or surgical gloves.

Comment and Analysis

Antiseptics (and later asepsis) solved the problem of infection. This, combined with the use of anaesthetics (see p.20) to stop pain, improved British surgery — many deaths were prevented as a result of antiseptics and anaesthetics.

Asepsis reduced the need for Nasty Chemicals

Since the late 1800s, surgeons have changed their approach from killing germs to making a germ-free (aseptic) environment.

1) Instruments are carefully sterilised before use, usually with high temperature steam (120 °C).
2) Theatre staff sterilise their hands before entering — and wear sterile gowns, masks, gloves and hats. Surgical gloves were invented by William Halsted in 1889.
3) The theatres themselves are kept scrupulously clean and fed with sterile air. Special tents can be placed around the operating table to maintain an area of even stricter hygiene in high risk cases.
4) Aseptic surgery reduced the need for a carbolic spray, which is unpleasant to get on your skin or breathe in — many doctors and nurses didn't like to use it.

Make a Lister them facts — then germ up on them...

REVISION TASK

Write a paragraph summarising whether you think anaesthetics or antiseptics were a greater breakthrough for 19th century surgery.

Case Study: Cholera in London

The industrial revolution began in the 18th century. Lots of people moved into cities like London to work in the factories. The places they lived were cramped, dirty and great for spreading diseases like cholera.

Towns had no proper Water or Waste facilities

1) Before the Germ Theory was published, people didn't understand the need for clean water or good sewerage systems. Most houses had no bathroom — they instead shared an outside toilet, called a privy.
2) Each privy was built above a cesspit. Cesspit and household waste was collected by nightmen, who threw the waste into rivers or piled it up for the rain to wash away.
3) Water companies set up water pumps in the streets, which were shared between many houses. The pump's water supply was often contaminated by waste from the cesspits or rivers.

Cholera epidemics Killed Thousands of people

1) Cholera reached Britain in 1831. By 1832, it was an epidemic — over 21,000 people in Britain died of cholera that year. The epidemics recurred in 1848, 1853-54 and 1865-66.
2) Cholera spreads when infected sewage gets into drinking water. It causes extreme diarrhoea — sufferers often die from loss of water and minerals. Both rich and poor people caught the disease.
3) At the time people didn't know what caused cholera — the best theory was miasma (see p.7). The government started regulating the burial of the dead, but this did little to halt the spread of cholera.

Snow linked Cholera to Contaminated Water

John Snow was a London doctor who showed that there was a connection between contaminated water and cholera. For a long time he had suspected that the disease was waterborne, but had very little proof.

1) When cholera broke out in the Broad Street area of London in 1854, Snow set out to test his theory. He interviewed people living in Broad Street and made a map of the area showing where cases of the disease had been. This is some of the information he collected, published in 1855 in his report 'On the Mode of Communication of Cholera':

'There were only ten deaths in houses situated decidedly nearer to another street pump. In five of these cases the families of the deceased persons informed me that they always sent to the pump in Broad Street, as they preferred the water.'

'There is a Brewery in Broad Street, near to the pump, and on perceiving that no brewer's men were registered as having died of cholera, I called on Mr. Huggins, the proprietor... He is quite certain that the workmen never obtained water from the pump in the street. There is a deep well in the brewery.'

'[A cholera victim in the West End] had not been in... Broad Street for many months. A cart went from Broad Street to West End every day, and it was the custom to take out a large bottle of the water from the pump in Broad Street, as she preferred it.'

2) Snow's investigations showed that all victims used the same water pump on Broad Street. He convinced the local council to remove the handle from the pump. This brought the cholera outbreak to an end.
3) It was later discovered that a nearby cesspit had a split lining — its waste had leaked into the pump's water supply.

Comment and Analysis

Snow's findings took a while to make an impact — it was not until the Germ Theory was published that his theory became widely accepted. But eventually Snow's findings helped lead to a change in attitudes — people realised that waterborne diseases like cholera needed a government response in order to clean up the streets and waterways. This contributed to the 1875 Public Health Act. Like Jenner (see p.17), Snow was also important for using observation and evidence to support his theory.

If anyone knows the cause of cholera, John Snows...

'John Snow's discovery in 1854 was an important turning point in the prevention of disease in Britain during the period 1700-1900.' Explain how far you agree with this statement. [16]

The Public Health Act, 1875

Before 1875, there was little effort to improve public health — people didn't know what caused disease, and they believed the government shouldn't do anything about it. The Public Health Act of 1875 changed this.

Earlier attempts to improve Public Health had Limited Success

1) In 1842, Edwin Chadwick published a report suggesting that poor living conditions caused poor health.
2) Chadwick's report led to the 1848 Public Health Act. The Act set up a central Board of Health and let local councils set up their own boards of health.
3) In 1858, sewage in the River Thames made a 'Great Stink' in the middle of London. This forced the government to plan a new sewer system, which opened in 1865.

The 1848 Act's impact was limited — towns could set up health boards but very few chose to, and those that did often refused to spend any money.

Public Opinion began to Change

For most of the 19th century, people believed in a laissez-faire style of government — they thought the government shouldn't intervene in public health. But then things began to change.

1) Snow's discovery of the link between dirty water and cholera (see p.22) and Pasteur's Germ Theory (see p.18) showed that cleaning up towns could stop the spread of disease.
2) In 1867, the Second Reform Act was passed. It gave an additional 1 million men the vote, most of whom were industrial workers.
3) Writers like Charles Dickens and philanthropists like Octavia Hill helped change attitudes towards the poor, who suffered the worst conditions.

Comment and Analysis

Now that they had the vote, workers could put pressure on the government to listen to concerns about health. For the first time, politicians had to address workers' concerns in order to stay in power.

The 1875 Act improved Public Health

In the 1870s, the government finally took action to improve public health.

1) In 1871-72, the government followed the Royal Sanitary Commission's proposal to form the Local Government Board and divide Britain into 'sanitary areas' administered by officers for public health.
2) In 1875, the government of Benjamin Disraeli passed another Public Health Act. It forced councils to:
   - Appoint health inspectors and sanitary inspectors who made sure that laws on things like water supplies and hygiene were being followed.
   - Maintain sewerage systems to prevent further cholera outbreaks.
   - Keep their town's streets clean.
3) The 1875 Public Health Act was more effective than the one passed in 1848 because it was compulsory.
4) In 1875, Disraeli also brought in the Artisans' Dwellings Act, which let local councils buy slums with poor living conditions and rebuild them in a way that fit new government-backed housing standards.
5) Other important reforms included the 1876 River Pollution Prevention Act, which stopped people from dumping sewage or industrial waste into rivers.

Comment and Analysis

Just as the government used the work of Jenner to make vaccination compulsory (see p.17), the 1875 Act built on the work of several individuals, including John Snow and Louis Pasteur. The scientific proof these individuals provided, combined with a change in attitudes towards the role of government, helped put pressure on the government to act.

Turns out laissez-faire had made things less fair...

Including your knowledge of the 1875 Public Health Act, explain why there was an improvement in the prevention of disease in Britain during the 19th century. [12]

Modern Ideas about the Causes of Disease

The Germ Theory (see p.18) was a major breakthrough in identifying the causes of disease, but identifying bacteria couldn't explain every disease. Viruses, genetics and lifestyle were all found to impact on health.

Viruses were discovered at the turn of the century

Despite their successes with bacteria, Pasteur and Koch (see p.18) were unable to find the cause of some diseases, as they were caused by microbes called viruses, which were too small to see under a microscope.

1) In 1892 the Russian microbiologist Dmitry Ivanovsky investigated mosaic, a disease that was killing tobacco plants. He found that the cause was an extremely small microbe that remained in water even after bacteria were removed. In 1898, the Dutch scientist Martinus Beijernick found that these microbes had different properties to bacteria — he labelled these microbes viruses.
2) The discovery of viruses led to their successful treatment. Unlike bacteria, viruses aren't destroyed by antibiotics (see p.26). Instead, doctors can prescribe antiviral drugs, but they only prevent a viral infection from growing — only the body's immune system can destroy a virus for good.

DNA has given an insight into Genetic Conditions

1) Genes are the chemical 'instructions' that plan out human characteristics, like sex and hair colour. They are stored in cells as DNA. Your DNA is a mix of your parents' DNA.

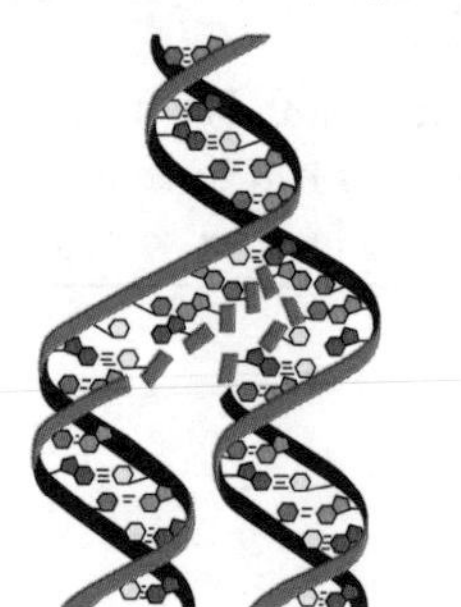
The structure of DNA is a double helix.

2) The structure of DNA, a double helix (a kind of spiral) that can reproduce itself by splitting, was first described in 1953 by Francis Crick and James Watson.
3) Watson and Crick's discovery allowed other scientists to find the genes that cause genetic conditions — diseases that are passed on from one generation to another. These include cystic fibrosis, haemophilia and sickle-cell anaemia.
4) Knowledge of genetic conditions has improved diagnosis and treatment of them. Scientists can now produce a synthetic protein to replicate the work of a faulty gene and treat inherited conditions using techniques like gene therapy.

One of the biggest breakthroughs in genetic research was made in 2003 with the completion of the Human Genome Project — this identified all the genes in human DNA.

Lifestyle Factors can increase the Risk of some Diseases

A healthy diet, exercise and other lifestyle factors have long been suggested as ways to prevent illness, but it was only in the 20th century that lifestyle choices were linked to particular health conditions:

1) Smoking has been shown to cause lung cancer (see p.31).
2) Obesity increases the chance of getting heart disease or diabetes.
3) Drinking too much alcohol has been shown to cause liver disease.
4) Overexposure to ultraviolet radiation (e.g. from sunlight) can cause skin cancer.

Comment and Analysis

The advances in science and technology since 1900 have shown that there is not just one cause of disease. In addition to bacteria, we now know that disease can be caused by viral infections, genetic mutations and our lifestyle choices. This makes their treatment and prevention even more complex — with so many different causes, treatment needs to be more targeted to the specific disease.

Watson and Crick described DNA — they're gene-iuses...

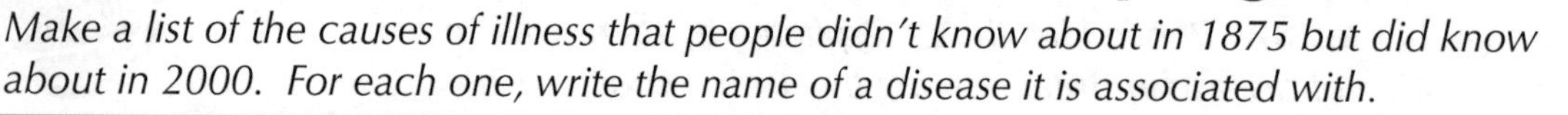
Make a list of the causes of illness that people didn't know about in 1875 but did know about in 2000. For each one, write the name of a disease it is associated with.

Developments in Diagnosis

New causes of disease demanded new ways of diagnosing them. These new methods were introduced rapidly in the 20th century, due to innovations in science and technology, from computers to X-rays.

Blood Tests allow doctors to Diagnose more illnesses

Blood tests were first introduced to test blood groups before blood transfusions (see p.28). Since then, blood tests have been used to test for a range of diseases.

1) Blood tests can be used to check a patient's cholesterol level. This can help diagnose their chance of suffering a heart attack or stroke.
2) Blood tests can be used to check a patient's DNA (see p.24). This can help diagnose a genetic condition, like haemophilia or cystic fibrosis.
3) Some blood tests can be used to show whether a patient has a certain type of cancer, including ovarian cancer, prostate cancer and breast cancer.

Blood tests make diagnosis more accurate, providing doctors with clearer information of what is wrong. This means they can be more confident when deciding how best to treat their patients.

Doctors can see more of the body with Medical Scans

1) The use of medical scans began in 1895 when Wilhelm Röntgen discovered X-rays. They pass easily through soft flesh, but less well through bone. They also affect photographic film. These factors allowed simple X-ray images to be produced by directing X-rays at a body part in front of a photographic plate.
2) Advances in computers allowed doctors to use ultrasound scanning — this uses high frequency sound waves, which bounce off the patient's organs and other tissues to create an image of them on the computer.
3) Computed Tomography (CT or CAT) scans were invented in 1972 by Godfrey Hounsfield. They use X-rays and a computer to make detailed images of parts of the patient's body.
4) Magnetic Resonance Imaging (MRI) scans were initially invented in 1970s but became widely used in the 1980s. These use extremely powerful radio waves and magnetic fields to construct images.

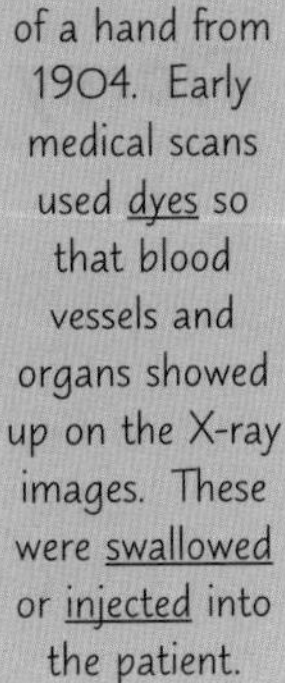

An X-ray image of a hand from 1904. Early medical scans used dyes so that blood vessels and organs showed up on the X-ray images. These were swallowed or injected into the patient.

Comment and Analysis

Improvements in technology, like medical scans, have given doctors a much more detailed picture of what's going on inside their patient's body. This has enabled them to intervene much earlier, before the disease has become too advanced. Early treatment is generally more effective and has a higher chance of success.

Patients can now Monitor their own bodies

Since around 1900, devices have been introduced to allow doctors and patients to monitor the body.

1) Blood pressure monitors were invented and developed in the 1880s and 1890s. They let doctors and patients see whether disease, lifestyle factors or medicines are causing high blood pressure, which can cause damage to the heart.
2) Blood sugar monitors were introduced in the mid 20th century. They allow those with diabetes to make sure their blood sugar is at the right level.

An important change in the 20th century is the use of monitoring devices by people in their own homes — this has allowed individuals greater control over their own health.

I've taken an X-ray of my pet — I call it a cat scan...

In the exam, you only have a limited amount of time to answer each question. If you're spending too long on one question, write a conclusion then move on to the next question.

EXAM TIP

Case Study: Penicillin

In the 1800s, Pasteur discovered that bacteria cause disease. But it wasn't until the 1900s that doctors were able to treat bacterial diseases. This was partly due to the discovery penicillin, the first antibiotic.

Fleming discovered Penicillin — the first Antibiotic

1) Alexander Fleming saw many soldiers die of septic wounds caused by staphylococcal bacteria when he was working in an army hospital during the First World War.
2) Searching for a cure he identified the antiseptic substance in tears, lysozyme, in 1922 — but this only worked on some germs.
3) One day in 1928 he came to clean up some old culture dishes on which he had been growing staphylococci for his experiments. By chance, a fungal spore had landed and grown on one of the dishes.
4) What caught Fleming's eye was that the colonies of staphylococci around the mould had stopped growing. The fungus was identified as Penicillium notatum. It produced a substance that killed bacteria. This substance was given the name penicillin.
5) Fleming published his findings in articles between 1929 and 1931. However, nobody was willing to fund further research, so he was unable to take his work further. The industrial production of penicillin still needed to be developed.

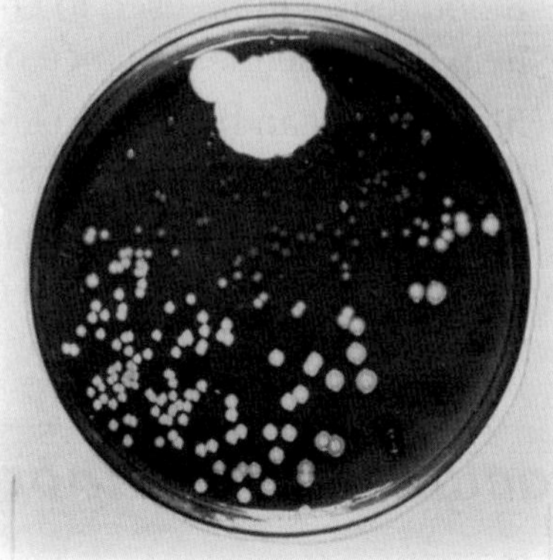

The original plate on which Fleming first observed the growth of Penicillium notatum.

Florey and Chain found a way to Purify Penicillin

1) Since it is a natural product, penicillin needs to be purified. A breakthrough was made by Howard Florey's team in Oxford between 1938 and 1940. Ernst Chain, a member of the team, devised the freeze-drying technique which was an important part of the purification process.
2) At first Florey and Chain didn't have the resources to produce penicillin in large amounts. They made penicillin for their first clinical trial by growing Penicillium notatum in every container they could find in their lab. Their patient began to recover, only to die when the penicillin ran out.

Florey took penicillin to America for Mass Production

Florey knew that penicillin could be vital in treating the wounds of soldiers fighting in World War II. British chemical firms were too busy making explosives to start mass production — so he went to America.

1) American firms were also not keen to help — until America joined the war in 1941. In December 1941, the US government began to give out grants to businesses that manufactured penicillin.
2) By 1943, British businesses had also started mass-producing penicillin. Mass production was sufficient for the needs of the military medics by 1944.
3) After the war, the cost of penicillin fell, making it more accessible for general use.
4) Fleming, Florey and Chain were awarded the Nobel Prize in 1945.

Today, penicillin is used to treat a range of bacterial infections, including chest infections and skin infections. Other antibiotics were discovered after 1945, including treatments for lung infections, acne and bacterial meningitis.

Comment and Analysis

While individuals (like Florey, Chain and Fleming) were important in making the discovery of penicillin, it was large institutions like governments that funded its mass production.

Penicillin isn't just mould news — it's still used today...

How far do you agree that Alexander Fleming's discovery of penicillin was the most important moment in medicine since c.1900? Explain your answer. [16]

Modern Treatments

Scientists have found a range of other treatments for diseases, besides penicillin.
These include magic bullets, which use chemical and synthetic substances to kill bacteria.

Paul Ehrlich discovered the first Magic Bullet — Salvarsan 606

Antibodies were identified as a natural defence mechanism of the body against germs. It was known that antibodies only attacked specific microbes — so they were nicknamed magic bullets. In 1889, Paul Ehrlich set out to find chemicals that could act as synthetic antibodies.

1) First, Ehrlich discovered dyes that could kill the malaria and sleeping sickness germs.
2) In 1905, the bacterium that causes the sexually transmitted disease syphilis was identified.
3) Ehrlich and his team decided to search for an arsenic compound that was a magic bullet for syphilis. They hoped it would target the bacteria without poisoning the rest of the body.
4) Over 600 compounds were tried, but none seemed to work.
5) In 1909, Sahachiro Hata joined the team. He rechecked the results and saw that compound number 606 actually appeared to work. It was first used on a human in 1911 under the trade name Salvarsan 606.

Gerhard Domagk found the second Magic Bullet — Prontosil

1) In 1932, Gerhard Domagk found that a red dye, prontosil, stopped the streptococcus microbe from multiplying in mice — without being poisonous to the mice.
2) In 1935, Domagk's daughter pricked herself with a needle and caught the disease. Afraid she would die, Domagk gave her a large dose of prontosil. The girl turned bright red, but recovered.
3) The active ingredient of prontosil was identified as a sulphonamide. A whole group of drugs based on sulphonamides followed, including M&B 693, which worked on pneumonia without turning you a strange colour.
4) Sadly more serious side-effects were discovered. Sulphonamide drugs can damage the liver and kidneys.

Streptococcus caused blood poisoning which was often fatal, and which could be contracted from very minor wounds. Many surgeons contracted it after cutting themselves in the operating theatre.

Comment and Analysis

The discovery of magic bullets showed that synthetic, targeted treatments for specific diseases were possible. Since Paul Ehrlich's first discovery, a huge pharmaceutical industry has grown, dedicated to the research and production of new treatments.

Treatments have been introduced to fight Cancer

1) The first successful treatment against cancer that didn't involve surgery was radiotherapy, introduced after the discovery of radiation in 1896-1898 by Antoine Henri Becquerel, Marie Curie and Pierre Curie. Radiotherapy involves killing cancer cells using targeted X-rays and gamma rays.
2) Chemotherapy is the treatment of cancer using drugs. It was discovered in World War II when doctors found that nitrogen mustard (a chemical in mustard gas) could be used to reduce cancer tumours. Other drugs were later discovered, including a compound in folic acid that blocks the growth of cancer cells.
3) Since the late 1990s, targeted therapy has been used to fight cancer. This uses drugs to prevent cancer from spreading.

When it comes to magic bullets, Ehrlich hit the mark...

Write a paragraph describing the changes in treatment during the 20th century. Explain whether you think individuals or advances in technology were the most important factor.

Modern Surgery

Surgery improved rapidly during the 20th century. The discovery of blood groups made blood transfusions more successful, and even heart transplants are now possible. Nowadays the emphasis is on precision.

Blood Transfusions have solved the problem of Blood Loss

The idea of blood transfusions was known from the 17th century, but they were rarely successful because the blood of the recipient often clotted. Blood also clotted if it was stored outside the body.

1) In 1900, Karl Landsteiner discovered blood groups. Certain blood groups can't be mixed as the blood will clot, clogging the blood vessels. He found that transfusions were safe as long as the patient's blood matched the blood donor's.
2) In 1914, during World War I, doctors found that sodium citrate stopped blood clotting so it could be stored outside the body. In 1917, this discovery was vital when the first ever blood bank was set up at the Battle of Cambrai.
3) In 1946, the British National Blood Transfusion Service was established.

Patients always suffer some blood loss during surgery. If a lot of blood is lost, this can be fatal. Blood transfusions helped to prevent this cause of death by allowing surgeons to replace any blood lost during surgery.

Transplants have been made more Successful

1) In 1905, the first successful transplant of the cornea of the eye was performed. During the First World War, surgeons developed techniques for skin transplantation.
2) The first complete organ to be successfully transplanted was the kidney. Livers, lungs, pancreases and bone marrow can now also be transplanted.
3) The first successful heart transplant was carried out by the South African surgeon Christiaan Barnard in 1967. The patient only survived for 18 days — he died of pneumonia.

The problem for transplants is rejection. The immune system attacks the implant as if it were a virus.

- The success of early transplant operations was limited because doctors lacked effective immunosuppressants — drugs that stop the immune system attacking.
- Since the 1970s, researchers have developed increasingly effective immunosuppressants, making transplants safer and more likely to be successful.

Keyhole Surgery and Robot-assisted Surgery increased Precision

1) Keyhole surgery is a technique (developed in the 1980s) which makes surgery less invasive — it leaves patients with smaller scars and allows them to recover more quickly.
2) A type of surgical camera called an endoscope is put through a small cut, letting the surgeon see inside the body. Other surgical instruments are then introduced through even smaller cuts in the skin.
3) Keyhole surgery is useful for investigating the causes of pain or infertility. It's also used for vasectomies, removing cysts or the appendix, mending hernias and other minor operations.

Robot-assisted surgery has also improved precision.

- The first surgical robot was introduced in 1985 but robot-assisted surgery only became widely used after 2000 with the launch of the da Vinci system.
- Robot-assisted surgery allows surgeons to make smaller cuts. This means less scarring, less infection and quicker healing of wounds.

These new types of surgery have made it safer for patients by limiting the possibility of infection and blood loss, as well as reducing the shock and trauma of surgery.

All you need to do is transplant these facts into your brain...

EXAM QUESTION

Explain why there were a lot of improvements in surgery between the end of 19th century and the end of the 20th century. [12]

The National Health Service

Advances in science and technology improved the quality of healthcare during the 20th century. But it was only with the founding of the National Health Service that everyone in Britain felt the benefits.

Before the NHS, access to Healthcare was Limited

1) At the start of the 20th century, access to healthcare was severely limited. This was particularly the case for poor people, who couldn't afford to go to the doctor or buy medicine.
2) This meant that people's health was poor. For example, in 1901 there were 140 infant deaths for every 1000 births — today it's less than 5. When the Boer War broke out in 1899, army officers found that 40% of volunteers were physically unfit for military service.
3) In 1911, the Liberal government introduced the National Insurance Act, which gave some workers health insurance to pay for medical attention. But World War I drained Britain's resources, and several economic slumps in the 1920s and 1930s meant the government couldn't expand healthcare provision.

The NHS was established in 1948

1) The Second World War (1939-1945) changed people's attitudes towards healthcare:
   - The raising of a mass army made powerful people take notice of the health problems of the poor.
   - Air raids, especially the Blitz of 1940, prompted the government to set up the Emergency Medical Service. This provided a centralised control of medical services and offered free treatment to air raid casualties. It proved successful under great pressure.
2) In 1942, the social reformer William Beveridge published a report. The report called for government provision of social security 'from the cradle to the grave'. The report became a bestseller.
3) In 1945, the Labour Party was elected with a mandate to implement Beveridge's proposals, primarily by founding the National Health Service (NHS) in 1948.
4) Aneurin Bevan was the Minister for Health who introduced the NHS. Bevan wanted the NHS to be free at the point of use — he set up a system of compulsory National Insurance to pay for it.
5) Bevan wooed doctors and dentists with a fixed payment for each registered patient. They were also allowed to continue treating private fee-paying patients. By 1948 nearly all hospitals and 92% of doctors had joined the NHS.

Aneurin Bevan.

Comment and Analysis

The founding of the NHS showed that government intervention could make a positive impact on people's health. However, it took a change in public attitudes (backed up by greater scientific knowledge) to make it happen.

The NHS has improved Access to Healthcare

1) The NHS increased the number of people with access to healthcare — the number of doctors doubled between 1948 and 1973 to keep up with demand.
2) Today, the NHS provides a range of health services, most of which are free and accessible to everyone. They include accident and emergency care, maternity care and major surgery, as well as pharmacies, dentists, mental health services, sexual health services and general practitioners (GPs).

The NHS has encountered some problems in providing access to care. The 1980 Black Report suggested that the NHS hadn't improved the health of the very poorest. Patients also had to suffer long waiting times during the 1990s. In 2000 the government drew up an 'NHS plan' to deal with waiting times among other areas.

Beveridge Report — nothing to do with your favourite drink...

EXAM QUESTION

Explain how people's attitudes towards government intervention were different in the 20th century compared to the period c.1700-1900. [4]

The Government's Role in Healthcare

Since 1900, the government's role in improving people's health has grown and grown.

Vaccination Campaigns have eradicated some Diseases

Since 1900, the government has launched several national vaccination programmes to prevent people from catching deadly diseases. These have been successful in reducing the number of deaths from such diseases.

Diphtheria is a contagious disease that is caused by bacteria in the nose and throat. It can eventually attack the heart muscles, causing paralysis or heart failure.

- Before the 1940s, diphtheria was a major killer disease — in 1940, there were over 60,000 cases of the disease and over 3,000 deaths.
- After fears that wartime conditions could lead to the spread of the disease, the government started a vaccination campaign in 1940.
- The government ran publicity campaigns, using posters, newspaper advertisements and radio broadcasts.
- The campaign was a success — by 1957, the number of diphtheria cases had dropped to just 38, with only six deaths.

In 1940, the easiest way to reach children was through schools, so 5-15 year olds were vaccinated more than the youngest children who were most vulnerable. The establishment of the NHS in 1948 (see p.29) allowed the government to vaccinate all children by their first birthday.

Polio is an infection that can attack the digestive system, bloodstream and nervous system. The disease can cause paralysis, and particularly affects children.

- In the late 1940s and early 1950s, Britain suffered a series of polio epidemics — the disease made over 30,000 children disabled between 1947 and 1958.
- The first vaccine was introduced in Britain in 1956 alongside a national campaign, aiming to vaccinate every person under the age of 40.
- The campaign was successful, with the disease all but eradicated by the late 1970s. In the period 1985-2002, only 40 polio cases were reported in Britain.

Lifestyle Campaigns aim to improve people's Health

In the 20th century, scientists showed a link between people's lifestyle choices and their health (see p.24). The government ran several campaigns to make people aware of the dangers and to change their lifestyles.

1) In 1952, a Great Smog caused by coal fires resulted in 4,000 deaths in London. It showed the dangers of air pollution, which can cause breathing conditions like asthma and bronchitis. The government passed laws in the hope of limiting air pollution.
2) An increase in less active lifestyles has led to an increase in obesity. In 2009, the government launched the Change4Life campaign, with the aim of improving diets and promoting daily exercise.
3) Excessive alcohol intake has been linked to several diseases, most notably liver cirrhosis. Alcohol intake rose between 1950 and 2004, but has since fallen. This may be due to the government's Drinkaware campaign, launched in 2004. The Drinkaware logo appears on many alcohol advertisements.

Comment and Analysis

These campaigns mark a big shift in the government's approach from the foundation of the NHS, and an even bigger shift from the laissez-faire attitudes of the 19th century, when people thought government shouldn't intervene at all in public health. Not only is the government trying to treat and vaccinate against known diseases, it is now intervening in people's lives in order to stop them getting particular illnesses in the first place.

My free speech campaign is getting everybody talking...

Draw a mind map of all of the ways the government has tried to improve health and medicine in Britain since 1900. Include vaccinations, lifestyle campaigns and the NHS in your diagram.

Case Study: Lung Cancer

Lung cancer is a disease that was much more common after 1900 than before. The battle against lung cancer is an example of science and technology and government campaigns working side by side.

Lung Cancer can be caused by Smoking

1) Lung cancer was a rare disease in 1900, but became common by the 1940s. Today, around 20% of all cancer deaths in the UK are due to lung cancer. Approximately 43,500 people are diagnosed every year.
2) Scientists have estimated that around 90% of lung cancer cases can be linked to tobacco smoking. The popularity of smoking increased in the First World War, particularly among soldiers. Smoking soon became popular among women too.
3) In 1950 the link between smoking and lung cancer was proven by Richard Doll and Austin Bradford Hill.

Lung cancer Diagnostics and Treatment have Improved

Advances in science and technology have made it easier to diagnose and treat lung cancer.

- Chest X-rays are the first means of diagnosing lung cancer. The X-rays can't show whether the patient definitely has cancer, but can show if there is anything on the lung that shouldn't be there.
- CT scans (see p.25) can be used to give a more detailed image of the lungs.
- Doctors can now use bronchoscopy to diagnose lung cancer. This involves putting a thin tube into the lungs to take a sample of the suspected cells. It requires a local anaesthetic to numb the throat.

- Lung cancer can be treated using surgery, for example by removing the affected lung.
- Modern treatments like radiotherapy and chemotherapy (see p.27) are also used to treat lung cancer. Radiotherapy involves directing radiation at the lungs. Lung cancer chemotherapy uses a combination of several drugs, which are normally injected directly into the bloodstream.

Government Campaigns have reduced smoking

When the link between smoking and lung cancer became clear, the government warned people of the risks.

1) In 1962 the Royal College of Physicians recommended a ban on tobacco advertising. Shortly afterwards, in 1965, cigarette adverts were banned from television. In 1971 tobacco companies were forced to put a health warning on cigarette packets.
2) In recent years, the government has put a ban on smoking in public places — this was introduced in Scotland in 2006, and in England and Wales in 2007.
3) Recent government campaigns have focused on helping people to give up smoking and on discouraging smoking in cars, homes and in front of children.
4) In March 2015 Parliament passed a law requiring all cigarette companies to use plain packaging on boxes of cigarettes.

These measures have contributed to a decline in smoking. The percentage of men who smoke cigarettes has fallen from 65% in 1948 to around 20% in 2010 and for women it's dropped from 41% to 20% in the same period.

Comment and Analysis

Lung cancer prevention is a good example of an area of health where the government has been increasingly active — the large number of television campaigns and pieces of legislation show that the government is now taking health seriously, which is in contrast to its attitude before 1900.

Dreams of a healthy lifestyle went up in smoke...

EXAM QUESTION

'Lung cancer is more common now than it was in 1900. This shows that there has been little improvement in medicine in the 20th century.' Explain how far you agree with this statement. [16]

Revision Summary

Well, that was a healthy amount of information to revise. Now treat yourself to these revision questions.

- Try these questions and tick off each one when you get it right.
- When you've done all the questions for a topic and are completely happy with it, tick off the topic.

c.1250-c.1500: Medicine in Medieval England (p.6-10)

1) Give two supernatural causes of disease believed by people in medieval England.
2) Describe two rational causes of disease believed by people in medieval England.
3) Name six treatments for disease used by people in medieval England.
4) List three types of people you might visit if you felt ill in medieval England.
5) Give three ways people tried to prevent the Black Death.

c.1500-c.1700: The Medical Renaissance in England (p.11-16)

6) Explain why Thomas Sydenham was important in renaissance medicine.
7) What was Vesalius' discovery and why did it help improve surgery?
8) What did Harvey discover and why did he have a limited impact on diagnosis and treatment?
9) Describe the impact of the printing press on people's understanding of medicine.
10) How did the Royal Society change perceptions of medicine?
11) List five ways in which there was continuity between medieval and renaissance medical treatments.
12) List five treatments and five prevention methods people used against the Great Plague in 1665.

c.1700-c.1900: Medicine in 18th and 19th Century Britain (p.17-23)

13) Describe how Edward Jenner proved the link between smallpox and cowpox.
14) List three reactions by Parliament to Jenner's discovery of the smallpox vaccine.
15) In what year did Louis Pasteur publish the Germ Theory?
16) Explain how Florence Nightingale changed nursing.
17) Name the year that chloroform was discovered and explain why it led to a higher death rate initially.
18) What is the difference between antisepsis and asepsis?
19) Describe John Snow's 1854 investigation and explain what he showed.
20) Give three things that the 1875 Public Health Act forced local councils to do.

c.1900-Present: Medicine in Modern Britain (p.24-31)

21) Describe three causes of disease that have been discovered since Pasteur's Germ Theory.
22) What did Watson and Crick discover in 1953 and how did it help medical diagnosis?
23) When were X-rays discovered? How are they used in medical diagnosis?
24) Explain how the following individuals or institutions contributed to the production of penicillin: Fleming, Florey and Chain, the United States government.
25) Name the first two magic bullets, who discovered them and the dates they were discovered.
26) Give three advances in surgery since 1900 and explain how they have made surgery safer.
27) List five factors that led to the founding of the National Health Service (NHS) in 1948.
28) Describe two government vaccination campaigns.
29) Give five ways in which lung cancer diagnosis and treatments have improved.
30) List four ways that the government has tried to reduce smoking.

Trench Warfare on the Western Front

Between 1914 and 1918, the Allies (including Britain, France and Belgium) fought the German Imperial Army in Belgium and France — the area where the fighting happened was called the Western Front.

The War on the Western Front was mostly Fought in Trenches

In the autumn of 1914, the Germans and the Allies realised that they couldn't beat each other outright. Instead of retreating, they built a line of trenches that stretched through northern France to the coast of Belgium. These trench lines were developed throughout the war, but their position mostly stayed the same.

1) In July 1916, the British tried to break through the German line in an area called the Somme — lots of lives were lost during this offensive.
2) In 1917, mines were used at Arras and Ypres to break through the enemy line (see p.34) — the aim was to avoid losses like those at the Somme by making it easier for the infantry to attack the enemy trenches.
3) The army also tried to improve medical care after the casualties of the Somme overwhelmed medical staff. In 1917, more medical posts were set up to prepare for casualties before a big offensive on the Ypres Salient.

On the first day of the Battle of the Somme, there were almost 60,000 British casualties — 20,000 of these were killed. There were only 174 Medical Officers treating tens of thousands of serious casualties in the first week of the battle. Many men died because they had to wait for days before being treated.

During the Third Battle of Ypres, from July to November 1917, there were over 200,000 casualties. This time, there were 379 Medical Officers, so many men were treated earlier than those at the Somme.

A salient is where one side's line pushes into the other side's line — their territory gets surrounded by the enemy on three sides.

4) By April 1917, the Germans had retreated to the Hindenburg line. In November 1917 at the Battle of Cambrai, the Allies broke its defences with tanks, but they lost this ground again later. There were about 45,000 British casualties — fewer than at the Somme, but still a high number.

Before the Battle of Cambrai, a blood bank was set up by Captain Robertson (see p.38) — he realised that it would be easier to save lives during the battle if they had a ready supply of blood.

Ypres
BELGIUM
The Ypres Salient
Arras
The Hindenburg Line
Cambrai
FRANCE
The Somme

The Western Front in 1916-1917

Trenches were Designed to Protect Soldiers from Enemy Attack

1) Most trenches were dug down into the ground and their upper level was fortified with sandbags. In wet areas, trenches were built upwards using sandbags full of clay — these were called 'breastworks'. Ideally, trenches were about six or seven feet deep.
2) Trenches were constructed by 'entrenching' (lots of soldiers in a line digging straight into the ground), 'sapping' (one man digging outwards from the end of the trench) or 'tunnelling' (like sapping, but a layer of earth was left along the top of the trench until it was finished).

Mounds of earth were built from the side of the trench to split it into sections — these were called 'traverses'.

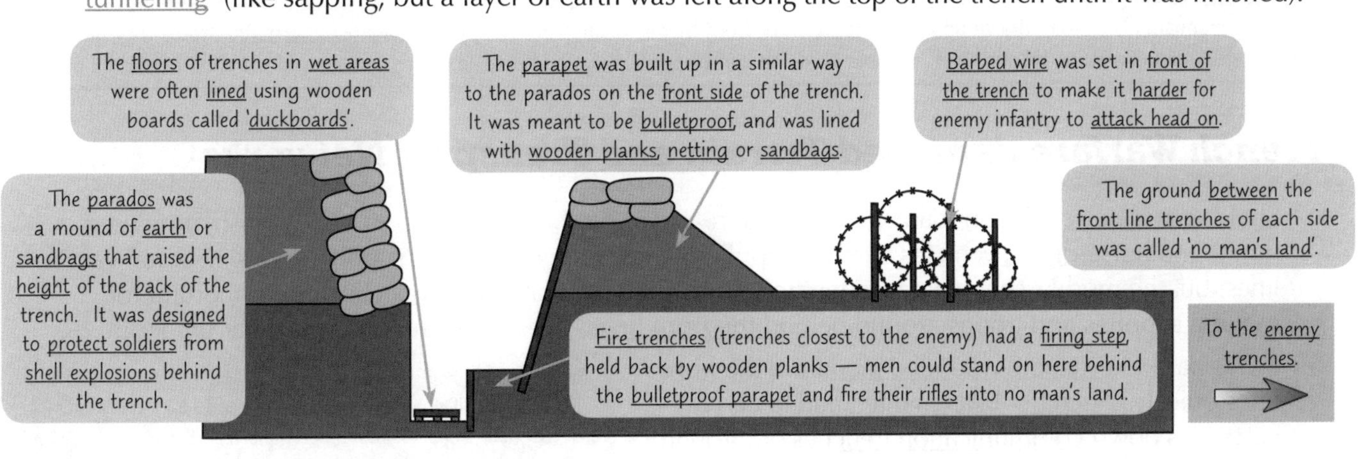

Trench warfare was new to everyone...

Write down a quick description of the following features and explain how they helped to protect soldiers from the enemy: breastworks, parapet, parados, firing step, barbed wire.

Trench Warfare on the Western Front

Trench systems were expanded during the war — this had a big impact on the terrain of the Western Front.

Trenches were often Organised in Parallel Lines

According to one 1916 training manual, trenches were ideally built in three parallel lines.

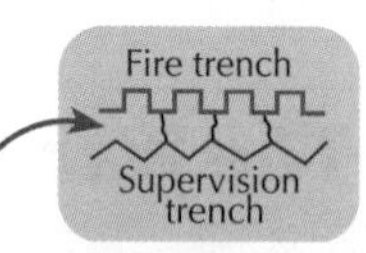

'Saps' were small trenches that pushed out into no man's land.

The front line had two trenches. The 'fire trench' faced the enemy. The 'supervision trench' was used to move along the line behind the fire trench. They had zig-zag or step-shaped sections separated by traverses (p.33). This stopped enemy infantry from firing along the trench, and contained explosions from shells in small areas.

The 'support trench' was about 60 to 90 metres behind the front trench — this protected it from shell bombardment aimed at the front line. It was connected to the front line trench by communication trenches — soldiers could retreat to the support trench, and the support trench reinforced the front line.

Communication trenches connected the trench lines to each other and to local roads and army depots behind the lines.

The 'reserve trench' was about 350 to 550 metres behind the front line. It was made up of dugouts (shelters that protected 4 to 6 men) or lines of trenches. Reinforcements waited here so they could counter enemy attacks.

Comment and Analysis

This image shows an ideal trench system. In reality, building such organised trenches was hard — they might be built quickly as troops advanced. Terrain had to be considered too. Trench maps drawn during the war show that the lines were often far more complicated.

Underground Warfare was a Key Feature of the Western Front

Both sides tunnelled under no man's land to reach enemy trenches. It was dangerous for tunnellers, who could be buried, suffocate or meet the enemy, but it was less costly than a normal infantry attack through no man's land.

In 1916, the Allies built a tunnel network under Arras by extending existing caves, quarries and mines — it had electricity, accommodation and a hospital (p.35). In April 1917, it was used to hide 24,000 men before the Battle of Arras. Tunnels were dug up to the German line so men could reach the enemy trenches in safety — the entrances were blown open with mines at the start of the battle. Lots of ground was won on the first day. However, the British suffered over 150,000 casualties during the battle.

At the Battle of Messines on the Ypres Salient in June 1917, 19 mines were blown up under the German line. Around 10,000 German soldiers died instantly. Two of the mines were used to destroy defences on hills — Hill 60 and the Caterpillar. They would have been hard to attack head on without heavy losses.

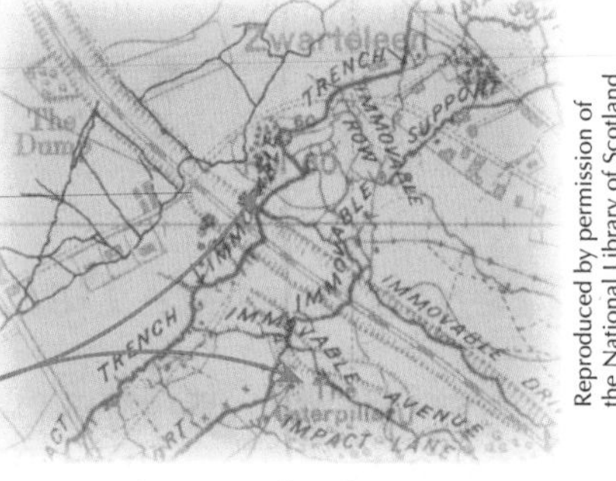

A trench map of Hill 60 and the Caterpillar in April 1917. German trenches are red and British are blue.

Comment and Analysis

Trench maps are a good source for studying the layout of trenches and their defences. They're more realistic than the ideal layout in training manuals. They were drawn up using photos taken from the air. Teams on the ground collected information too. They don't always give the full picture, though. For example, machine gun placements were often deliberately hidden and could be missed by planes.

Trench Warfare damaged Terrain and Transport Networks

1) Shelling and entrenchment damaged roads and terrain on the Western Front. The British army used motor and horse-drawn vehicles to move supplies towards the Front from 'supply dumps' near railway lines, but the muddy, shell-damaged terrain was hard to negotiate. Railways became important for moving supplies and troops around behind the front lines, but they weren't always near the Front.

By 1917, the British had built a light railway network behind the lines (other Allied armies had done this already). This made it easier to move supplies, ammunition and men through muddy and damaged terrain, and to evacuate wounded men from the Front.

2) It was hard to evacuate wounded men from the front lines quickly. Stretcher bearers often had to carry casualties down communication trenches or through a series of relay posts — this delayed wound treatment.

I'll never complain about potholes again...

Write down the advantages and disadvantages of using trench maps to study trench systems.

The RAMC and the FANY

The fighting on the Western Front disrupted local transport networks. The British Army were supported by various medical units who treated wounded men and evacuated them from the front line.

The Royal Army Medical Corps (RAMC) ran Field Ambulances

1) Moving casualties away from the Front to be treated was a problem — the terrain had become very muddy.
2) The RAMC Field Ambulances (these were units, not vehicles) set up mobile medical stations. Stretcher bearers carried casualties through a series of relay posts until they reached a medical post or somewhere they could be moved by road, rail or river.

Field Ambulance transport included:
- Teams of stretcher bearers.
- Horses, wagons and carts.
- Motor ambulances (the RAMC started using these in 1915).

The RAMC Field Ambulances created the Chain of Evacuation

Men were more likely to survive if their wounds were treated quickly. The RAMC developed a system to move wounded men who had a chance of surviving to medical areas — this was called 'the Chain of Evacuation'.

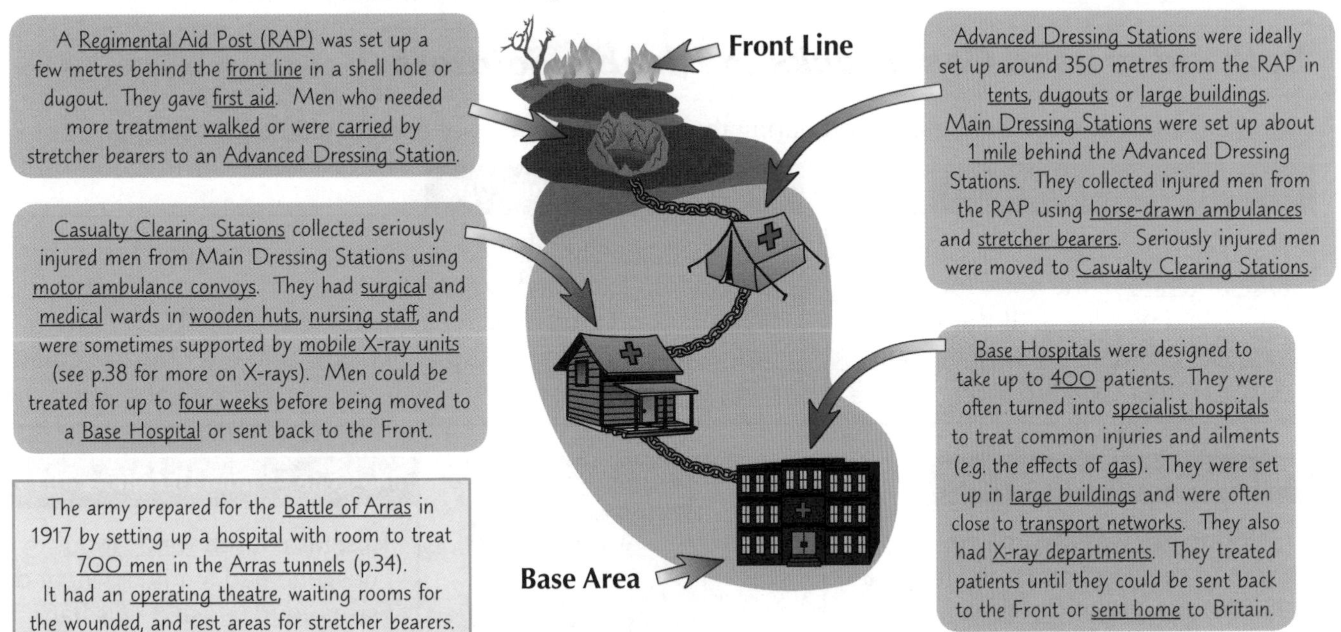

A Regimental Aid Post (RAP) was set up a few metres behind the front line in a shell hole or dugout. They gave first aid. Men who needed more treatment walked or were carried by stretcher bearers to an Advanced Dressing Station.

Advanced Dressing Stations were ideally set up around 350 metres from the RAP in tents, dugouts or large buildings. Main Dressing Stations were set up about 1 mile behind the Advanced Dressing Stations. They collected injured men from the RAP using horse-drawn ambulances and stretcher bearers. Seriously injured men were moved to Casualty Clearing Stations.

Casualty Clearing Stations collected seriously injured men from Main Dressing Stations using motor ambulance convoys. They had surgical and medical wards in wooden huts, nursing staff, and were sometimes supported by mobile X-ray units (see p.38 for more on X-rays). Men could be treated for up to four weeks before being moved to a Base Hospital or sent back to the Front.

Base Hospitals were designed to take up to 400 patients. They were often turned into specialist hospitals to treat common injuries and ailments (e.g. the effects of gas). They were set up in large buildings and were often close to transport networks. They also had X-ray departments. They treated patients until they could be sent back to the Front or sent home to Britain.

The army prepared for the Battle of Arras in 1917 by setting up a hospital with room to treat 700 men in the Arras tunnels (p.34). It had an operating theatre, waiting rooms for the wounded, and rest areas for stretcher bearers.

The FANY provided Transport Services to the Allied Armies

1) The women of the First Aid Nursing Yeomanry Corps (FANY) were trained in first aid, veterinary skills, signalling and driving. They mainly worked as a field ambulance, moving wounded men between base hospitals, medical posts, trains, barges and hospital ships. The FANY staffed two key ambulance convoys — the Calais Convoy and the St. Omer Convoy.

One FANY driver called Beryl Hutchinson who was part of the St. Omer Convoy described her role in her memoirs. She had to pick up wounded men from trains and drive them to base hospitals or to boats that would take them back to Britain. The driving skills of the FANY were pretty useful when it came to transporting men who were very badly wounded — they had to drive as smoothly as possible so that the men wouldn't be jolted around. Canal barges were used to move the worst cases.

The driving skills of the FANY were very useful to the army, as they needed to move supplies, wounded men and rations between coastal ports and the front line.

2) The FANY had many roles. They ran a mobile soup kitchen and a mobile bathing vehicle, staffed hospitals and convalescent homes, ran a hospital canteen and organised concerts for the troops.

The army really liked their acronyms...

You need to know the system that the army used to move men away from the Front. Scribble down a quick diagram of the Chain of Evacuation and label it.

Conditions in the Trenches

Life in the trenches exposed soldiers to lots of illnesses and infections — they were also at risk of gas attacks.

Bad Conditions in the Trenches caused Illness

1) Soldiers were exposed to the weather in the trenches. Many suffered from exposure to the cold and frostbite, especially in the cold winter of 1916-17.
2) Trench foot was a condition caused by standing in flooded trenches for too long. Skin and tissue on the feet broke down. It could become gangrenous (infected) — doctors used amputation to stop the gangrene from spreading.
3) Dysentery caused diarrhoea and dehydration. Dirty water and unhygienic latrines (holes about 4 or 5 feet deep that served as toilets) helped this disease to spread.
4) The trenches were also full of vermin that spread diseases, like rats, lice, maggots and flies. Trench fever and typhus were spread by body lice — it could take 12 weeks to recover.

Trench foot was more common at the start of the war. By 1915, there were fewer cases, as soldiers had to change their socks frequently. They also put whale oil on their feet to create a waterproof layer.

Doctors didn't make the link between lice and trench fever until 1918. Delousing stations were set up to try and stop outbreaks of these diseases, but they weren't always successful. It was hard to remove lice eggs from soldiers' clothing.

Both sides used Gas Attacks to Disable Soldiers

Four main types of gas were weaponised during the war — the effects of each could be devastating.

Lachrimatory Gas — from 1914

Also known as tear gas. It caused inflammation of the nose, throat and lungs, and blindness. It was meant to disable soldiers or force them to retreat, rather than kill them.

Mustard Gas — from July 1917

A 'blistering agent' that caused blisters, burning and breathing difficulties. Extended exposure to mustard gas could cause blindness and lung infections. It ate away at the body from the inside, and it could take up to five weeks to die. The gas could cling to clothes for hours, which put medical staff at risk too.

Chlorine Gas — from April 1915

Chlorine gas was the first deadly gas used on the Western Front. It was a 'killing agent' that slowly suffocated its victims. A medical officer for the French described its effects at Ypres.

"...I felt the action of the gas on my respiratory system; it burned in my throat, caused pains in my chest, and made breathing all but impossible. I spat blood and suffered from dizziness. We all thought we were lost."
(April 1915)

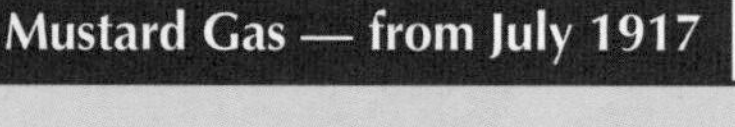

Phosgene — from December 1915

This gas caused suffocation. Phosgene had a mild scent and was colourless, so it was hard to detect. It could take over 24 hours for symptoms to set in.

Trench Warfare could also cause Emotional Trauma

1) In the trenches, soldiers were exposed to lots of death, destruction and artillery bombardment. Living in these harsh conditions could cause a psychological illness called shell shock.
2) Symptoms of shell shock could include tiredness, blindness, hearing loss, shaking and mental breakdown. Doctors disagreed over whether it was caused by unseen physical injuries or by emotional trauma.

Comment and Analysis

'Shell shock' meant two different things:

1) When an explosion shocked the central nervous system, causing brain damage.
2) An emotional disorder caused by the traumatic trench environment.

After the Battle of the Somme in 1916, there was an increase in shell shock cases — doctors started to evacuate these cases to specialist hospitals. However, the emotional trauma caused by trench warfare wasn't really understood until later in the war — even then, many with shell shock were seen as cowards.

The trenches were pretty horrific...

You'll need to be able to explain how you'd use sources to study a historical problem. Think about the kind of sources you could use to study the effects of gas attacks and how they're useful.

Wounds and Injuries

Trench warfare caused horrific injuries on a scale doctors had not seen before the war.

Soldiers were often Wounded by Gunfire and Shell Explosions

1) Machine guns and rifles caused gunshot wounds, bruises, fractured bones and organ damage.
2) Trenches often protected the body, but the head was exposed — the army were alarmed at the number and severity of head injuries. They saw injuries like shrapnel embedded in the brain, skull fractures, large scalp cuts and brain damage. In 1915, metal 'Brodie' helmets were issued. Before this, many head injuries were fatal. The helmets gave soldiers a better chance of surviving, but treatment was still limited.

American surgeon Dr Harvey Cushing treated head injuries during the war. He pioneered new surgical techniques that were still being used in the 1970s. His techniques halved the number of deaths caused by brain surgery during the war. He used X-rays to find shrapnel in the brain and drew it out using magnets. His efforts were limited by slow evacuation and lack of brain imaging techniques.

3) Shrapnel (metal objects and fragments from explosions) caused horrific facial injuries and could kill instantly. Shrapnel shells were blown open in the air using a small fuse — they were filled with bullets and metal balls which flew out and hit soldiers. Other shells were designed to explode violently — the cases of these high explosive shells broke into large jagged pieces of shrapnel that tore through flesh.

Dr Harold Gillies, a British surgeon, treated serious facial injuries at Queen Mary's Hospital in Sidcup during and after the war. He developed a plastic surgery technique called the tube pedicle, which made skin grafting and facial reconstruction more effective.

4) Soldiers could also get concussions from shell explosions, be hit by flying debris, buried under collapsed buildings and trenches or poisoned by carbon monoxide from blasts which then collected in air pockets.

Wound Infection was a Big Problem

1) Many trenches were dug in farmland, which was covered in bacteria from fertilisers. In Flanders, drainage ditches had been destroyed by shelling, so trenches were often waterlogged and bacteria thrived.
2) The ground was also infected by unhygienic latrines and thousands of bodies that were left to decompose or were buried in shallow graves near the trenches.
3) Wounded men often had to lie in the contaminated mud of trenches or no man's land for hours or days before being picked up by stretcher bearers. They were at risk of getting serious infections like tetanus and gas gangrene — these were fatal without treatment. Infections could also cause sepsis.

"...there were numerous dug outs, and these so filthy that our men could not occupy them, the bottom of the trenches were paved with dead all German so far as we could learn, and very badly decomposed..."
Extract from the 10th Canadian Battalion's war diary describing conditions in a French trench on the Ypres Salient in April 1915.

"...every gunshot wound of this war in France and Belgium is more or less infected at the moment of its infliction... mud and dirt pervade everything; and bacteriological investigations of the soil, of the clothing, and of the skin demonstrate the presence of the most dangerous pathogenic organisms in all three."
Extract from a 1916 lecture by British Army surgeon Sir Anthony Bowlby.

Comment and Analysis

Doctors like Bowlby realised that every wound was likely to be infected. This was a big problem for the army, as those with only minor injuries were still at risk of dying from a fatal infection.

There were a Few Ways to Fight Infection at the Start of the War

1) Anti-tetanus serum was given to injured soldiers on the front line to prevent tetanus.
2) Wounds were thoroughly washed in an antiseptic solution called carbolic lotion, closed up and wrapped in bandages soaked in carbolic acid.
3) A paraffin paste called Bipp was used to cover wounds to prevent infection.
4) Before antibiotics were discovered in the 1920s, amputation of wounded arms, legs, hands or feet was a common way to stop life-threatening infections from spreading.

I'm feeling a bit squeamish now...

How useful are the Canadian war diary entry and the account of Sir Anthony Bowlby for studying illnesses and infections that were linked to living conditions in the trenches? [8]

Developments in Surgery and Medicine

During the war, doctors developed new techniques for dealing with serious injuries and infections.

The number of Deaths from Wound Infection was Reduced

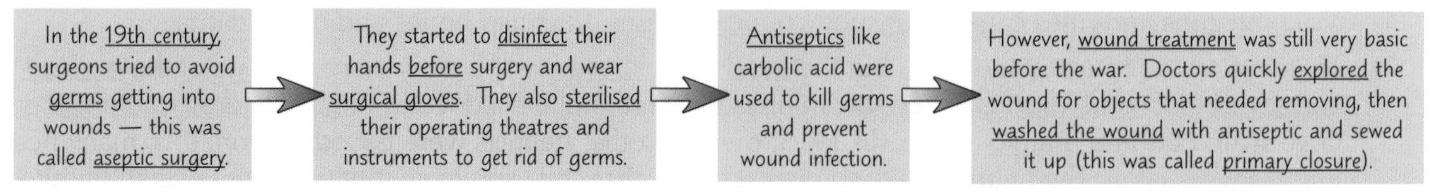

During the war, a Belgian doctor called Antoine Depage developed a better way to treat wounds. He treated every wound as if it was already infected. There were two main steps in his treatment:

1) The wound was properly and thoroughly explored and objects like shrapnel or bits of clothing were removed. Depage also realised that removing all damaged tissue and then washing the wound with antiseptic decreased the chance of infection.
2) Depage left the wound open to the air for about 24 to 48 hours. Next, he looked at a swab of the wound under a microscrope to check for bacteria. If the wound wasn't infected, then he closed it up — this was called delayed primary closure.

In 1915, Alexis Carrel and Henry Dakin developed a new way to prevent infection. Dakin created an antiseptic solution that could be flushed into a wound using rubber tubes before closure — this technique was called irrigation. Depage used this method as part of his wound treatment.

Comment and Analysis

These improvements in wound treatment saved many men from having amputations just to stop infections from spreading. Allied surgeons also used these techniques to improve the chances of surviving an amputation.

Fracture Treatment was improved by X-Rays and Splints

1) Wilhelm Roentgen discovered X-rays in 1895. During the war, hospitals used X-ray machines to find broken bones and shrapnel.
2) The British had 528 X-ray units — 14 of these were mobile units. They took mobile X-ray machines and radiographers to casualty clearing stations, so men could be treated closer to the front line.

Before X-ray machines, surgeons had to look for shrapnel by hand, putting their patients at risk of infection. X-ray machines made aseptic surgery more effective, because the surgeon didn't have to touch the wound to find shrapnel and bone fragments.

3) At the start of the war, 80% of men who suffered a fractured femur (thigh bone) in the trenches died. A surgeon called Robert Jones treated this injury using the Thomas splint.
4) The Thomas splint was strapped around the broken leg before the casualty was moved. This stopped the leg from moving, so that it was protected from more damage. By 1915, only 20% of soldiers with this kind of injury died.

In 1917, Robert Jones released a book (influenced by his war experience) advising doctors in Britain on how to treat complicated shoulder, leg, arm, spinal and pelvic fractures. It explained how to use splints to treat certain fractures.

Blood Transfusions were used to treat Blood Loss

1) Blood loss caused many deaths during the war. British doctors transfused blood from one person to another (direct transfusion), but it was a slow process and not always successful.
2) A new method called the syringe-cannula technique was developed. Doctors took blood from a donor using a needle and syringe and transfused it into their patient quickly. It was tricky to carry out, as blood could clot in the syringe.
3) In 1917, a US Army doctor called Captain Oswald Robertson argued that it would be better to collect blood before it was needed. As a result, the first blood bank was set up in preparation for the Battle of Cambrai in 1917.

In 1914, it was discovered that adding sodium citrate to blood stopped clotting so it could be stored. In 1916, blood was added to a citrate glucose solution, so it could be stored on ice for about 10 to 14 days.

War doctors set the stage for modern medicine...

Describe two characteristics of the treatment of infected wounds on the Western Front. [4]

EXAM QUESTION

Revision Summary

You've made it through the whole section — now it's time to test your mettle on some revision questions.

- Try these questions and tick off each one when you get it right.
- When you've done all the questions for a topic and are completely happy with it, tick off the topic.

Trench Warfare on the Western Front (p.33-34)

1) Name four key places on the British sector of the Western Front.
2) Give three defensive features of a trench.
3) What was a traverse?
4) What were communication trenches used for?
5) Give two features of a reserve trench.
6) Why were mines used at the Battle of Messines to destroy Hill 60?

The RAMC and the FANY (p.35)

7) Give three types of transport used by the RAMC.
8) Why was it hard for the RAMC to move wounded men away from the front line?
9) Write down two features of Casualty Clearing Stations.
10) Where was the underground hospital that was built by the Allies?
11) Name three things that the FANY did during the war.

Conditions in the Trenches (p.36)

12) Name three illnesses caused by poor conditions in the trenches.
13) Why was trench foot less common by 1915?
14) Describe the effects of mustard gas.
15) How did phosgene kill?
16) Name one place where chlorine gas was used during the war.
17) Give three symptoms of shell shock.

Wounds and Injuries (p.37)

18) Why were Brodie helmets issued in 1915?
19) What did Dr Harold Gillies work on during the war?
20) Name three kinds of injuries that might be caused by a shell explosion.
21) Give two reasons why soil on the Western Front was contaminated.
22) Name two serious wound infections that soldiers were at risk of on the Western Front.
23) How was carbolic acid used as an antiseptic?

Developments in Surgery and Medicine (p.38)

24) What was aseptic surgery?
25) Describe Depage's two-step approach to wound treatment.
26) Why did X-ray machines improve aseptic surgery?
27) What was the Thomas Splint?
28) Name two methods of blood transfusion used during the war.
29) What did Captain Oswald Robertson do before the Battle of Cambrai?

Exam Skills

Now you've made it through all of the horrible details (phew!), it's time to think about how to use all of your lovely knowledge in the exam. This page tells you what you can expect in the exam and how to deal with it.

You'll be asked to Write About the Key Features of your Site

In the exam, you'll need to be able to identify and talk about the key features of your site.

Key features of a historical site are any details, characteristics or unique features that stand out and make the site, or part of it, special. They are the main or most important characteristics of the site. For example, the layout and organisation of the trenches, trench conditions, illnesses and injuries caused by trench warfare, and the chain of evacuation are all key features of the Western Front.

1) You'll be asked to describe two different features of a certain aspect of the Western Front.
2) To get all four marks, you'll need to identify two features and then give a little bit of extra information that's relevant to each one.

You only need to talk about two key features — writing about more won't get you any extra marks.

Give a description of **two** features of Base Hospitals on the Western Front. [4 marks]

Base Hospitals could treat up to 400 men at a time. They were set up in big buildings in towns.

Identify a feature, then add some supporting information that gives a bit more detail.

Base Hospitals were set up near major river and railway networks. They collected men from trains and barges.

Make sure your supporting information is linked to the feature that you've talked about.

There'll also be a Question about the Usefulness of Sources

In the exam, you'll be given two sources and asked to decide how useful they are for answering a question about your historic site. Here are some tips on how to analyse the usefulness of a source.

Have a look at p.40-41 for more tips on answering the source questions in the exam.

1) Think about the source's provenance (where it's from) and how that might affect its usefulness. There are three main things to think about when you're analysing provenance.

Nature — what is the source (e.g. a photo, a document)? What can it tell us?
Origin — where and when was the source created? Is it contemporary?
Purpose — who created the source and why did they create it?

2) Think about the strengths and weaknesses of each source. Some sources are more useful than others, depending on their provenance and the kind of information that you're trying to find out.
3) Analyse the sources by picking out key details and explaining what each source can and can't tell you. Think about how useful these details are for answering the question.
4) Use your knowledge of the historic site to put the sources into context — use what you know to decide how typical the information in the source is.
5) Make a judgement about how useful the sources are for answering the question. Base your judgement on the results of your analysis and your own knowledge.

Don't just bring in random bits of information — make sure you stick to stuff that's relevant to the question.

In 2008, a man broke 46 toilet seats with his head in one minute...

Random facts are fun, but they're also pretty useless if you're trying to pick up marks in the exam. Study all of the key features of your site — it'll help you to answer the questions with the most relevant examples.

Types of Sources

When you're talking about the usefulness of sources, it's a good idea to think about what that source can and can't tell you. Some types of sources will give you information that other types of sources don't.

Different Types of Document have different Uses

Documents are written sources that contain information or evidence.

1) Documents like official records or government reports are useful if you're looking for statistics or factual information about your site and the people who used it.
2) There's often a date attached to official documents too, so you can tell exactly when the source was written. This is useful if you're looking for evidence that's linked to a particular time in your site's history.
3) Documents can be quite one-sided, and it's not always obvious who wrote them, so it can be hard to decide how reliable they are. This affects how useful the source is, as it's hard to judge how reliable the facts in the document are.

Documents
- Official Records
- Government Reports
- Diaries and Letters

Documentary sources for the Western Front include diaries, letters, medical records, official reports written by RAMC and army officers, hospital admission records and government reports.

4) Record collections are useful if you're trying to spot patterns or work out how typical a piece of evidence you've found might be. Lots of records are based on forms that ask for certain facts or information about a person, so they're really useful for comparing the experiences of different people.

Field Ambulance hospital admission records were based on forms. They sometimes used a wound classification code to show what type of wound a soldier had — these records are useful for working out which kinds of wounds were the most common.

First-hand Accounts can be More Personal

1) First-hand accounts are really useful for finding out what it was like to live in a particular place. They often reveal details about a historic site that less personal sources don't mention.
2) It's important to look at the provenance (p.39) of first-hand accounts.

A trench map can't tell you what it felt like to be on the front line, but a diary entry or memoir extract that describes life at the Front can give a really good idea of how it felt. Personal accounts can be one-sided, though, so they're only useful as evidence of the experiences of the person who wrote them.

- A diary entry written as events were happening might be more accurate than a memoir or autobiography written years later, as it's easy to forget details, or focus on some more than others.
- An official account has a different purpose to a personal account. They're more useful if you're looking for technical details or if you want to know about the priorities of the people in charge.

First-hand Accounts
- Diaries or Memoirs
- First-hand Reports
- Autobiographies
- Oral Accounts

Image Sources can Show what a site Looked Like

1) Maps and plans are useful sources for looking at how a site was laid out and organised. Maps covering large areas are useful for putting the site into a wider context. Maps of a specific part or physical feature of a site can give a detailed picture of how the site looked and worked.
2) Photos give a snapshot of what a historic site looked like at a particular time. Photos don't always tell the whole story, though. Every photograph is taken by a photographer who chooses what to focus on and what to leave out.

Image Sources
- Photographs
- Maps
- Plans
- Diagrams
- Artwork

Some photos of soldiers on the Western Front were posed so that journalists could use them in magazines. They showed an idealised version of life in the trenches. When you're analysing a photo to decide how useful it is, it's a good idea to use your own knowledge to decide whether it's giving a typical or accurate picture.

Some sources are more useful for putting on chips...

Different types of source are better for answering certain questions. Think about what the source was originally designed to do or say — this'll help you to decide how useful it is for answering your question.

Analysing Sources

This page shows you how to analyse a source for usefulness — there are a few key things to remember.

You'll be given Two Sources and asked to Analyse their Usefulness

In the exam, there'll be a question that asks you to analyse two different sources and decide how useful they are for carrying out an enquiry. Both of the sources will be contemporary and at least one will be written.

How useful are these two sources for studying the problems involved in managing wound infection on the Western Front? [8 marks]

The question will sound something like this.

Analyse the Provenance of the Sources and Say Why It Matters

It's important to look at provenance (p.39), as it can affect the usefulness of a source:

1) Knowing who wrote a source and why will help you to decide how reliable it might be. If the author had a reason to lie, leave out details or exaggerate them, then the usefulness of the source is affected.
2) It's important to work out the original purpose of the source — think about what kind of information it was meant to get across and whether this limits its usefulness for answering your question.

For example, a medical article about wound infection in British hospitals might be useful for understanding different types of wound infection, but it might not give any information about the specific problems that were caused by the conditions on the Western Front. This would limit its usefulness.

Talk about the Strengths and Weaknesses of Each Source

A key strength of Source A is that it's a diary that incudes dates. It says when the soldier was diagnosed with a septic cut, and when he was in hospital, which shows how long it took for him to be moved to a place where his wound infection could be treated.

Source A

Apl 27 Germans sent over gas shells which burst 200 yards away. Sent out thick yellow smoke which rolled along like a fog bank, the wind driving it away. Went to doctor to see about a cut on the ankle. He said it was septic and sent me to hospital.
Apl 28 In hospital. Plenty of company, wounded coming in all the time.

From the war diary of John French, written in 1916

A weakness of this source is that it only shows one man's personal experience of being treated for wound infection. It doesn't tell you very much about the wider treatment of wound infection throughout the Western Front.

Use your Own Knowledge to put Key Details into Context

This extract talks about an infection that caused problems on the Western Front — gas gangrene. It was written two years after Alexis Carrel and Henry Dakin developed their irrigation technique to treat wound infection.

Source B

That the septic character of wounds is disastrous is also well known. During the early hours, or the first few days, the wound is exposed to the danger of gas-producing infection. Later are developed the various infections, which, either in the seat of fracture, in joints laid open, or in extensive lacerations of soft parts, sometimes give rise to lesions leading to amputation or to death.

Extract from 'The Treatment of Infected Wounds', written by Alexis Carrel and Georges Dehelly in 1917

Bring in some relevant knowledge, then use it to make a judgement about the source.

The source is useful, as it shows that wound infection was still a big issue in 1917, even after Carrel and Dakin's efforts.

Barbecue sauce has no weaknesses...

Source analysis might sound a bit complicated, but it's not so bad once you've practised the skills on this page. Make sure you support the points you make with your own knowledge and stuff from the sources.

Historical Enquiries

In the last bit of the exam, you get to use all of your lovely source analysis skills to design a historical enquiry.

The Last Question will ask you to Plan a Historical Enquiry

1) Once you've decided how useful your two sources are (p.41), then you'll be asked to explain how you'd use one of the sources to find out more about the issue in the first part of the question.
2) You'll be asked for four pieces of information — you'll get a mark for each one.

Identify a Detail in the Source that you'd like to Investigate

How could you follow up Source A to find out more about the problems involved in managing wound infection on the Western Front? [4 marks]

Source A

Apl 27 Germans sent over gas shells which burst 200 yards away. Sent out thick yellow smoke which rolled along like a fog bank, the wind driving it away. Went to doctor to see about a cut on the ankle. He said it was septic and sent me to hospital.
Apl 28 In hospital. Plenty of company, wounded coming in all the time.

From the war diary of John French, written in 1916

Read the question and work out what it wants you to investigate — this'll help you to pick your detail.

This bit of the source is a good starting point if you want to follow up on the topic of wound infection — it mentions a small septic wound, but it doesn't give very much information about it.

Decide what Questions still need to be Answered

1) Next, you'll need to create a question that will help you find out a bit more information about the detail that you've picked out.
2) Your question should help you to follow up on the issue that's been identified in the exam question.

Was infection in small wounds a big issue for hospitals on the Western Front?

Make sure your question is linked to the detail that you identified.

Identify which Type of Source you'd use to Answer your Question

After you've written a question, you'll need to say which type of source you could use to answer it.

1) Start by thinking about what kind of information you need to answer your question.
2) For example, the question above is designed to find out how common infection in small wounds was — in other words, it's questioning whether the soldier's experience in Source A is part of a bigger problem.
3) To answer this, you need to know how many soldiers were sent to hospital with septic wounds. A good source to use would be hospital admission records that say why each soldier was admitted to hospital.

Explain How the Source will help you to Answer the Question

It's a good idea to think about the strengths of the source and why it would be useful for your enquiry.

This source would show how common it was for soldiers to be admitted to hospital with small infected wounds, which would help me to see how much pressure this put on Western Front hospitals.

Hospital admission records would be very useful for finding out how many men were admitted to particular field hospitals with septic wounds. You could use these records to work out whether septic wounds were a big issue compared to other medical problems and injuries.

Be a historian for a day...

This question is like being a historian for a day (well... okay... more like for a few minutes). It's a bit more straightforward than the source analysis question — follow the four steps on this page and you'll ace it.

Exam Skills for the Period Study

These two pages are all about how to tackle the period study section of your exam.

Period Studies are all about how Events Unfolded

1) The period study covers a short period of history — usually around 50-60 years. It focuses on the different events that took place during that time, as well as why events unfolded in the way they did.
2) You'll have to know all about the key turning points of the period you're studying, and the actions of key individuals.
3) You should also have a good knowledge of the context in which these events happened — for example, the nature of the societies involved, and what problems people faced. This will give you a better understanding of what happened, and help you to make judgements about the importance of events.
4) You'll be expected to make connections between events. You must have a good grasp of cause and effect — you'll need to know what led to significant events and what their consequences were.

There are Three basic types of exam question

1) You'll be asked to explain two consequences of an important development during the period, for example a significant event or a treaty.

The First Transcontinental Railroad was completed in 1869. Explain two consequences of this event. [8 marks]

2) The next question will ask you to write an account of something — this means you'll have to describe what happened and analyse the links between the various events that took place — e.g. causes, consequences and change.

Give an account that analyses the key events between 1985 and 1989 that led to the fall of the Berlin Wall. [8 marks]

In question type 2), you'll be given some 'stimulus points' — hints about things you could include in your answer. You don't have to include details about these stimulus points, so don't panic if you can't remember much about them. Even if you do write about the stimulus points, you must add other information too — if you don't, you can't get full marks.

3) The third question will always ask you about the importance of particular developments in relation to wider issues. Think about what changed as a result of the development and how it influenced attitudes. You'll need to write about two developments out of the three that are listed in the question.

Explain how important the formation of NATO (1949) was to relations between the Soviet Union and the USA. [8 marks]

Each part of Question 3 is worth 8 marks, so you can earn 16 marks in total.

Remember these things for All the questions

1) For all these questions you need to show how particular aspects of the period helped contribute to the events you're describing.
2) Always use detailed and relevant information to support any point you make. Including specific dates, names and statistics shows the examiner you have a good knowledge and understanding of the period.
3) Your answer should be well organised and structured — each of your points should lead clearly to your conclusion. For question type 2) you should show the sequence of events that led to an outcome.

For more general advice on how to answer exam questions, see p.135.

Exam Skills for the Period Study

Here are some sample answers to questions in the period study section of your exam.

Have a look at this Sample Answer

This sample answer will give you an idea of how to explain the consequences of a development from your period study. The comments below will help you to structure your answer.

The First Transcontinental Railroad was completed in 1869.
Explain two consequences of this event. [8 marks]

One consequence of the completion of the First Transcontinental Railroad was an increase in buffalo hunting. The railroad allowed hunters quick access to the Plains, where they shot buffalo for sport or their hides. The railroad also enabled these hunters to transport the hides back to the east coast to be sold, encouraging more people to make money from hunting buffalo. This increase in buffalo hunting angered the Native Americans, shown by the fact that the US army had to build forts to protect the railroads from Native American attacks.

This first sentence directly addresses the question.

This explains how the consequence was caused by the development of the railroad.

Giving more detail shows a good knowledge of the period.

This is a shortened example — in the exam, you'll need to describe a second consequence.

Here's another Sample Answer to help you

This sample answer will give you an idea of how to write an analytical narrative account. Look at the way it's structured and how the links between different events are explained.

Give an account that analyses the key events between 1985 and 1989 that led to the fall of the Berlin Wall. [8 marks]

In 1985, Mikhail Gorbachev became General Secretary of the Communist Party and fundamentally changed Soviet policy. He created closer ties with US President Reagan, e.g. at the Geneva Summit in 1985, and began withdrawing Soviet troops from Afghanistan in 1988. This helped to reduce tensions between East and West, and brought hope that relations could improve further.

In 1988, Gorbachev abandoned the Brezhnev Doctrine, which had promised that the USSR would intervene in any country where communist regimes were threatened. This meant that countries in Eastern Europe no longer had to fear Soviet aggression if they chose to turn away from communism.

As a result, Hungary felt it could open its border with Austria in May 1989 without fear of military consequences. This caused chaos for the East German government, as thousands of East Germans crossed the border to travel to West Germany. Public opposition to the government grew — in October 1989 there were anti-communist protests in East Germany. As the USSR was now unwilling to give support to struggling communist regimes, the government was forced to give in to public pressure, and opened the Berlin Wall in November 1989.

This evidence to backs up the point.

This analyses the impact of the event that took place by explaining how it affected other countries' attitudes.

This makes it clear that one event led to another.

It's important that you make connections between different events.

History — just one thing after another...

The period studies are pretty short, so you're expected to know lots of details. You'll find events easier to remember if you build up connections between them — plus, it'll get you more marks in the exam.

The Plains Indians

Central North America is dominated by the Great Plains. The Great Plains are mostly a huge, flat expanse of grassland. The Native Americans who lived there were known as the Plains Indians.

The Plains Indians lived in different groups called Tribes

1) The Plains Indians weren't a single group with a single culture — there were many different tribes, such as the Sioux, Comanche and the Apache.
2) Many tribes were nomadic, hunting the millions of buffalo that lived on the Plains. Other tribes were more settled and lived in one place, farming the land.

E.g. The Lakota Sioux, regularly moving from place to place, led a nomadic lifestyle. In contrast, the Mandans farmed and lived in permanent villages.

3) Tribal warfare was common. The aim wasn't necessarily to kill or seize land, but to perform acts of bravery such as stealing horses and counting coup (getting close enough to an enemy to touch him).

The Arapaho and the Kiowa often fought each other.

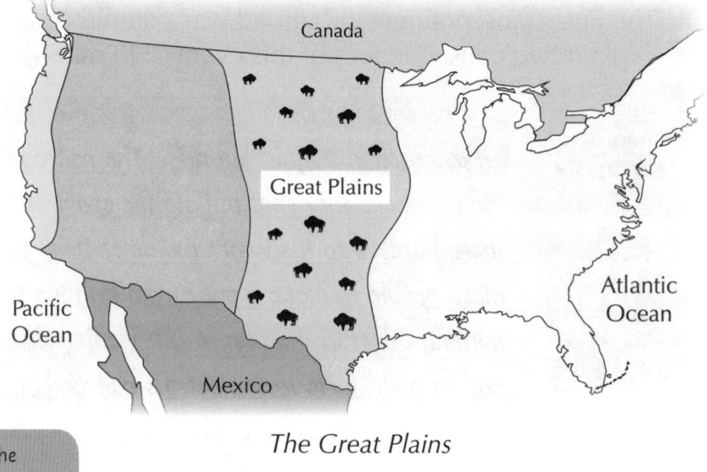

The Great Plains

The Plains Indians led Very Different Lifestyles to white settlers

1) Tribes were usually split into bands, and each band had a chief and a council of elders. The chief didn't have complete control, but he would have earned loyalty over the years by demonstrating courage and generosity — this gave him influence over the tribe.
2) The Native Americans didn't see land as something that could be bought and sold — land belonged to everyone. Even for more settled tribes, agricultural land belonged to the tribe as a whole.
3) Medicine men and medicine women were spiritual leaders of tribes. Native American religion was closely linked with nature — humans were believed to be part of nature, not masters over it. Most tribes believed in a Great Spirit which created the world, and that everything in nature contained spirits which they needed to keep on their side — ceremonies and dance rituals were performed to contact the spirits.
4) Women did most of the work in the village or camp, while the men hunted and fought. Although men were head of the family, women owned the tipi (the family tent) and its contents, which gave them status.

Many tribes practiced polygamy because the dangers of hunting and warfare meant there were often more women than men in tribes.

5) Buffalo were vital for the Plains Indians. They used almost every part of the animal — meat for food, skin for clothing and tents, and bones for weapons and tools.

Hunting became easier when the Plains Indians began to use horses, which were brought over by the Europeans in the 16th century.

Comment and Analysis

Settlers failed to understand the culture of the Plains Indians because it was so different to their own. This led to tension and conflict.

Learn some tribe names and facts about their lifestyles...

You'll need to show that you have a good knowledge of how the Plains Indians lived. You don't need to know all of the tribes — just a couple of examples will do nicely.

The Permanent Indian Frontier

The US government and its citizens wanted to settle the north American continent.
This meant that the Native Americans living on the land would need to be moved elsewhere.

Tribes living in the East were moved onto the Plains

1) US citizens initially lived only on the east coast. Over time, settlements moved westwards and by the 1830s settlers had moved just beyond the Mississippi river, attracted by the fertile farmland there.
2) Since the population was growing, the demand for more land was also increasing.
3) There was a growing belief in government and among US citizens that it was the USA's duty to expand westwards. Thomas Jefferson, a former president, believed that land ownership and farming would create a healthy, moral population. Extra land could only be gained by expanding further west. Expansion promised freedom, independence and opportunity.

A Permanent Indian Frontier was created

1) Some of the land that settlers wanted to farm was occupied by Native American tribes, such as the Cherokee, Creek, Choctaw, Chickasaw and Seminole.
2) Many US citizens saw the Native American way of life as inferior and uncivilised — they wanted them to be moved off the land so that it could be farmed and settled.
3) In 1830, the Indian Removal Act was passed under President Andrew Jackson — this authorised the president to grant tribes land on the Great Plains in exchange for their land in the East.

Before 1830, the government had pursued a policy of assimilating Native Americans in the East into white society — this means making them change their lifestyle to fit in with that of whites. Tribes such as the Cherokee had taken on aspects of white culture as a result — but people still didn't see them as equal.

Some tribes resisted removal. The Cherokees tried to resist through legal means, but they were eventually forcefully marched by US soldiers to the Plains in 1838 — it has been estimated that around 4000 out of 15,000 died on the journey. The Seminoles of Florida fought US soldiers from 1835-1842, but eventually surrendered and moved west.

4) By 1840, most of the eastern tribes had been moved onto the Plains — around 70,000-100,000 people in total.
5) The intention was that Native Americans would live on the Great Plains, while settlers farmed land in the East — the Plains would be like one large Indian reservation. The boundary between the two regions was known as the Permanent Indian Frontier.
6) At this point, white Americans viewed the Plains as 'The Great American Desert' — they believed that its harsh climate and lack of wood and water made it unsuitable for settling.

Settlers began to Encroach on the Plains

1) Gradually, settlers began to move across the Plains towards the west coast, and some began to settle on the eastern edges of the Plains themselves.
2) This created conflict between settlers and the Plains Indians. The Plains Indians didn't like settlers moving across their land, and the two groups couldn't live together — the nomadic culture of the Plains Indians clashed with the desire of settlers to fence off and settle the land.

'Here you are, you can have this lovely desert to live in...'

Make sure you use this page to understand the significance of the Permanent Indian Frontier. It was actually a lot less permanent than the name suggests... more about this later.

Wagons Roll

Settlers made the journey across the Great Plains to the west coast for different reasons.

People went to the west coast in Large Numbers from the 1840s

1) The first people to explore the West were mountain men who hunted animals in the 1820s and 1830s to sell their skins. They didn't settle in the West, but established westward trails that settlers would later use.
2) Missionaries were among the earliest settlers on the west coast in the 1830s. Their aim was to convert the Native Americans there to Christianity.
3) Later, larger groups of people who wanted to make new lives for themselves went to the west coast. The first of these was the Peoria Party in 1839. Others followed in the 1840s — their routes became known as the Oregon and California Trails.

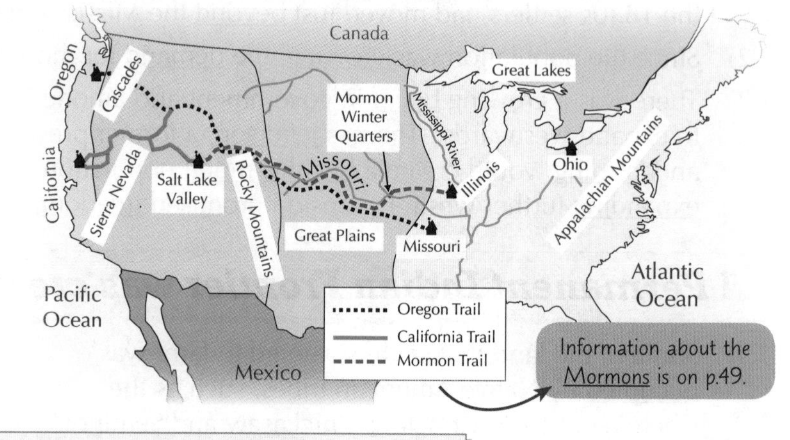

Information about the Mormons is on p.49.

They had many Different Reasons for heading west

The Great Migration of 1843 saw a sudden increase in settlers — a party of around 1000 people moved to the west coast. This was because life in the East was hard, and there was promise of better things in the West.

Problems in the East

- Economic problems — Recession in 1837 caused banks to collapse and businesses to fail. Wages and profits fell and unemployment rose.
- Overpopulation — High levels of European immigration, particularly from Ireland and Germany between 1846-1854, led to overcrowded cities, fewer jobs and a lack of land for people to farm.
- Disease — Overcrowding and poor sanitary systems led to epidemics of yellow fever and cholera.

Comment and Analysis

Reasons why people went west can be split into push and pull factors — things that pushed them out of the East and things that pulled them to the West.

Attraction of the West

- A new start — Land was fertile and cheap.
- Government encouragement — The government passed Acts which allowed settlers to claim land in Oregon — they wanted people to settle in the West to strengthen the USA's claim to the land there.
- Gold — Gold was found at John Sutter's sawmill in California in January 1848. In December, President Polk confirmed that there was gold in the area. In 1849 there was a Gold Rush, as tens of thousands of people made the journey to California, hoping to make their fortune.

In 1841, Congress passed the Distributive Preemption Act, which allowed settlers to buy 160 acres of land for a very low cost if they'd lived there for 14 months.

Only about 8% of early migrants to California during the Gold Rush were women. More followed later as their husbands and families settled in California.

Settlers also moved west because of a belief in 'Manifest Destiny':

- Many US citizens believed that they were destined to occupy and govern all of North America. They saw it as their god-given right.
- They believed they were superior to Native Americans and that they should civilise the continent.

The term 'Manifest Destiny' was coined by John L. O'Sullivan in 1845.

More facts you're destined to learn...

You should be able to make links between the reasons why people went west. For example, there wasn't enough land in the East, but there was promise of fertile land in the West.

EXAM TIP

Wagons Roll

Those crossing the Plains faced a difficult journey. Those who settled on the Plains also had challenges.

The journey to the west coast was Difficult

1) It took around 5 months to complete the 2000 mile journey to the west coast. The journey had to be completed before winter. People travelled in wagons and formed wagon trains with other settlers.
2) The journey was dangerous — as many as 10% would die on the way.
   - There were mountains and rivers to cross — this was difficult with heavy wagons.
   - People suffered from food and water shortages, and diseases such as typhoid and cholera.
   - Accidents were common, such as falling under wagon wheels and accidental shootings.
3) Half of the estimated 100,000 people who went to California during 1849 did so by sea. This journey also took around 5 months and had its own difficulties — crowded conditions, sickness and storms.

In 1846 the Donner Party, heading for California, tried a shortcut but they ended up trapped in deep snow in the Sierra Nevada mountains. Supplies were low and many starved to death. Of the 87 travellers, less than 50 survived... by eating those who had died.

The fact that people were willing to make such a dangerous journey shows how much they wanted to move west.

Mormons experienced Hardships too

1) The Mormons (members of 'The Church of Jesus Christ of Latter Day Saints') also travelled west. They didn't go as far as the west coast — they travelled around 1400 miles to Salt Lake Valley.
2) They left because of religious persecution — many Americans disliked Mormon practices such as polygamy (having more than one wife). The Mormons were attacked and driven from their homes in Ohio. They then fled to Missouri and on to Illinois (see map on p.48).
3) Their leader, Brigham Young, wanted to go further west to Salt Lake Valley to create an independent state where the Mormons could live freely. Conditions in Salt Lake Valley were dry and harsh, but he chose it because he believed that nobody else wanted to live there. It was also part of Mexico, not the US.
4) The Mormons planned to leave Illinois in the spring of 1846, but due to an increase in anti-Mormon violence they had to leave in February. This rushed departure meant that they left supplies behind and were disorganised. Conditions were hard — it was a cold winter and there was deep mud.
5) Their progress was very slow, so they couldn't complete the journey that year. They stayed in Winter Quarters by the Missouri River — by the spring of 1847, about 400 Mormons had died.
6) They set off again in April and organisation improved. They were divided into groups led by captains under the strict overall command of Brigham Young. They finally reached Salt Lake Valley in July.

Although the journey was hard, the Mormons planted crops and built way stations along the trail to feed and help later travellers.

Conditions at Salt Lake Valley were tough. There was a lack of rain, water and wood, and grasshoppers destroyed crops. However, Mormons adapted by digging irrigation ditches and building houses from sod (the top layer of soil, including the grass and its roots).

People began to Settle on the Plains

In the 1850s, people began to see the possibility of settling on the Plains — it wasn't quite the 'Great American Desert' they had thought. In 1854 the government opened up Kansas and Nebraska for settlement — settlers didn't have as far to travel, but living and farming on the Plains would be tough:

- The soil was fertile, but it was covered with a thick layer of sod which was too hard for light ploughs.
- There was little or no wood for building or fuel.
- Lack of water meant crops like maize failed and deep wells had to be dug.
- Wind, extremes of climate, grasshopper plagues and prairie fires often destroyed crops.

For the settlers, heading west was a big risk...

REVISION TASK

Make a list of the difficulties the early migrants faced on their journey west.
Then write a short summary of why the Mormons in particular decided to risk the journey anyway.

Early Reservations

As more and more settlers started to use the Great Plains, tension grew between them and the Plains Indians.

There was a Lack of Understanding between settlers and Indians

1) To settlers, it seemed that the Plains Indians had no system of government, that their warfare was cowardly and their religion just superstition (see p.46).
2) They had different views on land ownership. Native Americans believed that the land was for everyone, but settlers wanted to own, farm and exploit land.
3) Settlers thought that the Plains Indians' nomadic lifestyle was uncivilised and that they wasted the land. Native Americans thought that the settlers ruined the land.

Horace Greeley, a newspaper editor, wrote in 1859 that 'God has given this earth to those who will subdue and cultivate it.'

Native Americans and settlers Increasingly came into Contact

1) Significant numbers of settlers moved beyond the Permanent Indian Frontier and across the Plains to reach lands in the West from 1843. Many more came with the California Gold Rush of 1849.
2) The settlers disrupted buffalo herds which the Plains Indians relied on, and polluted water sources, bringing diseases such as cholera.
3) As a result, Plains Indians became more hostile. They sometimes attacked wagon trains, which increased the settlers' fear and distrust. The settlers also felt threatened by the Indians' inter-tribal conflict.

The Reservation System replaced the Permanent Indian Frontier

1) The government wanted to reduce conflict on the Plains. It decided to concentrate the Plains Indians onto specific areas called reservations — the Indian Appropriations Act (1851) allocated funds to allow this. The Act aimed to encourage the Native Americans to farm and build houses.
2) The Fort Laramie Treaty (1851) was the first attempt to use the Appropriations Act to concentrate the Plains Indians in certain areas. It defined the territory of each tribe to try to minimise inter-tribal conflict.
3) Tribes agreed to remain in their territory, allow settlers to cross the Plains, and allow the government to build roads and forts along the trails. In return, the government promised the tribes that they would have permanent rights to their lands, and that tribes would receive $50,000 of goods a year for 50 years.
4) Neither side kept to the treaty. Not all tribes agreed with it and many didn't even know it existed. The US government didn't keep its side of the deal either — it couldn't ensure settlers kept to the agreement, and in 1852 it reduced the yearly payments from 50 years to 10.

The government didn't allow existing treaties to prevent settlement it was in favour of — it simply negotiated new ones. For example, thousands of people encroached on Cheyenne land in Colorado during the Pike's Peak Gold Rush. The government then negotiated the Fort Wise Treaty, reducing Cheyenne land to make room for white settlers, while the Cheyenne were moved to poor quality land on the Sand Creek Reservation. Some Cheyenne later claimed that they didn't understand the terms of the treaty when they signed it.

5) The treaty had a large impact:
   - Settlement increased in California and Oregon.
   - Restricting Native Americans to their reservations, and the building of roads and forts in their territory, threatened their way of life.
   - Broken promises increased resentment among Native Americans towards government and settlers.

Comment and Analysis

The Fort Laramie Treaty is significant because it marked the end of the Permanent Indian Frontier — the Native Americans could no longer live freely on the Plains. It paved the way for further treaties in the 1850s and 60s which resulted in tribes losing land, e.g. in 1853 treaties were made with tribes in Kansas and Nebraska when these areas began to be settled (see p.49) — these tribes lost nearly 17 million acres.

Native Americans had been given the Great Plains when they were considered uninhabitable. This changed when settlers decided that they wanted the land.

Know the important events which created and built tension...

EXAM QUESTION

Explain why the Fort Laramie Treaty was important. [8]

Law and Disorder

Settlement of North America not only led to friction between the settlers and the Native Americans — there were also tensions among the settlers themselves. Law and order was a big problem in early settlements.

The growth of California during the Gold Rush caused Problems

1) Huge numbers of people moved to California during the Gold Rush which began in 1849. People came from all over the world — e.g. China, Mexico and South America, as well as from other parts of North America. The non-Native American population rose from around 14,000 to about 225,000 between 1848 and 1852.

Gold seekers who came to California during 1849 are known as the 'forty-niners'.

2) The rapid migration of mostly male gold seekers and quick development of mining towns meant that society was unstructured — there were no stable families or communities.
3) Keeping order could be a problem. Tensions grew in 1849 as rivers and streams where miners panned for gold became crowded and gold grew scarce — people known as 'claimjumpers' stole other people's claims to profitable land.
4) Criminals and professional gamblers were also attracted by the promise of wealth in California. Disagreements sometimes resulted in shootings and murder.
5) Living and working conditions were poor. There was little hygiene, disease was commonplace and nutrition among miners was poor. Miners who couldn't find gold worked for mining companies in dangerous conditions for low wages.
6) When not working, people turned to drinking and gambling which often led to trouble in mining towns.
7) There was frequent racial conflict. White Americans considered themselves to be superior and more entitled to the gold, especially when it began to grow scarce.

Comment and Analysis

Violence took over in the absence of law. Many miners had weapons and would have felt more free to use them in such a lawless place.

A miner panning for gold.

In 1850 a Foreign Miners Tax was introduced. When some foreign miners revolted, a vigilante army fired on them. There were assaults and beatings and many foreign miners were driven out.

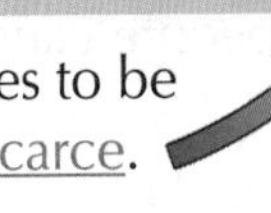

People tried to Solve law and order problems

1) Congress didn't establish a government in California until it became a state in 1850. Some army units were stationed there before this date, but they did not enforce law.

The US only acquired California, by treaty, from Mexico in 1848.

2) The US didn't have a national law regulating mining claims until 1866, so miners made their own laws. They created mining districts, elected representatives and settled disputes over mining claims. Claims officers patrolled mining areas to enforce the laws. Justice wasn't always fair — claims from foreigners were often ignored.
3) Many areas relied on vigilante justice — miners taking the law into their own hands. They held unofficial trials and handed out swift punishments, such as hanging. There were no prisons and no right to appeal. This sort of justice was rarely fair.
4) Mining areas were often remote, which made it difficult to enforce the law. Even after California became a state, law enforcers didn't have the means to police these areas effectively.
5) Law enforcement officials were sometimes unable to cope in areas with high levels of lawlessness. In 1851, a group of citizens in San Francisco took matters into their own hands by forming a vigilance committee — they targeted gangs who were accused of starting fires in the city and sentenced them to death, deportation and whipping.

Comment and Analysis

It would take time for proper systems of law and order to be effectively established in new settlements.

It's interesting how things panned out, isn't it...

It's likely that some exam questions will ask you to explain causes and consequences. Make sure you can explain why there were law and order problems in early settlements such as California.

The Civil War and Westward Expansion

The Civil War was a conflict between the Northern and Southern states of the USA between 1861-1865. Encouraged by the government, settlers moved west on to the Plains in greater numbers after the Civil War.

Westward expansion was a Cause of the Civil War...

1) The Northern and Southern states were very different. They disagreed mostly about slavery — the South used slave labour to grow cotton on plantations, whereas the North had abolished slavery.
2) As the USA expanded westward, the North and the South disagreed over whether new territories should become free states or slave states. Both felt threatened by the spread of the opposing labour system.
3) The South feared that if there were more free states than slave states, then the North would gain political power and would abolish slavery in all states. As a result, the southern states left the USA (seceded) in 1860 to form a new country — the Confederate States of America.
4) The North, under President Abraham Lincoln, wanted the states to stay united — this difference is what resulted in the Civil War. The North eventually won the war and abolished slavery. The period after the war from 1865-1877 is known as 'Reconstruction' — when the United States was being rebuilt.

The country had to be reunited and the South had to be physically rebuilt after the devastation of war.

... but the war also had an Impact on western expansion

Before the war, southerners in Congress opposed Acts which encouraged non-slave owning settlers to move into new areas. When the South seceded, the North was able to pass the following Acts:

The Homestead Act (1862)

1) The Homestead Act gave each settler 160 acres of free land, if they farmed it for 5 years. This opened up 2.5 million acres for settlement and was open to everyone, including immigrants, freed slaves and single women. Between 1862 and 1900 it has been estimated that 600,000 people claimed land under the Act.
2) The condition of farming the land for 5 years was meant to discourage speculators — those aiming to make a short-term profit on rising land prices rather than settling and living on the land. However, the Act was still affected by speculators and corruption.

Comment and Analysis

The Act was important because it opened up land ownership to ordinary people. Although there were problems, it helped to establish settlement on the Plains.

The Pacific Railroad Act (1862)

1) The government wanted to build a railway from east to west. They believed it would make migration into unsettled land easier and would create national unity by connecting the West to the East.
2) The Pacific Railroad Act approved the construction of the First Transcontinental Railroad, and work was completed in 1869. The railroad encouraged further settlement of the West:

- The government gave the railways land, which the railways sold to settlers cheaply to fund railway building. Promotional posters made exaggerated claims about the good life on the Plains.
- Economic development was made easier because the West was now linked with markets in the East.
- People could be transported more easily, as well as supplies which aided settlement, such as building materials and machinery.

Union Pacific Railroad advertisement for farming lands in Nebraska.

The Civil War was, to put it lightly, a significant event...

It was a significant event for many reasons — newfound freedom of slaves, the deaths of many soldiers... But you just need to concentrate on its impact on the development of the West.

Life Out West

The government was encouraging people to settle on the Plains, but homesteading was a tough life. As more people faced the difficulties of living and farming on the Plains, they found ways to survive.

Different Groups of people moved to the Plains

After 1865, thousands of people were willing to move to the Plains:

- Migrants from eastern states who moved because of growing population and high land prices.
- Immigrants who'd come to America to escape poverty and religious and political persecution.
- Slaves who had been freed after the Civil War, and ex-Civil War soldiers who wanted a new start.

Technology and Government Acts helped settlers farm the Plains

1) Conditions on the Plains made farming (and life generally) difficult (see p.49). But new developments in technology and crops helped:

- John Deere developed a stronger steel plough in the 1830s which could break through the tough soil. This was improved on by James Oliver who invented a lower cost iron plough called the 'sodbuster' in 1868.
- Windpumps increased the supply of water by pumping underground water to the surface.
- The introduction of barbed wire in 1874 meant that farmers could cheaply fence off their land to keep animals off their crops.
- Turkey Red Wheat was a hardy crop brought over from Russia in around 1874 which was well-suited to growing on the Plains. People also learned which crops were most suitable for growing on different types of land, e.g. people in Kansas and Nebraska realised that their land was more suited to growing wheat than corn.

Comment and Analysis

Farming was still hard. Not all settlers could afford new farming equipment.

2) The government helped people living in less fertile areas who struggled to make a living from the 160 acres given to them by the Homestead Act. For example, the Timber Culture Act of 1873 gave these settlers another 160 acres for free — as long as they planted trees on one quarter of the land. This meant that wood eventually became more widely available on the Plains.

Settlers had to Adapt to survive everyday life on the Plains

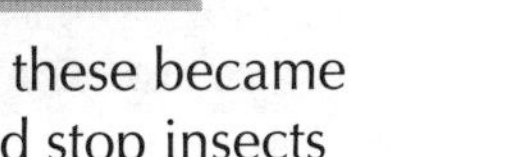

1) Because of the lack of wood, people originally had to make houses out of sod. But these became infested with insects and were unhygienic. Settlers whitewashed the walls to try and stop insects coming into the house through the walls.
2) Women were responsible for housework and their children's education. They had to collect buffalo dung for fuel and made a lot of what they needed, such as clothes and soap. They also nursed the sick and helped each other in childbirth.

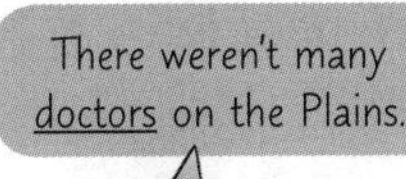

There weren't many doctors on the Plains.

3) Isolation was a constant problem for early settlers, as towns and neighbours were often far away. Women formed church groups and other social networks to combat the loneliness.
4) As more settlers arrived, communities formed. This eventually led to the building of schools and shops.

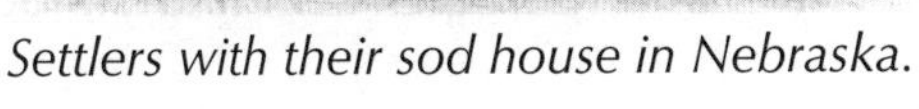

Settlers with their sod house in Nebraska.

Life on the Plains was... well... plain difficult...

Make two columns. In the first, make a list of the hardships faced by settlers on the Plains and in the second write down how people tried to overcome them. Use p.49 to help you with this.

Cattling and Cowboys

The popularity of beef in the 1850s led to the 'Beef Bonanza' — when the beef trade became very profitable. This was when ranchers started to drive their cattle along cattle trails to reach lucrative markets further north.

The Beef Bonanza began in Texas

Texas had been part of Mexico until 1845, when it became a US state. Many Mexicans were driven out, leaving their cattle to American ranchers.

1) The famous Texas Longhorn cattle was the result of interbreeding between Mexican cattle and cattle brought to the USA by Anglo-American settlers.
2) Numbers of Texas Longhorn grew massively during the Civil War. Many Texans left their ranches to fight, and while they were away, their cattle continued to breed. E.g. Charles Goodnight (who would later become a key figure in cattle ranching) left behind 180 cattle, but returned in 1865 to find he owned 5000.
3) Beef grew in popularity in the 1850s — there was a large demand for it in northern markets. So ranchers drove their cattle to the railroads, which then transported them to these markets.

Comment and Analysis

Railroads were very important in the growth of the cattle industry — they connected ranchers with lucrative markets. Railroads had become established by the end of the Civil War and continued to expand afterwards.

The great Cattle Trails linked supply with demand

1) The four main cattle trails were the Goodnight-Loving Trail, the Western Trail, the Chisholm Trail and the Shawnee Trail. Trails were between 1200 and 1500 miles long and progress of 15 miles was considered a good day's drive.
2) Early cattle drives followed the Shawnee Trail, where they would then be taken east by rail to Chicago.
3) However, Oliver Loving and his partner Charles Goodnight decided to target western markets. They established the Goodnight-Loving Trail in 1866, making it possible to drive cattle from Texas to Wyoming. They sold their beef in New Mexico to the army, to growing numbers of settlers and to the US government to feed Indians on reservations. They then drove the cattle up to Colorado to sell to miners.

1871 was the peak year for the cattle drives — 600,000 cattle were driven north.

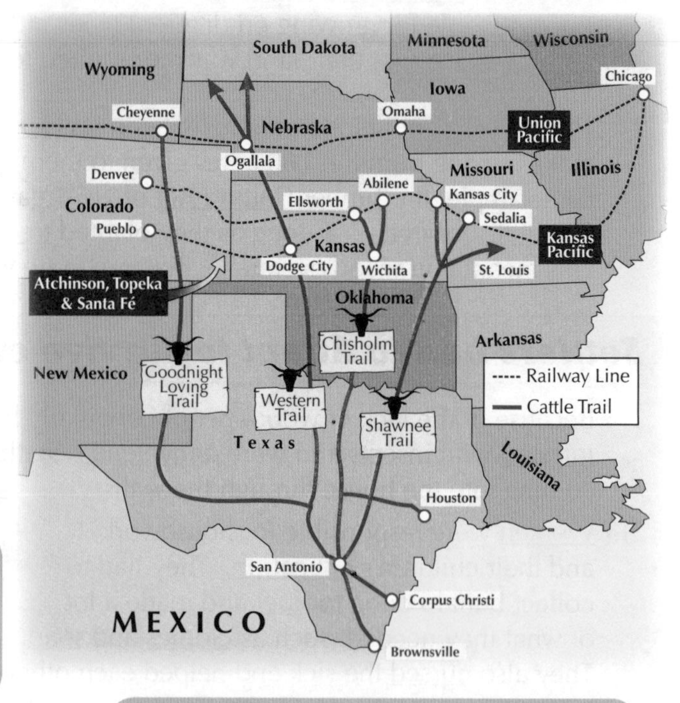

Some Indian tribes were being put on reservations in the 1860s (see p.57). Goodnight and Loving supplied beef to the Apache and Navajo Indian reservation at Fort Sumter in New Mexico.

4) Instead of driving their herds all the way north from ranches in Texas, some cattlemen decided that it would be more efficient to set up ranches on the Plains.
5) The first man to do this was John Iliff, who set up open-range ranching in Wyoming in 1867. In 1868, Goodnight drove cattle up to Iliff in Wyoming, which Iliff sold on to the transcontinental railroad construction gangs. Iliff also won a government contract in 1868 to supply beef to the Sioux reservation.

Open ranching meant there were no fences — cattle were free to graze where they liked.

Some ranchers were very successful and became known as cattle barons. John Iliff became a powerful rancher, with 35,000 cattle in Colorado and Wyoming.

I think that 'Cow Cornucopia' sounds better...

Make sure you know the key players and how they contributed to the growth of the cattle industry. You won't get any marks for getting your Goodnight-Lovings mixed up with your Iliffs.

Cattling and Cowboys

The cattle industry continued to develop and thrive with the emergence of cow towns. But it wasn't all plain sailing — cowboys had a tough job, and there was rivalry between ranchers and homesteaders.

The Cattle Trails led to the Cow Towns

The development of refrigerated rail carriages from 1878 meant that cattle could be slaughtered before transportation.

1) The Shawnee Trail (see p.54) was threatened when homesteaders in Kansas and Missouri objected to ranchers' cattle crossing their land.
2) Joseph McCoy, a livestock trader and entrepreneur, saw the potential of moving beef cattle by rail to the eastern cities and Indian reservations. He decided to create a cow town away from homesteaders' land where cattle could be driven. He chose Abilene to be his cow town — the Kansas Pacific railway had pushed westward to run past Abilene and it was away from settled areas.
3) In sixty days in 1867, McCoy built Abilene up to a fully equipped cow town, with a stockyard, hotel, and bank. It was soon connected to Texas via the Chisholm Trail — McCoy persuaded ranchers to drive their cattle to Abilene, where they would be sold and transported to northern markets.
4) In a few years, about 3 million cattle had passed through Abilene. Soon, other cow towns such as Wichita, Ellsworth and Dodge City emerged, as the railway continued to advance westwards.

The Cowboys' job was Very Tough and Badly Paid

1) The men who drove the cattle on the trails were called cowboys. Cowboys had a tough job — they had to contend with storms, river floods and, worst of all, stampedes on the trail.
2) Boredom and discomfort were also part of the job. Winters were spent watching the cattle from line camps on the edges of the ranch. Trail life mostly involved breathing dust and staring at cows.
3) Longhorn cattle are big and aggressive, so rounding them up by 'cutting out' the correct cattle from mixed herds on the open range took skill.

Many cowboys were Mexican or African Americans. Some were ex-soldiers from the Civil War, some were outlaws. Most cowboys were young and single with little time for a family life.

4) Cowboys sometimes came into conflict with other people on the Plains. Native Americans and other rustlers could steal or stampede cattle. Diplomacy would help deal with some situations, but others ended in violence, so cowboys had to know how to use a gun.
5) Cowboys had to work as a team on the trail to succeed. They were highly disciplined and were kept in line as much by each other as by their bosses.
6) Cowboys' pay was low but tended to come in one lump at the end of a drive.

The hardships of the trail led to many cowboys letting off steam and misbehaving once a cattle drive was over (see p.56).

The work of the cowboy changed as ranches became increasingly established on the Plains in the 1870s. It reduced the distance that cowboys had to drive cattle — the journey from Texas to the railroads could take up to two months, but from ranches on the Plains it could be done in around 35 days.

There was Rivalry between Ranchers and Homesteaders

1) Homesteaders living on the Plains weren't always delighted to see ranchers' cattle heading for their homes. The lack of wood on the Plains for fences meant that homesteaders' crops could be destroyed by the cattlemen's herds as they passed. Homesteaders' cattle sometimes died — the cattlemen's Longhorn herds carried a disease called Texas fever which they were immune to but homesteaders' cattle weren't.
2) Homesteaders used barbed wire as a cheap way to fence off their land from 1874, but this reduced cattlemen's access to water and made cattle drives much harder.
3) As ranches moved on to the Plains there were clashes with homesteaders over land ownership. This would lead to violent confrontations later on, such as the Johnson County War (see p.61).

Beef up your knowledge by making some mind maps...

Create a mind map of how the cattle industry developed. Make sure you have each of the main factors and then add detail to explain each one. You'll need to use the information from p.54 too.

Law and Order in the West

Law and order continued to be a problem as more people settled more areas of the West.

Settled areas became Territories, which then became States

1) As the USA expanded, it brought more land and people under the control of its government.
2) The USA has a federal system of government — there's a national government in Washington, and then each state also has a government of its own, which is responsible for things such as law and order.
3) As the West developed, it was carved up roughly into territories. The federal government controlled these, and took responsibility for law and order by sending a governor, a marshal and three judges into each territory. As the population increased, people could elect some of the lawmen, such as sheriffs.

Marshals sent in by the government looked after whole territories. They had deputy marshals to help them. Territories were split into counties and towns — sheriffs were in charge of counties and some towns elected town marshals.

4) Territories became states when the population reached 60,000. On becoming a state, law and order decisions could be made locally, instead of relying on the federal government a long way away.

Many Factors led to Crime on the Plains

1) **Gold** — Gold was discovered in Montana and Nevada in the 1860s and 70s. These areas had the same problems as California during the 1849 Gold Rush (see p.51). The areas grew quickly, and criminals were attracted by the potential riches, but it took time to establish systems of law and order.
2) **Cow towns** — Cowboys would go to cow towns such as Abilene and Dodge City at the end of long cattle drives. These places grew to provide lots of temptations for cowboys who wanted to relax after their hard work on the trail. There was drunkenness, gambling and gun fights.
3) **Homesteaders and cattlemen** — There was conflict as homesteaders and cattlemen clashed with each other (see p.55). They struggled to live side-by-side on the Plains.
4) **Gangs** — Outlaws formed gangs, which robbed trains and banks, and often committed murders. In the late 1860s, many of these men were ex-Confederate soldiers who turned to crime after the Civil War — the famous outlaw Jesse James and the other men in the James-Younger gang are examples.
5) **Racial tensions** — Different groups of people including African Americans, Chinese, Europeans and Mexicans, created the potential for conflict.

Many people carried guns — this created a culture of violence. Poverty and lack of stable communities to promote good behaviour in new settlements also contributed to lawlessness.

Policing these areas was Difficult

1) The West was a huge area of land, and transport was slow — it could take a long time for marshals to reach remote areas.

Comment and Analysis

The geography of America was an important cause of law and order problems.

2) Law officers such as sheriffs and marshals were sometimes criminals themselves. For example, Henry Plummer was elected Sheriff of the gold mining town of Bannack in Montana in 1863 while he was still the leader of a gang of robbers.

Plummer was caught and hung by vigilantes. Vigilante groups could do some good, but their justice was violent, quick and not always fair.

3) For lawmen such as sheriffs, the work was dangerous and they were poorly paid — this made it difficult to attract new recruits. There was also a shortage of money to train anyone who wanted to do the job.
4) This lack of formal law enforcement meant that vigilante groups often sprang up. These were made up of ordinary citizens who tried to keep law and order — often brutally.
5) The army also tried to police the West. 'Buffalo soldiers' were black soldiers whose job it was to keep order among settlers and fight Native Americans who raided white settlements.

These guys had worse problems than stolen wheelie bins...

Make a bullet point list of law and order problems on the Plains. Then write down the attempted solutions to these and how successful you think they were. Use evidence to back up your opinion.

REVISION TASK

The Indian Wars

The Plains Indians grew increasingly threatened as more people settled on the Plains — this led to conflict.

Railroads, Ranching and Gold angered the Plains Indians

1) Railroad companies often clashed with the Plains Indians. They encouraged the settling of the Plains as they expanded their networks and they frequently built railroads through Native American lands, even if it violated treaties.
2) Railroad companies also encouraged the hunting of buffalo — both to feed the railway construction gangs, and to make money by transporting hunters.
3) Buffalo were a hugely important resource for Native Americans (see p.46). So some tribes derailed trains and ambushed workmen. In response, the military built forts to safeguard the railroad.

Buffalo hunting became a popular sport (see p.64).

Sioux raiding a train on the Great Plains.

4) Ranchers clashed with the Plains Indians when their cattle drives went through Indian land and when they built ranches on Indian territories. Again, this disrupted buffalo herds, leading to Indian attacks on ranchers and the cattle drives. Oliver Loving (see p.54) died in 1867 after a fight with Comanches.
5) When gold was discovered in Montana in 1862, miners arrived in the area and prospected on Indian reservation land, breaking the treaties which had promised this land to the Native Americans.

Many Plains Indians were Unhappy with the Reservation Policy

1) More Indians were moved onto reservations as more settlers came to live on the Plains.
2) Life on reservations varied. The Navajos achieved peace and prosperity after 1868 when a treaty with the US allowed them sufficient reservation area in their homeland.
3) Other tribes were moved off their homeland and onto unfamiliar territory. They were encouraged to farm the land, which went against their culture and nomadic lifestyle.
4) Often reservation lands were insufficient and unsuitable for farming — some tribes faced starvation.
5) If the lands were good, they were often grabbed by settlers, despite the promises in the government treaties. Many chiefs also lacked the authority to make their tribes keep to the agreements.

Many Plains tribes were still able to hunt buffalo, but only within certain areas.

Many tribes wanted peace, but the situation had become intolerable. They were forced into conflict during the 1860s in a series of Indian Wars.

Comment and Analysis

It isn't surprising the Native Americans went to war. The government had given them the Great Plains (see p.47), but the government repeatedly broke their promises and forced tribes onto ever-smaller areas of land.

Little Crow's War was an uprising in Minnesota — 1862

1) The first major Indian War was Little Crow's War. Little Crow was the chief of the Santee Sioux, also known as the Dakota, who lived on a reservation in Minnesota.
2) They were peaceful and accepted reservation life. But they nearly starved as a result of Civil War shortages, a delay in their payment from the government, cheating by traders and a poor harvest.
3) In August 1862, four Dakota returning from an unsuccessful hunt murdered five settlers for a dare. Fearing retaliation on the entire tribe, Little Crow reluctantly led his warriors in an uprising. Hundreds of settlers and about 100 soldiers were killed, and the town of New Ulm was burned.
4) The uprising was ended when the Dakota were defeated at Wood Lake in September. 38 Dakota prisoners were hanged and most of the Dakota were expelled from what was left of their land.

Railroads didn't have a positive impact on everybody...

EXAM QUESTION

Give two consequences of the building of the railroads for the Plains Indians and explain them. [8]

The Indian Wars

More Indian Wars followed during the 1860s. This led the US government to try a more peaceful approach.

The Cheyenne Uprising and the Sand Creek Massacre — 1864

1) In 1863, the Cheyenne faced starvation because they couldn't grow enough food on their infertile reservation land at Sand Creek (see p.50) or find any buffalo. They decided to raid settlers' wagon trains for food. There was further violence between Indians and the army during 1864.
2) Chief Black Kettle, who wanted peace, moved his band to a camp where he believed they would be safe. But in November 1864, Colonel John Chivington attacked the camp while most of the band's men were out hunting. Of the 500 people left in the camp, at least 163 were killed — mostly women and children.
3) The Cheyenne, Arapaho and Sioux retaliated by attacking ranches and other settlements, and killing those inside, including women and children. The central Plains erupted into war.

Red Cloud's War and the Bozeman Trail — 1866-1868

1) The Bozeman Trail was established to link the gold fields in Montana with the Oregon Trail. However, this trail passed through the hunting grounds of the Sioux, which had been guaranteed to them by the Fort Laramie Treaty of 1851.
2) The Sioux attacked travellers who used the trail, so the army wanted to build forts to protect them. Talks were held with Red Cloud, a Sioux chief, to negotiate the building of these forts, but they were abandoned when the Sioux saw soldiers marching out to begin building before any deal had been made.
3) The Sioux began to attack the army. In a major incident known as Fetterman's Trap, the Sioux ambushed Captain W.J. Fetterman and his troops — Fetterman and all 80 of his men were killed.
4) As a result, the US army surrendered and abandoned the forts. This was a major defeat for the army.

Red Cloud.

- Red Cloud eventually signed the 1868 Fort Laramie Treaty, which created a large Sioux reservation on an area that included the sacred Black Hills of Dakota. The government also agreed not to rebuild their forts on the Bozeman Trail.
- Red Cloud promised never again to make war on the settlers — and kept his promise. But not all of the Sioux bands agreed with the treaty. Sioux chiefs Crazy Horse and Sitting Bull would be involved in future conflict after gold was discovered on the Black Hills of Dakota in 1874 (see p.63).

Policies of Separation and Assimilation were tried

1) The Indian Wars made it clear to the government that their Indian policy wasn't working. The government wanted to move away from aggressive military actions.
2) In 1867 the Indian Peace Commission tried to establish peace by negotiating the Medicine Lodge Treaty — this treaty moved southern Plains Indian tribes onto smaller reservations away from settlers.
3) Following on from this, President Grant established his 'Peace Policy' in 1868 — the aim was to assimilate the Indians peacefully into white society. But it was agreed that those who resisted the policy would face military action.
4) The policy failed — the Native Americans didn't want to give up their lifestyle and Grant didn't stop settlers encroaching on Indian land when gold was found on the Black Hills of Dakota in 1874. More conflict would follow (see p.63).

Many settlers and army officers such as General Sherman thought the Native Americans should be destroyed. Many politicians took a more humane view.

Comment and Analysis

Although the 'Peace Policy' had humane intentions, it still aimed to deny the Native Americans their way of life — many didn't want to be assimilated.

Remember that the Indian wars weren't just one war...

They were a series of conflicts fought against different tribes — not one united nation. Make sure you remember the key people involved on both sides and what they did.

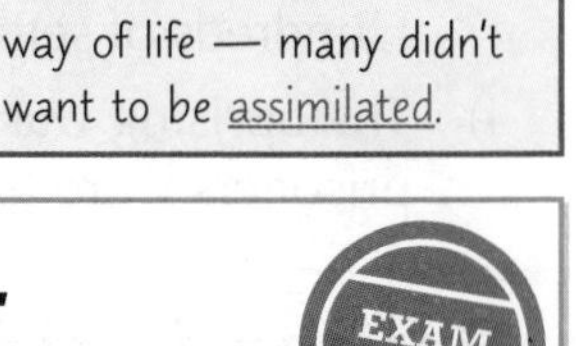

Changes in Farming

The 1860s to the 1880s were the ranchers' heyday — but sadly for them, the Beef Bonanza didn't last forever.

Changing Tastes and Hard Winters ended the Beef Bonanza

1) Eastern markets eventually began to demand a higher quality of meat than the Longhorn could provide. This led ranchers like Iliff and Goodnight to start crossbreeding Longhorns with Herefords — the meat from these cattle was better quality, but the cattle were less resistant to harsh conditions.
2) States passed quarantine laws because settlers were concerned about diseases carried by the ranchers' cattle (see p.55) — from 1885 Kansas shut its borders to Texas cattle between March and November.
3) Ranchers overstocked their cattle and after 1885 there was less demand for beef — herds grew very large and prices fell. The herds became too large for the grazing area and the drought of 1886 meant there wasn't enough grass to feed the cattle.
4) The over-grazed range meant that underfed cattle entered the terrible winter of 1886-1887 in weakened condition. Thousands of cattle died. Homesteaders' fences became death traps as cattle piled against them during blizzards. Average losses were perhaps 30%. Many cowboys also died.

Ranchers had become greedy — they wanted to take advantage of the high demand for beef, but they allowed their herds to grow too large.

Comment and Analysis

The winter of 1886-7 was the catalyst for change on the ranches.

The end of the beef bonanza Transformed cattle Ranching

1) Ranchers had to adapt when the cattle boom ended.
2) Businesses which survived the 1880s economised by raising better-quality animals on smaller areas of land, shifting towards a more managed environment.
3) More intensive ranching also favoured smaller scale operations — these were more likely to be family-owned than corporate.
4) Ranching now depended on the ability to feed livestock in winter. Ranchers grew crops such as hay so that they could feed their cattle and this meant that dependence on irrigation increased.
5) Ranchers, like homesteaders, began to use barbed wire enclosures to fence off their land — this allowed them to control their herds and look after them. Cattle could no longer roam freely — it was the end of the open range.

The bad winter of 1886/7 had shown ranchers the importance of caring for their cattle in harsh weather, including being able to feed and shelter them.

Windpumps made it easier for ranchers to fence off their land. Previously, cattle had moved around to find water sources, but this invention allowed water to be pumped from underground.

The end of the open range had a large Impact on the Cowboy

1) The change from the open range to fenced pastures changed the role of the cowboy.
2) The expansion of the railroads made long drives unnecessary. Round-ups (herding cattle together) occurred less often and involved much smaller herds of cattle. This meant that fewer cowboys were needed and those who remained spent less time roaming the Plains on their horses.
3) Cowboys became domesticated ranch hands with more mundane jobs, such as mending fences. As ranchers were growing more crops, cowboys became more involved in farming.
4) As a whole, their lives became more settled — their living conditions on ranches were more comfortable than life on the trail, they had to follow ranch rules and their hours were more regular.

Comment and Analysis

The end of cowboy culture and the cattle trails helped bring some order to the Plains.

The romantic image of the cowboy has remained strong in popular culture — it's a symbol of a wild and free existence.

The Cow Cornucopia was good while it lasted...

REVISION TASK

Make a list of the factors which resulted in the decline of the cattle industry and explain each one. Decide which you think is the most important factor and write a paragraph explaining why.

Changes in Farming

Living and farming on the Great Plains was still hard, but the area was eventually successfully settled.

People continued to Settle on the Plains...

1) Different groups of people were still helping to settle the West:

People had started to move onto even drier areas of the Plains by 1880.

- There were 10 million immigrants to America during 1865-90 — many of these helped settle the West, such as the Scandinavians on the Dakotas. By 1900 there were 500,000 farms on the Plains.
- At the end of the Reconstruction era in 1877, African Americans faced growing oppression in the South. As a result, thousands moved west — e.g. approximately 20,000 black migrants moved to Kansas in 1879. This mass migration is known as the Exoduster movement.

The effects of the Civil War were still being felt.

2) Government actions also helped:

- **The Desert Land Act 1877** — Farmers who lived on drier land could buy up to 640 acres at a low cost as long as they irrigated the land within three years.
- **The Oklahoma Land Rush of 1889** — The government opened up two million acres of land in Oklahoma to settlers in 1889 — this had previously been Indian territory (see p.47). Thousands of people rushed in to the territory to claim their land.

In 1893 another 6 million acres was opened up. This land was known as the 'Cherokee Strip' and had been promised to the Cherokees 60 years previously on their removal to the West.

3) By 1890, six railroads crossed the US from east to west. This helped to make the Plains a less isolated place and linked farmers on the Plains with wider markets.
4) People continued to adapt to life on the Plains. Towns developed and communities grew, as more people settled the Plains. Life was made more comfortable by luxury goods brought by railroads from the East.
5) There were still hardships though, and the failure rate for new farms was high. There were severe droughts in the 1870s and 1880s, and problems caused by overgrazing. Some people got into debt and lost their farms, while others gave up and moved on.

... and Farming continued to Develop

1) Farmers began to learn techniques to cope with the low rainfall and retain the moisture in the soil, e.g. 'dry farming' involved turning the soil after rain.
2) Machinery — such as reapers, binders and harvesters — was developed and improved to harvest grain faster.
3) Initially only farmers making good profits could afford to buy new machinery, but it eventually became more widespread as it became more affordable. The railroads gave farmers greater access to machinery by transporting it to the Plains from the East.
4) Bonanza farms were established. These were large farms which grew and harvested wheat on a large scale.
5) The Great Plains helped the US become a major world wheat producer. In 1895, the US grew around three times as much wheat and corn as it did in 1860.

Farmers who could afford to were using steam-powered tractors by the 1890s.

Steam-powered wheat thresher, 1878.

This image shows the productivity of the Plains and the growing use of new machinery.

Comment and Analysis

By the 1890s, farming was becoming increasingly mechanized — farm work took less time, required less labour and became more productive.

Settle down at the back — there's a lot to plough through...

EXAM TIP

A lot of the problems faced by homesteaders had been solved by 1895. Make sure you can give specific examples in the exam of the technology and farming methods which helped settlers.

Wild West

It was known as the Wild West for a reason. Lawlessness was still a big issue.

A 'Western Civil War of Incorporation' or just lawlessness?

1) The violence in the late 1800s in the American West was partly due to changes in society. Cattle barons, railroads and other corporations — using the power and influence that their size gave them — were taking over from the homesteaders, small ranchers and prospectors. Some historians call the violence it sparked the 'Western Civil War of Incorporation'.
2) Outlaws were treated as heroes by some for standing up for ordinary people.
3) The brutal James Younger gang, led by Jesse James, acquired a Robin Hood reputation because their victims — banks and the railway companies — were institutions hated by many.

Comment and Analysis

These outlaws have often been romanticised in books and films, but they frequently committed violent crimes.

The Range Wars were conflicts over Land and Power

The Lincoln County War — 1878

1) The Lincoln County War was a conflict between established cattle barons Lawrence Murphy and James Dolan, and John Tunstall who tried to set up a rival business.
2) Tunstall was threatened by Murphy and Dolan, and was later killed by people working for Sheriff Brady (a supporter of Murphy and Dolan). To get revenge for his murder, a group of men formed a gang called the Regulators. One of the members was Billy the Kid, an outlaw who had been involved in robbery and cattle rustling — he later became a famous figure of the Wild West.
3) The Regulators took the law into their own hands — they killed Sheriff Brady and his deputy. The killing then escalated — it's been estimated that around 19 men died during the conflict.
4) Billy the Kid survived and went on the run. He was arrested by Sheriff Pat Garrett and charged with Brady's murder in 1881. He was sentenced to hang, but he killed two guards and escaped from jail.

The Johnson County War — 1892

1) Homesteaders in Johnson County, Wyoming, felt that the cattle barons were stealing their land. Cattle barons felt that homesteaders were blocking their use of the open range and accused them of rustling (stealing) their cattle. Vigilantes who worked for the cattle barons dealt out 'justice'.

In 1889 a wealthy rancher called A.J. Bothwell wanted land claimed by a storekeeper called James Averill. Averill lived with a prostitute called Ella Watson who had some rebranded cows. Bothwell accused them both of rustling and a lynch mob murdered Watson and Averill in front of their cabin. There were more murders of alleged rustlers in 1891.

2) In 1892 the Wyoming Stock Growers Association (who represented the cattle barons) mounted a huge vigilante raid into Johnson County. The Union Pacific Railroad laid on a special train for them.
3) The vigilantes killed two alleged rustlers, Nate Champion and Nick Ray, but a group of locals came out of Buffalo and laid siege to the vigilantes at a ranch called the TA.
4) More locals gathered, including Buffalo's sheriff, until there were about 250 men ready to kill the vigilantes. The Stock Growers Association had influence with the government via the Republican Party and the President. They used this to call out the army, who rescued the vigilantes in a bloodless truce.
5) Despite the efforts of the locals, there were no prosecutions. However, the cattle barons lost their power and influence and the war marked the end of the open range in Wyoming.

Range wars — unfortunately they weren't singing battles...

It's important to understand the causes of the range wars and what actually happened in them. Write summaries of the two wars on this page, making sure to include the key players and events.

Wild West

People tried to bring order to the Wild West. By 1895, the situation had improved for a variety of reasons.

Lawmen fought the Outlaws

1) A career as a lawman in the Wild West was open to all sorts of people. Wyatt Earp was a natural recruit for the forces of incorporation (corporations and big businesses — see p.61) as he was a keen entrepreneur as well as an effective gunman:

He had been arrested in 1871 for rustling (horse stealing) in Missouri. Rather than stand trial, he fled the state, and the federal system did nothing to prevent his later career as a lawman.

- Earp, his brothers and Doc Holliday killed three men who were accused of cattle rustling and other crimes at the OK Corral in Arizona in 1881. The dead men were typical of the small ranchers/outlaws who opposed the growth of big business in the West.
- Some people believed that the violence wasn't justified — the Earps and Holliday were charged with murder, but this was later dropped.
- A bloody feud followed the shootout. When Wyatt's brother Morgan was killed, Wyatt got his revenge by killing the men he believed responsible.

As victor at the OK Corral, Wyatt Earp not only wrote the history of the shootout, but the screenplay as well — he worked as an advisor on early Hollywood westerns. Wyatt was seen as a hero.

Earp also took part in the so-called Dodge City War of 1883 — a faction fight between a saloon-keeper friend of Earp and a corrupt mayor. Dodge City had a reputation as the 'Wickedest City in America', but by 1886 the cattle trails had gone and Dodge had become a sleepy town.

Wyatt Earp (1848-1929)

Comment and Analysis

The OK Corral has become one of the most famous Wild West shootouts. It has come to symbolise the lawlessness of the Wild West.

2) Other lawmen had successes in hunting down outlaws. Pat Garrett, who was elected sheriff of Lincoln County in 1880, hunted down and shot Billy the Kid after he escaped from jail in 1881.
3) Some lawmen, such as Bill Tilghman, gained reputations for being respectable and honest. Unlike other lawmen, he wasn't quick to resort to violence. He became Deputy US Marshal in Oklahoma in 1892 and played a major part in stopping outlaw activity there.

Law and order in the West gradually Improved

1) The expansion of the railroads and improved communication (e.g. the telegraph) helped law enforcement — news travelled faster and lawmen could more easily reach areas where there was trouble.
2) More homesteaders arrived who wanted to make a successful life for themselves and their family — they demanded better law and order.
3) As towns developed, living conditions improved — towns and roads were planned properly, with better buildings and sanitation systems. This created a more civilised atmosphere and encouraged better behaviour.
4) More states were created, which meant more areas were becoming responsible for their own law and order rather than having to rely on a distant federal government. Seven more territories became states between 1876 and 1890, bringing the number of states up to 44.

Comment and Analysis

Law and order in the West was getting better by the 1890s, but conflicts such as the Johnson County War (see p.61) show that there was still progress to be made.

Learn it or lose marks — it's Earp to you...

The lines between who was right and wrong in the Wild West aren't that clear. When answering exam questions, remember that lawmen such as Wyatt Earp weren't squeaky clean.

EXAM TIP

The End of the Indian Wars

The Indians won a major battle in 1876, but it was too little too late. By 1890, the Indian Wars were over.

The Indians Won at Little Bighorn but it made things even Worse

1) In 1874 troops under Lt. Col. George Custer confirmed the presence of gold in the Black Hills of Dakota and a gold rush began. The US government tried to buy the Black Hills from the Sioux, but they refused — the hills were sacred to them and had been guaranteed to them by the Fort Laramie Treaty of 1868.
2) The government ordered the Sioux to return to their reservation — and if they didn't, the government and military would regard them as hostile. The Sioux refused, and by the start of 1876 Sitting Bull and Crazy Horse had raised the largest Native American force ever seen (about 4000 warriors).
3) The Army was sent to oppose this uprising, with Custer taking charge of some of the government soldiers. Custer was ambitious and wanted to attack the Indians alone, so he didn't wait for the rest of the army to arrive. They were outnumbered and didn't even have the advantage of technology — many of the Indians had repeating Winchester rifles, while Custer's soldiers had single-shot Springfields.
4) Custer and all 225 of his command were killed. This was the greatest Native American victory in battle against the US army. However, this only strengthened the resolve of the US army to defeat the Indians:

- The army launched a winter campaign against the Sioux in 1876-77. Facing hunger and the loss of their horses, the Sioux surrendered and were forced onto reservations. Crazy Horse surrendered in May 1877 and was later killed by a US soldier while resisting arrest.
- Sioux reservations were put under military control and, in 1877, the Black Hills were opened to white settlement.
- Sitting Bull retreated to Canada, but returned and surrendered in 1881.

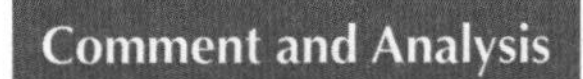

Little Bighorn was only a short term victory for the Native Americans. It wasn't enough to turn their fortunes around and the army's determination to defeat them increased following the battle.

The Wounded Knee Massacre marked the End of the Indian Wars

1) Some armed resistance continued during the 1880s, but was finally suppressed in 1890 with the Wounded Knee Massacre. This was to be the last confrontation between Native Americans and the army.
2) A Native American spiritual leader named Wovoka taught that a special Ghost Dance could raise the dead and bring a new world, free from the settlers. He was opposed to violence, but ghost dances built the dancers up into a frenzy — this unsettled whites who feared that the dance would lead to rebellion.
3) Tensions peaked at the Pine Ridge Reservation in Wounded Knee Creek, South Dakota. Troops tried to disarm a band of Sioux led by Chief Big Foot, but when a warrior fired a shot, the troops replied with a volley, killing 52. Survivors went on to fight by hand.
4) The battle escalated when more warriors from nearby heard the gunfire and swarmed out, shooting at the soldiers, then disappearing into the prairie.

- The Battle of Wounded Knee cost the lives of some 150 Sioux — about 60 of them women and children — and 25 soldiers.
- It marked the final suppression of Native Americans by armed force. By mid-January 1891 the dispersed warriors had all surrendered.
- Some Sioux followers of the Ghost Dance movement had believed that special shirts would protect them from the bullets of the Americans. The sight of Ghost Dance shirts pierced by bullets after the battle destroyed the tribes' faith in a magical restoration of the old way of life. The reservation was reluctantly accepted as home.

A terrible end to the Native American fight for freedom...

Little Bighorn and Wounded Knee are very important in the history of the American West. For both of these events, write a summary explaining their role in the defeat of the Native Americans.

A Way of Life Destroyed

It seems as though the Indians had always been fighting a losing battle against land-hungry settlers.

Buffalo Slaughter forced Native Americans to accept Reservations

1) Millions of buffalo had once roamed the Plains. They were vital to the Native Americans' survival (see p.46) and were sacred to them.
2) Buffalo were slaughtered in large numbers by white settlers (see p.57). They were killed to feed soldiers and railroad construction workers. People also killed them for their skins — there was a demand for buffalo robes in the East from the 1850s, and from 1871 a process was developed to make buffalo hides into leather. Others just killed them for sport — men would shoot the animals from the windows of trains.
3) As a result of this, buffalo numbers decreased rapidly — it has been estimated that there were 13 million buffalo on the Plains in 1865, but by the end of the century they were almost extinct.
4) The effect on the Plains Indians was devastating — their main source of food was gone, as well as a major part of their culture. This caused many Indians to accept life on the reservations — they feared starvation.
5) It's not clear whether there was an official policy to exterminate the buffalo, but many people recognised that destroying them would help defeat the Indians.

General Sheridan is quoted as saying, 'let them kill, skin and sell until the buffalo is exterminated as it is the only way to bring lasting peace and allow civilisation to advance'.

A buffalo skinner. Buffalo skins were much in demand. The rest of the animal would be left to decay on the Plains.

Reservations destroyed their Culture

1) The formerly nomadic Plains Indians, now confined to smaller areas, could no longer feed or clothe themselves without government aid. Living on hand-outs, they became demoralised and there were high rates of alcoholism.
2) Many tribes were moved off their culturally significant ancestral lands and on to reservations elsewhere. Influence of chiefs declined because reservations were run by Indian agents, undermining tribal structure. Hostile tribes were sometimes put on reservations in close proximity.
3) Many children were taken away to be educated, for example at the Carlisle Indian School in Pennsylvania (founded in 1879). Polygamy (having more than one wife) and religious practices such as the Sun Dance, were banned. The threat of withholding rations was used to enforce cooperation.

Comment and Analysis

The government had always wanted the Indians to assimilate. As Indians living on the reservations were now dependent on the state, there was a way to force them to abandon their own culture.

Native Americans were Unable to fight back Successfully

It's debatable whether the Plains Indians could ever have protected their traditional way of life. There were many factors at work against them:

1) The US army usually had better weapons than the Native Americans — repeating rifles, machine guns and cannons.
2) The system of forts gave the US army control on the Plains. The railroads and telegraph system provided fast transport and communication.
3) Divisions between Native American nations meant that they had no organised resistance. Reservation life also made it more difficult for them to resist.

Comment and Analysis

It seems that nothing could halt the tide of white settlers — and broken government promises failed to protect the Indians from it.

Not a particularly proud moment in American history...

Give an account that analyses how the Native American way of life was destroyed. [8]

EXAM QUESTION

End of the Frontier

A lot had changed by 1895. Settlers had claimed so much land that the American frontier — the line separating settlements from unsettled land — no longer existed.

The government decided to Break Up the reservations

1) Government policy from the 1850s had been to move Native Americans onto reservations away from settlers. In the late 1880s, the government decided to split up the reservations into smaller units. These would be given out to individual tribe members to own and farm — the aim was to convert tribesmen into independent farmers.
2) It was believed that this would help destroy tribal bonds and the power of tribal leaders — and that this would finally lead to the assimilation of Native Americans into white society.

Comment and Analysis

Native Americans could no longer be separated from white society on reservations — there was no more land to move them onto as settlers continued to claim more and more of it.

The Dawes Act (1887) Parcelled Out tribal lands

1) The Dawes Act broke reservations up into allotments. Each head of family was assigned 160 acres, each single adult 80 acres, and each minor 40 acres. US citizenship was also part of the deal.
2) When all the inhabitants of a reservation had been assigned their holdings, the remaining surplus land was thrown open to white settlement. Indian schools were established from the sale of this surplus land.
3) The Act was a disaster for the Native Americans:
   - Their tribal communities were broken up and their culture almost destroyed — the idea of land ownership went against Native American tradition.
   - The creation of allotments led to Indians losing their land — down from 138 million acres in 1887 to 78 million acres in 1900. They also lost land granted to them under the Act (nearly two thirds of it between 1887 and 1934) as a result of being cheated by land speculators.
   - Lands belonging to five tribes on Indian territory (Cherokee, Chickasaw, Choctaw, Creek and Seminole) were exempt from the Dawes Act, yet through forced sales they too were eventually lost.
   - In 1934, the government repealed the Dawes Act and encouraged tribal identities. But by that time, Native Americans had lost over 60 per cent of their original reservation lands and were suffering from high rates of poverty, alcoholism, illiteracy and suicide.

Some reformers supported the act because they wanted to stop Indian suffering on reservations. Some believed that reservation life encouraged idleness and reliance on government hand-outs. Others just wanted to open up reservation lands to settlers.

Men found it difficult to adapt to farming — this had traditionally been seen as a woman's role. In Indian schools, Children had to dress like white Americans and weren't allowed to speak tribal languages.

Comment and Analysis

While many reformers may have believed they had good intentions, their actions were based on their prejudiced belief that Native Americans needed to be introduced to Christianity and western civilisation to improve themselves.

Americans became aware of the End of the Frontier

1) In 1890, census results revealed that, unlike in 1880, there was no longer a definable Western frontier of settlement. The frontier was declared officially closed.
2) This didn't mean that there was no more land available for settlers, but what remained was in isolated pockets and the best areas had been taken.
3) Settlers occupied land from the East all the way to the West. Manifest Destiny had been fulfilled.

The Native Americans were no longer a barrier to settlement — they'd been subdued and were in the process of being assimilated into white society.

The frontier closed — and the West is history...

To sum up — settlers in, Indians out. It's all very well knowing all the little facts about this period of American history, but you've got to know how they fit together too.

Revision Summary

Well, that was the American West — but now you need to see how well you've taken it all in.

- Try these questions and tick off each one when you get it right.
- When you've done all the questions for a topic and are completely happy with it, tick off the topic.

The Early Settlement of the West, 1835-1862 (p.46-51)

1) Why were the buffalo important to the Plains Indians?
2) Summarise the Plains Indians' beliefs about land and nature.
3) What was the Permanent Indian Frontier? Why was it created?
4) Give three reasons why settlers went to the west coast.
5) What difficulties did the Mormons face on their journey to Salt Lake Valley?
6) Why did people start settling on the Plains?
7) Explain why the culture of the Plains Indians clashed with that of the settlers.
8) Why did the US government introduce the Indians Appropriations Act in 1851?
9) Give three consequences of the 1851 Fort Laramie Treaty.
10) Give three reasons why there were law and order problems in California.

Development of the Plains, 1862-1876 (p.52-58)

11) Explain the impact of the Civil War on westward expansion.
12) Name three things which helped settlers live and farm on the Plains.
13) Why did the cattle trails develop?
14) What was the role of Joseph McCoy in the growth of the cattle industry?
15) Explain why there was rivalry between ranchers and homesteaders.
16) What did the government do to try and bring law and order to new settlements?
17) Why did many Native Americans dislike life on the reservations?
18) Describe the events of the Cheyenne Uprising and the Sand Creek Massacre.
19) What was agreed in the 1868 Fort Laramie Treaty?
20) Why was the 'Peace Policy' of 1868 introduced? Was it successful?

Conflicts and Conquest, 1876-1895 (p.59-65)

21) Why did ranchers begin to fence off their land?
22) What was the Exoduster movement?
23) How did changes in society contribute to lawlessness?
24) Describe the events leading up to the Johnson County War.
25) What role did Wyatt Earp play in enforcing law and order?
26) Why did the Native Americans go to war at Little Bighorn?
27) What happened at Wounded Knee in 1890?
28) What impact did the destruction of the buffalo have on the Native Americans?
29) The US government passed the Dawes Act in 1887.
    Why was it introduced? What effect did it have on the Native Americans?
30) In what year was the closure of the western frontier officially announced?

The Grand Alliance

The Grand Alliance was made up of the 'big three' allies from World War Two — Britain, the USA and the USSR. They were united by their desire to defeat Nazi Germany, but as the war ended, tensions emerged.

The 'Big Three' discussed Europe's Future at Tehran and Yalta

1) In 1943, the Grand Alliance held a conference in Tehran. The talks focused mainly on plans to defeat the Nazis. But the allies also started to discuss what would happen to Europe and Germany after the war.
2) Britain and the USA were politically very different from the USSR and there were tensions between the three allies. These were put aside during the war as they fought a common enemy (Germany).
3) The British Prime Minister Winston Churchill and US President Franklin D. Roosevelt agreed the USSR could claim a 'sphere of influence' in Eastern Europe after the war was over. Eastern European countries would be subject to Soviet policies and ideas.
4) The Grand Alliance made more decisions about the future of Europe at the Yalta Conference in February 1945:
   - Free elections would be held in previously occupied countries in Eastern Europe.
   - The United Nations (UN) would replace the failed League of Nations.

The USSR (Union of Soviet Socialist Republics) was also known as the Soviet Union.

Comment and Analysis

The allies had different interpretations of a 'free' election. To the USA and Britain, it meant lots of political parties competing for votes. But Stalin (the leader of the USSR) believed only communist parties should run in elections as they were the only parties that truly represented the people.

Potsdam revealed the First Cracks in the Grand Alliance

After Germany surrendered in May 1945, the allied leaders met again at Potsdam over July and August. They wanted to work on the finer details of their plans for Germany and Europe.

Some important agreements were made at Potsdam...

- The new boundaries of Poland were agreed.
- The 'big three' plus France would divide Germany and Berlin between them.
- Nazi leaders would be tried for war crimes at Nuremberg.

1) Some things remained undecided. For example, Germany would be divided into four zones (one each for Britain, France, the USA and the USSR) — but the allies didn't decide if, or when, the zones could rejoin and form a country again.
2) Tensions were high. Roosevelt had died and Harry Truman had succeeded him as US President — Truman was more suspicious of the USSR and less willing to compromise.
3) Britain and the US were also alarmed by Stalin's actions in Poland — he had installed a government consisting of only pro-communist members. Britain and the US felt this went against the Yalta agreement.

Britain also had a new leader — Clement Attlee replaced Churchill mid-conference.

The USA and the USSR had very Different Ideologies

The tension between the USA and the USSR was partly caused by their very different beliefs — the USSR was communist, while the USA was capitalist. Both countries also feared the other's intentions.

1) Communism meant state control of industry and agriculture. The USA, by contrast, valued private enterprise — the 'American Dream' was that anyone could work their way to the top.
2) The USSR only allowed one political party — the Communist Party. The USA valued political freedom.
3) Communism aimed at world revolution, and so it was seen by Americans as a danger to their democracy. However, the communists also feared worldwide American influence.

'East' and 'West' had different perspectives...

Summarise the tension in the Grand Alliance between 1943 and July 1945.
Include how the allies' relationships altered and why their attitudes changed.

REVISION TASK

The Two Superpowers

The USSR and the USA emerged from the Second World War as the two biggest powers in the world. But they were very suspicious of one another, and began to interpret each other's actions as threats.

The USA kept their Atom Bomb a Secret

1) Japan was on Germany's side in the war, and continued to fight after Germany surrendered in May 1945. In August 1945, the USA dropped two atom bombs on Japan — destroying the cities of Hiroshima and Nagasaki.
2) The atom bombs meant that military help from the USSR wasn't needed to defeat Japan. President Truman also refused to allow the USSR to take part in the US occupation of Japan.

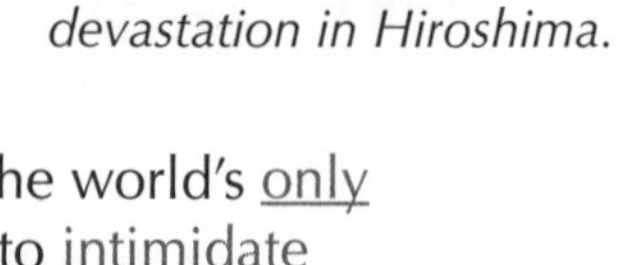

The atom bomb caused devastation in Hiroshima.

3) The USA had kept the exact nature of the atom bomb a secret from the USSR at Potsdam in July 1945 (although Stalin's spies had passed on many details).
4) These nuclear weapons boosted the status of the USA. For four years it was the world's only nuclear power. Stalin saw the development of the atom bomb as an attempt to intimidate the USSR, and was angry that the USA had managed to surpass Soviet technology.
5) The atom bombs increased the rivalry between the USA and the USSR. The USSR sped up the development of its own atomic bomb, starting an arms race between the two countries (see p.71).

The USSR became Influential in Eastern Europe

1) At the end of the Second World War, the Red Army (the USSR's army) occupied Eastern Europe. These countries would pass into the USSR's sphere of influence after the war.
2) Between 1945 and 1948, Stalin installed pro-Soviet 'puppet' governments in Poland, Hungary, Romania, Bulgaria and Czechoslovakia.

- For a while it seemed that Czechoslovakia might remain democratic. But when the Communist Party seemed likely to lose ground in the next election, it seized power in February 1948.
- The exception to Soviet domination was Yugoslavia, which had freed itself from the Germans without the Red Army. Yugoslavia was communist but more open to the West. Its leader, Tito, argued with Stalin over political interference. Stalin cut off aid but didn't invade.

There was an 'Iron Curtain' between East and West

1) Increasing tensions between the USA and the USSR became known as the 'Cold War'. There was no direct fighting — both sides were afraid of another war, especially after 1949, when the USSR had its own nuclear weapons.
2) Countries in Western Europe tended to support the USA. Most countries in Eastern Europe were dominated by the USSR. In a famous speech in 1946, Winston Churchill warned there was an 'Iron Curtain' dividing Europe.

Comment and Analysis

Churchill's 'Iron Curtain' speech demonstrates the breakdown of the Grand Alliance — Britain and the USA now viewed the USSR as a threat, not an ally.

Countries under the influence of the USSR became known as its 'satellite states' (in pink).

My two favourite superpowers — flying and being invisible...

EXAM TIP

In the exam, try to explain people's actions by considering the way they would have looked at a situation. Here, each country is acting for reasons that made sense to the people in charge.

Mutual Suspicion

The Cold War was a period of international tension — with each side suspicious of the other.

The 'Long' and 'Novikov' telegrams were detailed Reports

By 1946, tensions between the superpowers were high. Each country issued secret telegrams about the other.

1) The telegrams were detailed reports describing the motivations and intentions of the other country.

The Long Telegram (February 1946)

- Issued to President Truman about the USSR.
- It said that Stalin had given a speech in favour of the destruction of capitalism.
- It warned of the USSR trying to weaken and divide Western powers, while building the strength of its own military.

The Novikov Telegram (September 1946)

- Issued to Stalin about the USA.
- The report claimed that the USA was pursuing world supremacy.
- It warned that the USA was trying to limit the influence of the USSR in Europe.

2) Neither country seemed to know for certain what the other was thinking. The reports panicked the Russian and American governments and accelerated the Cold War — the findings seemed to confirm their worst fears.

Truman Acted to Contain the Communist Threat

President Truman was extremely worried about the spread of communism to Western Europe. Many countries were undergoing economic hardships, which he thought might make communism look more appealing. The USA decided to intervene in Europe to try and contain the spread of communism.

The Truman Doctrine (announced March 1947)

The USA pledged to support any nation threatened by a communist takeover. This support could be diplomatic, military or financial. For example, the USA gave $400 million of aid to Turkey and Greece to stop communism spreading.

The Marshall Plan (announced June 1947)

This promised $17 billion of aid to European countries to help rebuild their economies — the areas of Germany under Western occupation benefited massively. Stalin, however, ordered all of his satellite states to reject the plan. He believed the USA was using economic incentives to lure Eastern European states away from the USSR.

The USSR Reacted by creating the Cominform

Stalin felt threatened by the Truman Doctrine, and reacted by strengthening and uniting his allies.

1) **The Cominform** (Communist Information Bureau) was set up in 1947. The organisation brought together all European communist parties and placed them under the control of the USSR.
2) **The Comecon** (the Council for Mutual Economic Assistance) was established in 1949. It countered the Marshall Plan by nationalising industries, collectivising agriculture and offering economic aid.

Stalin hoped this would encourage economic development in Eastern Europe and discourage trade with the West. It also appeased the countries that had been ordered to refuse Marshall aid.

Comment and Analysis

Marshall Plan aid ensured that a lot of Western Europe became allied with the USA. Stalin's retaliation — his creation of the Cominform and, later, the Comecon — strengthened his alliances in Eastern Europe.

The Cold War was tense — but preferable to a hot one...

In your own words, summarise what the USA and the USSR believed about each other after the Long and Novikov Telegrams were sent, and how this might have affected their actions.

The Berlin Crisis

Tension over the division of Germany had been building since the Potsdam Conference, and finally spilled over in the Berlin crisis in 1948. It resulted in an even larger rift between the two great powers.

In 1948 the USSR and the West Clashed over Berlin

Berlin was in East Germany. The French, British and US sectors formed West Berlin, while the Soviet sector was called East Berlin.

1) Immediately after the war, there were four zones of occupied Germany, and four zones in Berlin. In 1947, the USA and Britain agreed to combine their zones to form 'Bizonia'. The next year, the French agreed to add their zone.
2) The new western zone had a single government, and in June 1948 introduced a new currency to help economic recovery.
3) This alarmed the USSR. Stalin did not want a unified western zone on his doorstep. West Berlin's strong capitalist economy embarrassed the USSR, and made communism look weak.
4) As a result, Stalin decided to blockade Berlin to try to force the West to withdraw from West Berlin.
5) In June 1948, he ordered that all road, rail and canal links between West Berlin and the outside world should be cut off.

Comment and Analysis

Stalin wanted to force the West to withdraw from Berlin altogether. The Western powers believed that if this happened, the Soviet Union would be tempted to invade West Germany.

The Western powers wouldn't give up West Berlin...

- The West decided to bypass the blockade and fly in supplies. This became known as the Berlin Airlift, and lasted for 318 days.
- By 1949, 8000 tons of supplies were being flown in each day.
- Tegel airport was built in West Berlin to accommodate the large volume of flights. It meant supplies could be delivered in even greater numbers.

After the crisis, Germany was Divided in Two

1) When it became clear that the West was determined not to withdraw from Berlin, Stalin had to lift the blockade. It was also clear that Germany would remain divided.
2) In 1949, two separate states were formed — West Germany (Federal Republic of Germany) and communist East Germany (German Democratic Republic).

Comment and Analysis

The end of the Berlin blockade increased tensions as Stalin hadn't lifted the blockade willingly. The allies appeared strong, and had discredited and humiliated Stalin.

The Two Powers formed Military Alliances

1) Stalin's blockade during the Berlin crisis showed how unprepared the West would be if there was a conflict with the USSR.
2) As a consequence, the Western Powers decided to form a military alliance. In 1949, NATO (the North Atlantic Treaty Organisation) was created.
3) All members of NATO agreed to respond together if any member of the alliance was attacked.

The USSR saw the formation of NATO as a real threat.

- In 1955, the USSR established the Warsaw Pact to rival NATO. All the USSR's satellite states (except Yugoslavia) became members.
- Its main aims were to improve the defensive capability of Eastern Europe and strengthen relations.
- There were now two power blocs in Europe — NATO and the Warsaw Pact.

Members of the Warsaw Pact formed the so-called 'Eastern Bloc'.

The West had made Stalin look weak...

Explain how important the Berlin Crisis was for relations between the US and the USSR. [8]

The Arms Race

In the Cold War, the USA and the USSR tried to gain an advantage by forming military alliances and developing ever more powerful weapons. The aim was to 'look strong' to deter the other from attacking.

The USA and the USSR began an Arms Race

1) During the Cold War, the USA and the USSR worked to develop the most powerful weapons they could — there was an arms race.
2) Neither side really wanted to use these weapons, but both felt the other couldn't be allowed to gain an advantage. The fear was that if either gained a significant military advantage, that country might be tempted to trigger a war to take advantage of it.
3) Instead, a stand-off developed where both countries didn't dare act against the other, but didn't dare get 'left behind', either.
4) This competition sometimes spilled over into other areas. For example, when the USSR launched the first satellite into space, the USA quickly developed one of its own. This 'space race' led to the USSR sending the first man into space in 1961, and to the USA sending astronauts to the Moon in 1969.

Both countries developed Nuclear Stockpiles

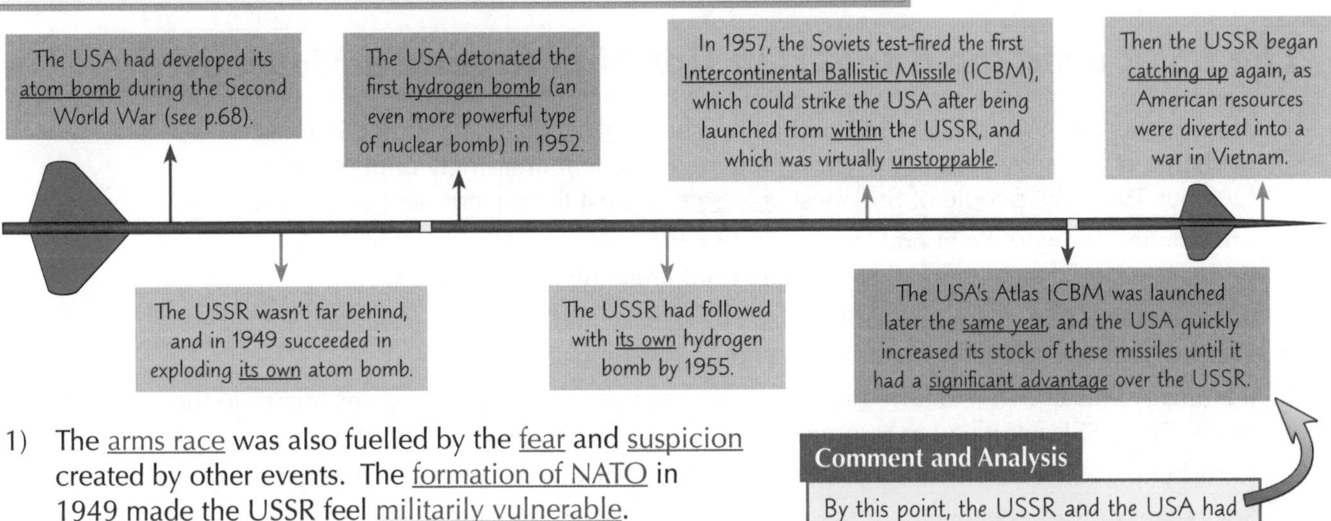

1) The arms race was also fuelled by the fear and suspicion created by other events. The formation of NATO in 1949 made the USSR feel militarily vulnerable.
2) In February 1950, communist China and the USSR signed a treaty of alliance, which strengthened Western fears that the USSR was planning communist domination.

Comment and Analysis

By this point, the USSR and the USA had the power to destroy each other multiple times over. As tensions increased, the threat of nuclear war became a real possibility.

Khrushchev raised hopes of 'Peaceful Co-existence'

In 1953, Stalin died and another member of the Communist Party, Nikita Khrushchev, took power.

Comment and Analysis

Because Khrushchev continued to develop weapons, the West still felt threatened and the arms race didn't slow down.

1) Khrushchev said he wanted 'peaceful co-existence' with the West. His words brought hope that there would be a 'thaw' in the Cold War.
2) But Khrushchev remained very competitive with the USA.
3) He wanted communism to spread, but thought the best way to achieve this was to clearly demonstrate its superiority — not defeat the West in a war.

The rivalry between the USA and the USSR kept on going...

When answering an exam question, always remember to give evidence to back up your points. For this page, you could use the sequence of 'tit for tat' weapons development to show how neither side dared fall behind in the arms race.

Divisions in Eastern Europe

Not all of the USSR's satellite states had willingly accepted communism, and the USSR soon faced unrest.

Unrest began to Stir in the Eastern Bloc

1) When Khrushchev came to power, he made a speech criticising Stalin's policies and brought in measures to 'de-Stalinise' the USSR. These included the abolition of the death penalty and the freeing of political prisoners jailed under Stalin's regime.
2) Some satellite states hoped that their countries would also become 'de-Stalinised'. Khrushchev abolished the Cominform (see p.69), meaning that states in Eastern Europe would have more political and economic freedom from the USSR.

Communism created a lot of economic hardship — poor living conditions increased anti-Soviet sentiment.

Comment and Analysis

Khrushchev wanted the Eastern Bloc to remain communist — he just didn't agree with Stalin's approach to communism. He thought that giving satellite states more economic independence would stabilise their communist regimes, but his plan backfired.

3) These moves allowed tensions in the satellite states to rise to the surface. Not all states had chosen communism, and saw the changes as a chance to loosen ties with the USSR.
4) In 1956, there was an uprising in Poland. The USSR threatened to intervene, but eventually allowed the new government to follow their own version of communism. This encouraged other states to consider revolt.

The USSR used the Hungarian Uprising to send a Message

1) After the Second World War, the USSR helped put Mátyás Rákosi, a brutal Stalinist, in charge of Hungary. His authoritarian regime became increasingly unpopular. In October 1956, the people of Budapest protested against the government of Rákosi.
2) Khrushchev allowed the liberal Imre Nagy to take over from Rákosi as Hungarian Prime Minister. Nagy hoped that Hungary could be a neutral state.
3) In November 1956, Nagy announced that Hungary would withdraw from the Warsaw Pact and hold free elections — ending communism there.
4) If Hungary was allowed to turn away from communism, other satellite states might do the same. The USSR felt it had to respond with force and make an example of Nagy.
5) Khrushchev, who had only held power for two years, also wanted to use the crisis to assert his authority.
6) Soviet tanks invaded Hungary in November 1956. Thousands of Hungarians were killed or wounded. Nagy was arrested and hanged. János Kádár became Prime Minister and ensured loyalty towards the USSR.

The crisis Strengthened the USSR and Discredited the West

1) Khrushchev's brutal response to Hungary demonstrated to satellite states that disloyalty wouldn't be tolerated. It also showed the Western powers that the USSR was still in control.
2) It was a turning point for Khrushchev — his actions reasserted his authority over the satellite states and destroyed any illusions in the West that his leadership signified a 'thaw' in the Cold War.

Western Reactions

- There was a lack of intervention from Western countries. They condemned the USSR's actions, but thought that helping Hungary would risk a nuclear war.
- The UN asked the USSR to withdraw from Hungary, but Kádár refused to take part in discussions. The situation remained unresolved.

Comment and Analysis

The Western powers' reputation as upholders of democracy was discredited. Their inaction sent a clear message to Eastern Europe that they wouldn't receive Western help to move away from the USSR. The UN was shown to be weak.

The USSR kept a tight hold on its satellite states...

Explain the significance of the Hungarian uprising as a factor in keeping the Eastern European satellite states loyal to the USSR. [8]

The Berlin Question

The 1950s saw more communication between the two superpowers, but underlying tensions remained.

There were some Steps to Improve East-West Relations...

President Eisenhower succeeded President Truman in January 1953, while Khrushchev came to power in September. This provided an opportunity to create a fresh start — there were several encouraging steps towards defusing tensions between the two powers:

- The USA and the USSR met in Geneva in 1955 and agreed to communicate more openly.
- In 1955, the USSR officially recognised the Federal Republic of Germany (West Germany) as a state.
- Khrushchev also freed some prisoners and reduced censorship in the USSR.

...but Berlin remained a Source of Tension

1) After the Berlin crisis in 1948 (see p.70), West Berlin was a unified zone and continued to develop economically, benefiting from a new currency and American (Marshall Plan) aid.
2) The situation in East Berlin was very different — the USSR had drained it of resources and its economy was slow to develop. Many people wanted to leave and go to the more prosperous West Berlin instead.

By 1961, at least 3 million East Germans had emigrated from East Berlin to West Berlin.

3) The situation was hugely embarrassing for Khrushchev, as it suggested that people preferred life under capitalism to communism.
4) It also threatened East Germany's economy, as many of those who left were skilled workers in search of a better life.
5) The refugee crisis in Berlin led Khrushchev to issue his 'Berlin Ultimatum' in 1958. He demanded that US, British and French troops leave West Berlin within six months. West Berlin would become a free city.
6) Eisenhower refused the ultimatum. Khrushchev took no further action, but the Berlin issue wasn't solved.

The Soviet attitude towards Berlin...

- The USSR felt threatened by the economic success in West Berlin.
- East Berlin had become dependent on trade links with West Berlin.
- The USSR worried the West was trying to use its strong economy to interfere in Eastern Europe.

The Western attitude towards Berlin...

- After the Berlin Airlift, West Berlin became a symbol of democracy — it had to be supported or the West would lose credibility.
- People fleeing from East Berlin suited the West — it was good propaganda because it made communism look weak.

Khrushchev and Eisenhower held a Summit in 1959

1) In 1959, Khrushchev became the first communist leader to visit the USA. The meeting symbolised a new spirit of co-operation and communication between the two powers.
2) At the meeting they discussed Berlin. Eisenhower still didn't agree to withdraw from West Berlin, but did agree to discuss the matter more deeply.
3) The leaders decided to meet in Paris the following year. Although no firm decisions had been made, the arrangement of another summit promised to continue the optimistic dialogue they had started.

Both powers refused to compromise on Berlin...

You need to show you understand how events are connected. Here you could show how the superpowers' attitudes towards Berlin were shaped by the Airlift or West Berlin's economic success.

The Berlin Wall

In 1961, around 2000 Germans crossed over from East to West Berlin every day. When it became clear that the situation wasn't going to be solved diplomatically, Khrushchev constructed the Berlin Wall.

Talks about Berlin Broke Down...

1) President Eisenhower and Khrushchev had agreed to discuss the Berlin question at the Paris Summit in 1960. Days before the summit was due to take place, the USSR shot down a U2 American spy plane over Soviet territory.
2) Eisenhower denied that it was a spy plane, but the USSR then produced the pilot (alive) and the plane's wreckage as evidence. When the USA refused to apologise, Khrushchev walked out of the Paris Summit.
3) The U2 incident hindered further negotiations about Berlin. Both countries met again at Vienna in June 1961 — by this time, John F. Kennedy had replaced Eisenhower as US President.
4) Kennedy vowed to take a tougher approach towards communism. He refused to compromise over Berlin, and no resolution was reached.

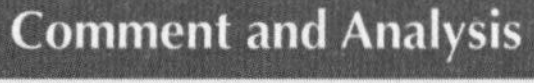

After the Vienna Summit, the USSR believed that problems in Berlin wouldn't be resolved by negotiation. This sparked the creation of the Berlin Wall.

...so the Berlin Wall was Put Up

1) Khrushchev felt he had to act to stem the flow of refugees out of East Berlin. On 13th August 1961, a 27-mile barrier was built across the city of Berlin overnight, separating East from West.
2) It was fortified with barbed wire and machine gun posts, and was later strengthened and made into a more permanent barrier. Military checkpoints policed any movements into or out of East Berlin.
3) Before the wall, East Berliners had entered West Berlin freely. After the wall, they could no longer go to work in West Berlin and were instantly separated from friends and relatives.
4) Citizens from East and West Berlin were rarely allowed through the military checkpoints and anyone who tried to escape East Berlin was shot.

© Mary Evans Picture Library/Imagno

A photo of the newly-built Berlin Wall.

The Berlin Wall helped Stabilise the situation in Europe

After the Berlin Wall was put up, Cold War tensions over Berlin stabilised.

'It's not a very nice solution, but a wall is a hell of a lot better than a war.' — President Kennedy, 1961.

The West condemned Khrushchev, but was actually relieved...

- Immediately after the Berlin Wall appeared, Soviet and Western troops were positioned either side of the wall, but then both powers agreed to back down.
- The USA condemned the building of the wall, but took no further military action.
- Kennedy was actually relieved — he'd been preparing for a confrontation of some sort.

1) The wall succeeded in stopping mass emigration to West Berlin. It also gave East Germany the opportunity to rebuild its economy, and strengthen itself as a communist state.
2) In the West, the Berlin Wall became a symbol of oppression and the failure of communism. In the USSR, it was seen as a sign of strength.
3) President Kennedy visited West Berlin in 1963 and gave a famous speech stating his solidarity with West Berlin and its people. He declared 'Ich bin ein Berliner' (I am a Berliner).

The wall cemented the divide between East and West Berlin...

Write a summary of the events that led to the construction of the Berlin Wall in 1961.

The Cuban Missile Crisis

As tension was increasing over Berlin, the USA also began to have problems closer to home. Cuba had long been the USA's economic ally, but revolution brought the communist threat to the USA's doorstep.

The Cuban Revolution in 1959 Worried the USA

1) Since 1952, Cuba had been ruled by Batista, a ruthless military dictator, who allowed American businessmen and the Mafia to make huge profits in a country where most people lived in poverty.
2) In 1956, a rebel called Fidel Castro began a guerrilla war. By 1959, he had enough support to take Cuba's capital, Havana, and successfully overthrew the government.
3) This revolution worried the USA. The USA had a long economic history with Cuba. It owned half of Cuba's land and held most of the shares in all Cuban industries.
4) The USA felt it had a right to be involved in Cuba's affairs. But Cubans had grown to resent American influence in their country — they didn't feel like an independent state.

In a 'guerrilla war', small military units use tactics like raids to fight a larger opponent.

The USA had occupied Cuba from 1898 to 1902. When Cuba became independent, the two countries maintained close economic ties.

The USA Accidentally pushed Castro Closer to the USSR

1) When Castro seized power in 1959, he nationalised US companies and increased taxes on goods imported from America. This angered the USA.
2) Eisenhower was concerned that Castro's drive towards public ownership showed that he was moving towards communism.
3) He threatened to stop importing Cuban sugar. Sugar was Cuba's main source of wealth, and the USA was sure that Castro would back down.
4) Instead, Castro signed a trade agreement with the USSR — the USSR promised to buy all sugar exports. All remaining American property in Cuba was confiscated.
5) In January 1961, the USA severed all diplomatic relations with Cuba — the new US President John Kennedy no longer recognised Castro's government.

'Nationalisation' means taking a privately owned industry and placing it under public ownership.

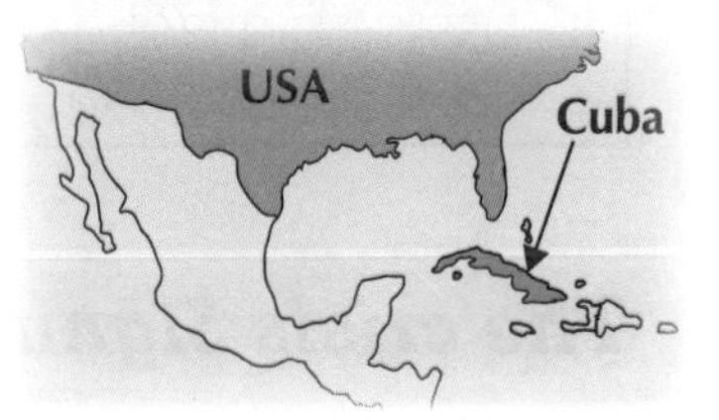

By 1961, Cuba had consolidated its ties with the USSR. As Cuba was only 100 miles from the USA, the communist threat had come dangerously close.

Comment and Analysis

Khrushchev wanted to help Castro, who was sympathetic towards communism. He also saw an opportunity to gain influence near US soil.

Rebels backed by the USA Invaded Cuba at the Bay of Pigs

Kennedy couldn't let a communist state emerge next to America — he intervened.

1) In 1961, Kennedy authorised an invasion of Cuba by anti-Castro rebels.
2) In April 1961, the rebels landed in the Bay of Pigs, but they were easily defeated and the USA didn't help — it was a bit of a fiasco.
3) The USA was humiliated, and had pushed Cuba even closer to the USSR.

Tensions continued to grow...

- The invasion led Castro to decide that Cuba needed Soviet military assistance to defend itself. This sparked one of the biggest crises of the Cold War — the Cuban Missile Crisis (see p.76).
- In December 1961, Castro publicly announced that he was a communist, confirming US fears.

The Bay of Pigs invasion wasn't Kennedy's finest moment...

In the exam you get marks for how well you organise your ideas. Make sure you've got a clear argument in your head before you start to write your answer — it's best to jot down a plan first.

The Cuban Missile Crisis

Khrushchev agreed to help Castro and began to build nuclear missile sites in Cuba.

Khrushchev planned to put Nuclear Missiles in Cuba

1) In September 1961, Cuba asked the USSR for weapons to defend itself against further American intervention. By July 1962, Khrushchev had decided to put nuclear missiles in Cuba.
2) Although Khrushchev already had missiles that could reach the USA, missiles in Cuba would allow him to launch a nuclear attack on all of central and eastern USA with very little warning.

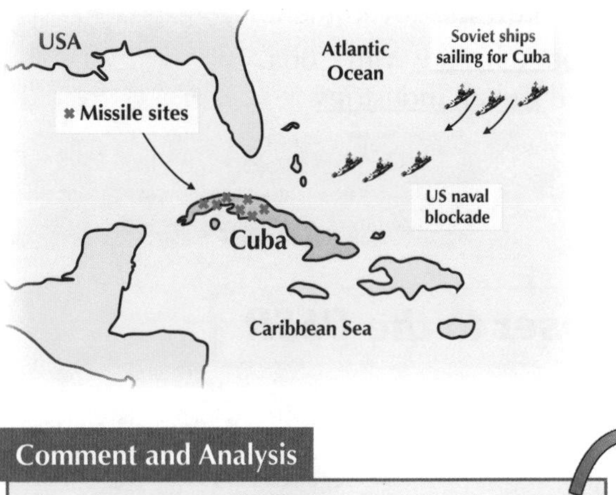

3) In October 1962, American U2 spy planes spotted that nuclear missile bases were being built in Cuba.
4) President Kennedy demanded that Khrushchev dismantle the missile bases and ordered a naval blockade of Cuba. All Soviet ships were to be stopped and searched to prevent missiles being transported to the island.
5) As tensions grew, US bombers were put in the air carrying nuclear bombs and the USA prepared to invade Cuba. The world was on the brink of nuclear war.

Comment and Analysis

The USA had placed missiles in Turkey right next to the USSR in April 1962. In Khrushchev's eyes, putting missiles in Cuba was a reasonable response.

On 27th October 1962, Khrushchev made a deal to dismantle the missile bases in Cuba and ordered his ships to turn around. In exchange the USA lifted the blockade, promised to not invade Cuba — and secretly agreed to remove their missiles from Turkey.

The crisis Significantly Altered the Course of the Cold War

The Cuban Missile Crisis was important because it forced everybody to face up to how quickly a tense situation could become an absolute catastrophe. In the short term, efforts were made to defuse tensions and improve communication between the powers.

- In 1963, a telephone 'hotline' was established between Washington and Moscow. This enabled the two superpowers to talk directly and more quickly in the event of a crisis.
- All nuclear missiles were removed from Cuba, and then from Turkey by April 1963.
- Kennedy emerged from the crisis as a hero who had stood up against the threat of communism.
- Khrushchev, however, was discredited — he'd forced the USA to remove their missiles from Turkey, but had agreed to keep the deal a secret. In the eyes of the public he'd failed and he resigned in 1964.

In the long term, the crisis prompted new measures to bring the build up of nuclear weapons under control.

1) **The Limited Test Ban Treaty** was signed by both powers in 1963. It stated that all future tests of nuclear weapons had to be carried out underground to avoid polluting the air with nuclear radiation.
2) **The Outer Space Treaty** was drawn up in 1967. It forbade countries (including the USSR and the USA) from placing weapons of mass destruction in space.
3) **The Nuclear Non-Proliferation Treaty** came into force in 1970. Both superpowers agreed not to supply nuclear weapons or related technology to countries that didn't already have nuclear arms. The treaty also encouraged nuclear disarmament, but it allowed countries to use nuclear technology for peaceful purposes (e.g. energy).

The Cuban Missile Crisis was one of the most dangerous events in the Cold War, but it also marked the beginning of a period of 'détente' (see p.79).

Signing that Non-Profiterole Treaty must've taken guts...

EXAM QUESTION

What was the significance of the Cuban Missile Crisis for the development of the Cold War? [8]

The Prague Spring

In 1968, discontent within the Soviet Eastern Bloc stirred again. Czechoslovakia wanted more freedom from Moscow, and decided to move away from Soviet influence in a rebellion known as 'the Prague Spring'.

There was Opposition to Soviet Control in Czechoslovakia

1) Tension had been building in Czechoslovakia. It had become a communist state in 1948 and its policies were heavily influenced by the USSR.
2) It was a member of the Warsaw Pact, which discouraged trade with countries outside the Eastern Bloc and promoted Soviet-style communism.
3) There was growing discontent about the extent of external control over Czechoslovakian affairs. In 1956, students and writers protested at the lack of free speech and free movement in the country.

Soviet policies such as collectivisation and centralisation slowed economic progress in Czechoslovakia.

Dubcek wanted to Move Away from Soviet policies

1) In January 1968, Alexander Dubcek became the leader of the Communist Party in Czechoslovakia. Dubcek wanted Czechoslovakia to follow its own version of communism.
2) In April 1968, he introduced a series of reforms that went against Soviet-style communism.

Dubcek's Reforms

- Travel to the West was made available for all.
- The border with West Germany was re-opened.
- All industry became decentralised.
- Trade unions and workers were given more power.
- Freedom of speech and opposition parties were allowed.

Decentralisation meant that companies were no longer controlled by Communist party officials — workers and local authorities were given more power.

3) Many of the reforms were aimed at improving the performance of Czechoslovakia's economy — partly by developing closer relations with the West.
4) This worried the USSR — it didn't want any Western involvement in its Eastern Bloc.
5) Even though some reforms moved away from Soviet policy, Dubcek was still a communist. He promised that Czechoslovakia would stay in the Warsaw Pact and remain a loyal ally to Moscow.
6) For four months, Dubcek's new policies were tolerated by the USSR, and Czechoslovakia enjoyed relative freedom. This period is known as the 'Prague Spring'.

The USSR was Under Pressure to Intervene

1) The USSR grew increasingly concerned about Dubcek's reforms. Dubcek promised he was still loyal to Moscow, but his new policies meant that the USSR had less control over Czechoslovakia.
2) The leader of the USSR, Leonid Brezhnev, was worried that Dubcek's reforms could lead to a rejection of communism in the Eastern Bloc and in the USSR itself. If Czechoslovakia pulled away, other satellite states might follow.

Events in August 1968 triggered a Soviet response...

- President Tito of Yugoslavia visited Prague. Yugoslavia had refused to sign the Warsaw Pact and had never accepted the USSR's version of communism. The trip was an ominous sign to Brezhnev that Czechoslovakia was no longer loyal to the USSR.
- The USSR received a letter from communists in Czechoslovakia, asking for help.

Dubcek wanted to reform Czechoslovakia peacefully...

In the exam, always read the question carefully and work out what it wants you to do. It's very easy to just describe what happened — but often you need to analyse events, too.

The Prague Spring

In August 1968, the USSR decided to intervene militarily. This led to a new pro-Soviet leader in power and Czechoslovakia returned to Soviet-style communism.

The USSR Invaded Czechoslovakia in August 1968

1) On 21st August 1968 500,000 Soviet troops invaded Czechoslovakia.
2) The Czechoslovakians responded with non-violent demonstrations — people took to the streets with anti-invasion banners, and in January 1969 a student burned himself alive in the street in protest.
3) In April 1969, Dubcek was forcibly removed from office, and replaced with Gustav Husak. Husak was loyal to Soviet-style communism, and would ensure that Czechoslovakia remained close with the USSR.

Czechoslovakia was keen to avoid the violence that erupted in the 1956 Hungarian uprising (see p.72).

Countries Criticised the USSR, but Didn't Act

There was an international outcry at the Soviet intervention in Czechoslovakia, but no action was taken.

Warsaw Pact forces enter Prague in August 1968.

- The UN denounced the invasion and proposed a draft resolution requesting the withdrawal of Soviet troops from Czechoslovakia. This was vetoed (rejected) by the USSR.
- Many countries condemned the Soviet action but didn't intervene. They were wary of interfering within the USSR's sphere of influence.
- Communist parties in the West criticised Brezhnev's reaction and sought to distance themselves from Soviet influence.

Comment and Analysis

Countries were wary of taking action against the USSR. The Prague Spring occurred at a time when the Cold War had thawed slightly. Nobody wanted to re-ignite tensions between the two superpowers.

The lack of reaction from the UN and the West made the Western powers appear weak.

The Prague Spring Strengthened the USSR

1) The USSR succeeded in returning Czechoslovakia to Soviet-style communism.
2) Brezhnev used the Prague Spring as an opportunity to establish his authority in the Eastern Bloc. He showed he was prepared to invade a friendly satellite state in order not to weaken the anti-Western alliance. He also proved to the USA that he was a strong and determined leader.

Brezhnev Doctrine

- After the invasion, Brezhnev announced that in future the USSR would intervene in any country where communism was under threat.
- The Brezhnev Doctrine was important because it strengthened the USSR's control over its satellite states.
- It also sent a message to the Eastern Bloc that giving up communism wasn't an option — the USSR would respond with force.

3) Soviet-American relations continued to be strained. Despite recent moves towards reducing the nuclear threat (see p.76), both countries still distrusted one another.
4) The incident reminded both superpowers that the Cold War wasn't over. Brezhnev had proved he was still willing to risk conflict to uphold communism in the Eastern Bloc.

The USSR regained control — the Cold War got chillier...

Look back at pages 73-78. Make a timeline of the main crises that occurred in the Cold War between 1958 and 1970, and summarise what happened in each one.

Détente — Easing of Tensions

In the 1970s there was a period of 'détente' — an easing in tension between the two superpowers.

The policy of Détente was Practical

Détente wasn't just goodwill — it was also a sensible policy for both countries.

1) The 1960s were marked by crises, including some of the most tense moments in the Cold War (p.73-78). Both the USA and the USSR wanted to avoid other near misses.
2) Boosting military power hadn't succeeded in reducing tensions. Both countries recognised that a new strategy was needed.
3) Both countries were also keen to reduce their military spending — the arms race was extremely expensive and led to falling standards of living.

Comment and Analysis

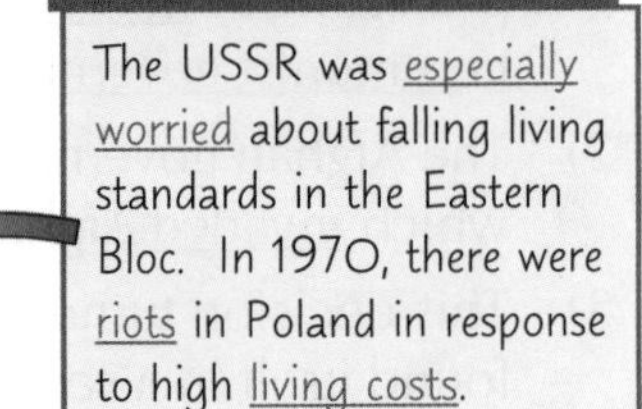

The Superpowers agreed to Reduce Arms and Cooperate

The two superpowers developed closer relations under détente. In 1975, Soviet and American spacecraft docked together in space. However, the most significant progress was achieved through diplomacy.

The First Strategic Arms Limitation Treaty (SALT 1) 1972

1) SALT 1 was a treaty signed in 1972 by the USA and the USSR. It limited the number of ABMs (anti-ballistic missiles) each country could have and placed a temporary limit on the numbers of ICBMs (Intercontinental Ballistic Missiles) on both sides.
2) ABMs were designed to intercept incoming missiles and had the potential to upset the delicate 'nuclear balance' between the USSR and the USA.
3) In the short term, the treaty was a success because it slowed down the arms race.

Comment and Analysis

By limiting the number of ABMs each country could have, SALT 1 reduced the likelihood of one country holding an advantage over the other.

If one side could use ABMs to destroy the other side's missiles then the threat of retaliation would be gone. The side with ABMs could launch a first strike and then just destroy the missiles that were fired back towards it.

The Helsinki Agreement 1975

1) The Helsinki Agreement in 1975 was a pact between the USA, the USSR, Canada and most of Europe. All countries agreed to recognise existing European borders and to uphold human rights.
2) Both superpowers accepted the division of Germany and the USSR's influence over Eastern Europe.
3) The West viewed the USSR's agreement to uphold human rights as great progress, but the USSR didn't stick to its word. It didn't grant freedom of speech or freedom of movement to its citizens. This undermined the Helsinki agreement and made the USA distrust the USSR.

The Second Strategic Arms Limitation Treaty (SALT 2) 1979

1) The SALT 2 Treaty was signed in 1979. The treaty banned the USA and the USSR from launching new missile programmes and limited the number of MIRVs (Multiple Independently targetable Reentry Vehicles) each country could have.
2) However the treaty was never ratified (approved) by the US Senate, so it didn't come into effect. See p.80 for more information.

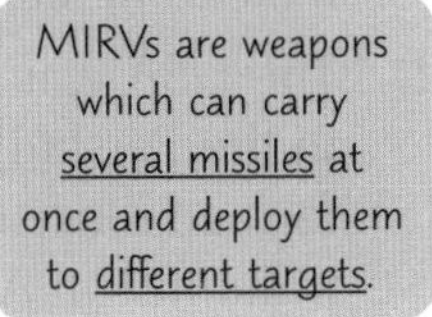

The superpowers took important steps towards limiting their nuclear arms during détente, but both countries continued to hold vast stockpiles of weapons.

You'd better learn this, or I'll put you in détente-tion...

1) *Jot down a quick summary of why both powers wanted to pursue détente.*
2) *Write out a table listing the successes and failures of détente.*

REVISION TASK

The Soviet Invasion of Afghanistan

The Soviet War in Afghanistan was a turning point for détente in the 1970s — it demolished the trust that had been so carefully built up between the USA and the USSR.

The USSR got bogged down in a War in Afghanistan

1) In 1978, a civil war broke out in Afghanistan. Rebels were protesting at new radical reforms brought in by the Afghan communist government, which had close ties to the Soviet Union.
2) The Afghan government requested help from the USSR, which invaded Afghanistan in December 1979.
3) This decision turned out to be a disaster — the USSR found itself in a seemingly unwinnable conflict.
4) It had to fight in difficult mountainous terrain against determined opposition, who were supplied with weapons by the USA.

Comment and Analysis

The USSR used the Brezhnev Doctrine (see p.78) to justify the invasion. It was also concerned by the idea of an anti-Soviet government in Afghanistan, as the countries shared a border.

Around 1 million Afghan civilians were killed and over 6 million became refugees.

The War was Disastrous for the USSR

1) 15,000 Soviet troops were killed and the government spent huge amounts of money, but the USSR couldn't win.
2) The Soviet-Afghan War led to a loss of public support in the USSR for the communist regime. The Soviet people were angry at falling living standards, which had deteriorated as a direct result of high spending in Afghanistan.

Comment and Analysis

When Mikhail Gorbachev came to power in 1985, he admitted that the USSR couldn't afford to keep fighting. In 1988, he began withdrawing Soviet troops from Afghanistan (see p.82).

It didn't work out too well for Brezhnev internationally, either...

- The war was an embarrassment for Brezhnev and undermined the USSR's strong military reputation, which was essential for keeping its satellite states under control.
- In January 1980, the UN condemned the invasion. It proposed a resolution demanding Soviet withdrawal, but the resolution was vetoed (rejected) by the USSR.
- In 1980, the USA and over 50 other countries (including Canada and West Germany) boycotted the Moscow Olympic Games, in protest at the Soviet-Afghan War.

The Superpowers began to Move Away from Détente

The war caused tension between the USSR and the USA to resurface. The situation was as dangerous as ever.

1) Soviet intervention in Afghanistan was interpreted by the USA as an act of communist expansionism. In 1979, US President Jimmy Carter was so alarmed he stopped the SALT 2 Treaty (see p.79) being debated by the US Senate, meaning it could never come into effect. Instead he called for an increase in the defence budget.
2) The USA was also worried that the USSR was trying to gain influence in the Persian Gulf, close to the Afghan border. The oil-rich area had formed close economic ties with the West, and Carter thought Soviet influence in Afghanistan threatened US interests there.
3) Carter warned that the USA would use force to prevent the USSR from gaining control of the Gulf region. This warning became known as the Carter Doctrine.

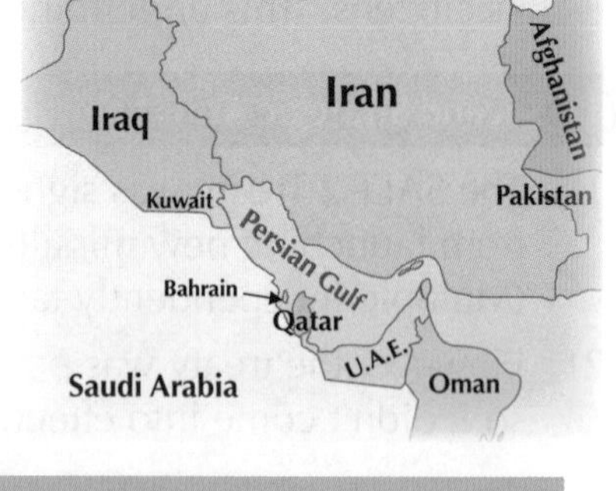

The Carter Doctrine was the first threat of aggression between the superpowers since détente.

The USSR bit off more than it could chew...

If you're asked about the importance of an event, think about its knock-on effects, e.g. the Soviet invasion of Afghanistan contributed to the end of détente and harmed Brezhnev's popularity.

The Second Cold War

Cold War tensions were resurrected during the 1980s, in a period now known as the 'Second Cold War'.

Reagan Boosted American Defences

After the Soviet invasion of Afghanistan, the policy of détente was badly damaged. It was in even more danger when US President Carter was succeeded by President Ronald Reagan in January 1981.

1) Ronald Reagan was a hardline anti-communist. His speeches were often full of anti-Soviet rhetoric and he called the USSR an 'evil empire'. This increased hostility between the two superpowers.
2) Reagan didn't believe in the policy of détente. He was willing to negotiate with the USSR, but only from a position of strength.
3) This meant he wanted to increase American defences. American intelligence gathered in 1976 also suggested that the USA had underestimated the USSR's nuclear strength, and the USA felt it had to catch up.

This worried the USSR — it couldn't afford to match Reagan's spending.

Reagan started the biggest arms build-up in American history...
- In the 1980s the USA spent $550 billion a year on conventional and nuclear weapons.
- Reagan also re-authorised some weapons programmes that had been abandoned during détente. The USA began to develop the neutron bomb, which was designed to cause maximum loss of life and minimum damage to property.

The USA Launched the Strategic Defence Initiative

Relations between the superpowers worsened when Reagan announced his Strategic Defence Initiative (SDI).

1) In March 1983, Reagan announced the development of the Strategic Defence Initiative, nicknamed 'Star Wars'.
2) The program would develop weapons that would be deployed in space and that could destroy nuclear missiles after they had been launched.
3) It would be the ultimate defence system — even nuclear missiles already heading towards the USA could be stopped.
4) If successful, the SDI would shift the balance of the Cold War in the USA's favour.
5) By 1983, détente was truly over.

Comment and Analysis

The SDI is a typical example of the differing perspectives that kept the Cold War going. For the USA, the SDI was a means of defence. But the USSR viewed it as an act of aggression — the USA would theoretically be able to attack the USSR without fear of retaliation.

There were anti-nuclear demonstrations as old fears resurfaced. This demonstration took place in Vienna in 1983. The banner reads 'create peace without weapons'.

Reagan's attitude Changed after 1985

Gorbachev's leadership brought about a thaw in Cold War tensions, and the return of détente.

1) When Mikhail Gorbachev became leader of the USSR in March 1985, Reagan reassessed his attitude towards the USSR.
2) Gorbachev proposed radical reforms and was far more open towards the West than previous Soviet leaders. Reagan recognised that the USSR was being steered in a new direction.
3) The USA realised that this change could be good. Although initiatives like the SDI weren't scrapped, Reagan thought negotiation was now the best way to protect American interests.
4) Importantly, the two leaders got on well, creating a better relationship between the superpowers.

In the early 1980s, the Cold War Rea-ganed momentum...

Give an account that analyses the role that Reagan's attitude played in the ending of détente. You could mention his fears about the USSR and the Strategic Defence Initiative. [8]

Gorbachev's 'New Thinking'

Mikhail Gorbachev came to power in the USSR and radically changed Soviet policies. This was one of the biggest turning points in the Cold War — it laid the foundations for the collapse of the USSR.

The Cold War created a Crisis in the USSR

1) The arms race with the USA and the war in Afghanistan were hugely expensive and the Soviet economy just couldn't support this level of spending.
2) Soviet goods were poor quality and Soviet farming was inefficient — there wasn't enough food and millions of tonnes of grain had to be imported from the USA.
3) The communist government was becoming more corrupt and was unable to give the Soviet people the same high living standards as people had in the West.

By the 1980s, Soviet citizens were becoming increasingly discontent.

Gorbachev introduced Radical Reforms

1) In 1985, Mikhail Gorbachev became General Secretary of the Communist Party. He was more open to the West than previous leaders and he admitted that the Soviet system had problems.
2) He introduced two major policies — 'perestroika' and 'glasnost'.

Perestroika and glasnost were part of what is known as Gorbachev's 'New Thinking'. Changes to foreign policy were part of it too.

Perestroika means 'restructuring'...
- Gorbachev wanted to make the Soviet economy more efficient.
- He moved away from the centralisation of industry — the government no longer told businesses exactly what they had to produce.
- Gorbachev also allowed private business ownership and allowed Soviet businesses to trade with the Western powers.

Glasnost means 'openness'...
- Gorbachev gave the Soviet people new rights.
- Thousands of political prisoners were released.
- Free speech was allowed and censorship was relaxed.
- In 1989, Gorbachev created the USSR's first elected parliament — Communist Party officials were chosen by the public for the first time.

Comment and Analysis

Gorbachev didn't want to end communism — he wanted to modernise it. He hoped that reform would revive the USSR's struggling economy, which was falling further behind the USA's.

Gorbachev changed Foreign Policy

1) Gorbachev improved relations with the West. He met with US President Reagan several times, for example at the Geneva Summit in 1985. Gorbachev's open attitude softened Reagan's hard approach.
2) In 1987, a disarmament treaty was signed — the INF Treaty (Intermediate-Range Nuclear Forces Treaty). The USA and the USSR agreed to remove medium-range nuclear missiles from Europe within three years.
3) The first missiles were dismantled in 1988. The INF Treaty was a milestone in American-Soviet relations — both countries actively reduced weapons for the first time.
4) Gorbachev reduced the scale of the USSR's commitments abroad. In 1988, he announced that all Soviet troops would withdraw from Afghanistan.
5) In 1988, he also announced the immediate reduction of the USSR's weapons stockpile and the number of troops in the Soviet armed forces.

Gorbachev's decrease in military spending and his decision to withdraw from Afghanistan greatly defused tensions between the superpowers.

In 1988, Gorbachev decided to abandon the Brezhnev Doctrine (see p.78). He told the United Nations that Eastern Europe now had a choice — the USSR wasn't going to control it any longer.

Gorbachev wanted to improve communism...

Draw a table with three columns labelled 'perestroika', 'glasnost' and 'foreign policy'. Put each of Gorbachev's 'New Thinking' policies into the table under the correct heading.

Eastern Europe Pulls Away

Gorbachev's 'New Thinking' was intended to modernise communism, but actually sparked its decline.

The satellite states No Longer Feared the USSR

Gorbachev's decision to abandon the Brezhnev Doctrine led to the USSR losing control of its satellite states.

- Gorbachev stated the USSR would no longer use force to uphold communism in its satellite states. In 1988, he announced the withdrawal of Soviet troops, tanks and aircraft from Eastern Europe.
- It was fear of Soviet military intervention that had kept opposition movements under control within the USSR's satellite states. Without it, they had a chance to act.

'New Thinking' Energised Opposition

1) The nature of Gorbachev's new policies encouraged reformist movements within Eastern Europe.
2) Gorbachev's 'New Thinking' also caused splits in the Soviet Communist Party, making control of Eastern European countries from Moscow more difficult.

Some members thought that Gorbachev's reforms weren't radical enough, and others worried they were too radical.

The Berlin Wall Fell in November 1989

1) In May 1989, communist Hungary opened its border with non-communist Austria. This let East Germans travel through Hungary to Austria, and then into West Germany.
2) Between August and September 1989, thousands left East Germany for West Germany. The East German government was unable to control the situation, and received no help from the USSR.
3) In October 1989, there were mass protests against the communist regime. The East German government finally agreed to open the border between East and West Berlin in November 1989. Free elections were promised and the wall was torn down.
4) The fall of the Berlin Wall showed that the relationship between East and West was transforming, and that the USSR was losing its grip over communist territory.

As news of the decision to open the wall spread, Berliners gathered at the wall. Here, East German officials wait for orders.

Communist governments in Eastern Europe started to Collapse

1) Free elections were also held in Poland in June 1989. In 1990, a new non-communist government came to power. The USSR didn't intervene.
2) In December 1989, communist governments collapsed in Czechoslovakia, Bulgaria and Romania. Hungary's Communist Party suffered a large defeat in free elections in March 1990.

In October 1990, communist East Germany and democratic West Germany rejoined to form a single state again. For many people this was a powerful symbol that the communist experiment was over.

Comment and Analysis

The reunification of Germany and the decline of communism in the USSR's satellite states symbolised a new thaw in the Cold War. Europe was no longer ideologically divided between East and West.

The satellite states eventually got a bit of space...

Look back at the information on Gorbachev's 'New Thinking' and the effect it had on Europe. Make a timeline of events between 1988 and 1990.

The Collapse of the Soviet Union

Despite the fall of communist regimes in Eastern Europe, the Cold War wasn't over until the USSR collapsed.

The Republics of the USSR Wanted Independence

As the USSR lost its grip on its satellite states, it was undergoing a national crisis.

1) In early 1990, some important regions in the Soviet Union demanded independence, especially the Baltic republics — Latvia, Lithuania, and Estonia.
2) They were encouraged by the recent success of revolutions across Eastern Europe (see p.83) and by Gorbachev's policy of 'glasnost' (openness), which gave greater power to individuals and encouraged constructive criticism of Soviet policy.
3) Gorbachev didn't want to lose the Republics. He granted them more power — but it wasn't enough.
4) The leaders of the Soviet republics no longer listened to Gorbachev, and he lacked the authority to make them comply with Soviet wishes.

The USSR was made up of 15 republics. Each republic had its own parliament, but was centrally controlled by Moscow.

- Lithuania declared itself independent in March 1990. Soviet troops were sent to Vilnius, the capital of Lithuania, in January 1991, and several civilians were killed in the violence that followed. But this only strengthened the independence movement.
- In April 1991, Georgia declared its independence, followed by the Ukraine's declaration in August.

Military intervention no longer deterred protests, it escalated them.

As Gorbachev's authority weakened, independence movements gained in strength.

There was a Political Crisis in the USSR

By 1990, Gorbachev faced opposition from within his own party and the public. The Communist Party was divided — some members wanted more drastic reform and others wanted a return to former Soviet policies. The public were unhappy because Gorbachev's reforms hadn't lived up to their high expectations.

1) More traditional Soviet communists were worried that the Communist Party was so divided it was going to split up.
2) They thought Gorbachev's reforms had gone too far and plotted a coup against the government in August 1991.
3) They arrested Gorbachev, tried to force him to resign, and sent tanks onto the streets of Moscow to deter protesters.
4) The coup didn't go to plan — it was condemned by Boris Yeltsin, a Soviet politician who opposed Gorbachev and wanted the USSR to adopt capitalism.
5) Yeltsin went onto the streets to rally opposition against the coup. There were mass protests in major cities, showing that Soviets had clearly rejected communism. The coup failed.

Economic reforms hadn't worked

- The USSR's economy hadn't improved, and in 1990 a quarter of its population was living below the poverty line.
- Economic corruption was still rife.
- Inflation was high and basic goods were in short supply.
- The huge costs of the arms race and the war in Afghanistan hindered the reforms too.

The Soviet Union Collapsed

1) On Christmas Day 1991, Gorbachev resigned.
2) The USSR was dissolved on the 26th December.
3) The republics that made up the Soviet Union had become independent states. These included Latvia, Lithuania, Estonia and Belarus.
4) The biggest of the republics was Russia. Yeltsin was elected leader and adopted capitalism.

As more and more countries declared their independence from the USSR, they also declared their intentions to pull out of the Warsaw Pact (p.70). This made it weaker and it eventually ended in July 1991.

The dissolution of the USSR marked the end of the Cold War...

Explain two reasons for the collapse of the Soviet Union. [8]

Revision Summary

That pretty much sums up the Cold War — now all you have to do is check it's all sunk in.

- Try these questions and tick off each one when you get it right.
- When you've done all the questions for a topic and are completely happy with it, tick off the topic.

The Origins of the Cold War, 1941-58 (p.67-72)

1) What was the Grand Alliance?
2) Describe the different ideologies followed by the USA and the USSR.
3) Why was the USSR in a position of influence over Eastern Europe after the Second World War?
4) What did Churchill mean when he said an 'Iron Curtain' divided Europe?
5) Why were the Long and Novikov Telegrams important?
6) What was the Truman Doctrine?
7) What was the Cominform? What did it do?
8) Describe the events of the Berlin Airlift.
9) Give two consequences of the 1948-49 Berlin Crisis.
10) What is meant by an 'arms race'?
11) What did Khrushchev mean by 'peaceful co-existence'?
12) Give two consequences of the Hungarian uprising.

Cold War Crises, 1958-70 (p.73-78)

13) Why was Berlin a source of tension between the superpowers?
14) Describe Khrushchev's 'Berlin Ultimatum' of 1958.
15) How did the Paris and Vienna Summits affect the USSR's attitude towards Berlin?
16) Give two consequences of the establishment of the Berlin Wall.
17) Describe the main events of the Cuban Missile Crisis. How did it alter the course of the Cold War?
18) Why did the USSR end the Prague Spring?
19) How did other countries react to the Soviet invasion of Czechoslovakia?
20) What was the Brezhnev Doctrine?

The End of the Cold War (p.79-84)

21) What does 'détente' mean?
22) Name three treaties signed by the superpowers in the 1970s.
23) How did the Soviet invasion of Afghanistan change relations between the USA and the USSR?
24) What was US President Reagan's attitude towards détente?
25) What was the SDI?
26) When did Mikhail Gorbachev become leader in the USSR?
27) What were 'perestroika' and 'glasnost'?
28) How did Gorbachev change Soviet foreign policy?
29) Why did opposition to communism rise in Eastern Europe after 1988?
30) Why was there a political crisis in the USSR by 1990?
31) Describe the events that led to the collapse of the Soviet Union from 1990-91.

Exam Skills for the British Depth Study

This page is for the British depth study section of the exam — for the modern depth study, see p.87-89.

British depth studies are about knowing a Period in Detail

1) The British depth study covers a short period of history (less than 50 years) in detail. It focuses on understanding how important features of the period (e.g. political, social, economic, religious and military issues) helped to shape events.
2) You'll need to have a detailed knowledge of the period, including an understanding of the important events that took place.
3) The study also encourages you to think about how different elements combined to bring about certain outcomes. For example, commercial rivalry increased existing tension between England and Spain, which eventually led to them going to war in 1585.
4) You'll also need to be aware of the consequences of events, and more general changes that took place.

There are Three basic types of exam question

1) You'll be asked to describe two features of the period you've studied. This is designed to test your knowledge of the period. Make sure the points you make are clear and accurate.

> Describe two features of education in Elizabethan England, 1558-88. [4 marks]

2) Another question will ask you to explain the reasons for a specific event or development. For every point you make, you need to back it up with evidence and explain why the evidence illustrates the point you're making.

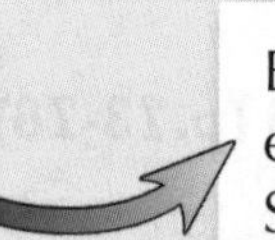

> Explain the reasons for the execution of Mary, Queen of Scots in 1587. [12 marks]

3) You'll then need to answer one more question, from a choice of two. Each will give you a statement and you'll be asked how far you agree with it.

> Explain how far you agree with this statement: 'The strength of England's naval tactics were the main reason why the Spanish Armada failed.' [16 marks]

- Decide your opinion before you start writing, and state it clearly at the beginning and end of your answer.
- Include evidence for both sides of the debate, and explain which factors are more important — these more important factors should be the ones backing up the opinion you've given.

In question types 2) and 3), you'll be given some 'stimulus points' — hints about things you could include in your answer. You don't have to include details about these stimulus points, so don't panic if you can't remember much about them. Even if you do write about the stimulus points, you must add other information too — if you don't, you can't get full marks.

Remember these things for All the questions

1) Using specific information like dates, names and statistics can help you get extra marks, but make sure all the information you include is relevant to the question.
2) Your answer should be well organised and structured — each of your points should lead clearly to your conclusion.

For more general advice on how to answer exam questions, see p.135.

This depth study stuff is pretty deep...

Some of these questions can be pretty specific, so don't get caught out. Make sure you know all the major features of the period you've studied. Check p.4 and p.45 for sample answers to similar questions.

Exam Skills for the Modern Depth Study

These pages are about the modern depth study section of the exam — for the British depth study, see p.86.

Modern depth studies are about Sources and Interpretations

1) The modern depth study looks closely at around 30 years of history. In some ways, it's similar to the British depth study, but it also considers different interpretations of key events and features of the period.
2) This means that you'll need to understand how historical sources or events can be interpreted in different ways by different people or at different times.

The First Part of the paper gives you One Source to analyse

1) The first question will ask you to infer something from a source — this means using details in the source to arrive at conclusions about an event or period.

> Infer two pieces of information from Source A about the role of von Papen and Hindenburg in Hitler's appointment as Chancellor in 1933. [4 marks]

2) The second question will ask you to explain the causes of a key event or issue that was important in the period you've studied.

> Explain why the creation of the Weimar Republic (1919) was unpopular in Germany. [12 marks]

The Second Part gives you Sources and Interpretations

1) You'll be given two sources and asked how useful they are for a particular historical investigation. Explain your answer, using both sources and your own knowledge.

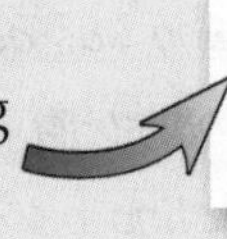
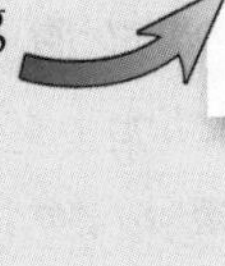

> Explain how useful Sources B and C are for an investigation into what the Nazi Party offered the German people. [8 marks]

For how to assess the usefulness of a source, see p.1.

2) You'll be asked to look at two different interpretations of an aspect of your period. You'll need to explain what the main difference is between the two views.

> Interpretations 1 and 2 provide different opinions on what Nazi Party offered the German people. Explain the main difference between these opinions. [4 marks]

3) You'll need to say why the two views are different. You'll have to use your own knowledge, but you can also refer to Sources B and C.

> Give one reason why these interpretations give different opinions. [4 marks]

4) Then you'll have to explain how far you agree with one of the interpretations. You must refer to both interpretations in your answer.

> Explain how far you agree with Interpretation 2 about what the Nazi Party offered the German people. [20 marks]

4 of the marks available for this question are for spelling, punctuation and grammar (see p.136-p.137).

Remember these things for All the questions

1) When working with sources, it's not just a case of describing what you see or read. You need to analyse the source and use it to draw conclusions about the period you've studied.
2) When you're evaluating interpretations, consider what information has been included (or emphasised), what has been left out, and the way the author has presented their view (e.g. whether they're describing things in a positive or negative way).

Exam Skills for the Modern Depth Study

Here's a sample answer to a question from the second part of the modern depth study section of your exam.

Here's a Sample Answer to help you

Source B

A German girl decorates a picture of Adolf Hitler with flowers. Photograph taken in Germany in 1935.

Source C

The German peasant has become impoverished... the social hopes of many millions of people are destroyed; one third of all German men and women of working age is unemployed... If the present parties seriously want to save Germany, why have they not done so already? Had they wanted to save Germany, why has it not happened?

Extract from a public speech made by Adolf Hitler July, 1932.

This sample answer will give you an idea of how to answer a source-based question, using the sources above.

Explain how useful Sources B and C are for an investigation into what the Nazi Party offered the German people. Use both sources, as well as your own knowledge. [8 marks]

Make it clear which source you're talking about.

Ask yourself about the source — who made it, when they made it, and where.

Use your own knowledge to look at the wider context of the source.

Remember to say how useful you think each source is.

Source B is partially useful because it shows that the Nazi party were offering the German people a strong leader who was admired and loved by his people. The photo was taken by an unknown photographer in 1935 — two years into Hitler's Chancellorship, when he was consolidating his dictatorship. By 1935, the Nazi Party had established a system of censorship to control the image of the party, so it is possible that this photograph was taken as a propaganda image, which limits its usefulness. The photo's suggestion that the Nazi Party offered a strong and loved leader, isn't necessarily false — Hitler's charisma and patriotism were undoubtedly a factor in the Nazi Party's popularity. However, it's unlikely that photos published at that time would challenge Nazi Party ideology, making Source B unreliable in showing what German people felt the Nazi Party offered them. Because of this, Source B is only partially useful.

Remember to write about both sources.

Use evidence from the source to support the points that you've made.

Think about when the sources were created, and how that affects their usefulness.

You can also think about what the sources don't include.

Source C is from a speech made by Hitler himself in July 1932. The fact that the speech was made by the leader of the Nazi party is useful because it shows what Hitler is directly offering the people of Germany. Hitler talks about the need to 'save Germany', which suggests that the Nazi Party wanted to be seen by the German people as offering hope. At this time, the Nazi Party was trying to appeal to as many people as possible before elections that November. This view is from the Nazi Party's perspective, and as a result is biased and only partly useful. Both sources focus on the impression the Party was trying to give — not on what Germans themselves believed. This means that both sources are only partially useful at best.

Exam Skills for the Modern Depth Study

Here are some more sample answers to questions from the modern depth study section of your exam.

Here's another Sample Answer to help you

Interpretation 1

To describe Hitler's thinking as an ideology is really to flatter it. It lacked coherence and was intellectually superficial and simplistic. It was not even a rational system of thought. It was merely a collection of ideas not very cleverly pieced together. Although the combination was unique, it was not in any positive sense original.

Extract from 'Access to History: Germany: the Third Reich 1933-45' 2nd ed., by Geoff Layton, published in 2000.

Interpretation 2

Nazism contained...wholly 'modern' types of appeal offering social mobility, a society of equal chances where success came from merit and achievement, and new opportunities to thrive and prosper through letting youth and vigour have its head at the expense of the old... and the decayed.

Extract from 'The Nazi Dictatorship: Problems and Perspectives of Interpretation', by Ian Kershaw, published in 2015.

This sample answer will give you an idea of how to explain the difference between interpretations.

Interpretations 1 and 2 provide different opinions on what Nazi Party offered the German people. Explain the main difference between these opinions. [4 marks]

Address the question directly in the first sentence.

A key difference between the two interpretations is that Interpretation 1 suggests that Nazi ideology wasn't offering anything 'original' — it was made up of old ideas, put together in a different way. However, Interpretation 2 states that the Nazi Party had a 'modern' type of appeal, suggesting that it offered the German people something new and original. This is supported by Interpretation 2's statement that the party would provide 'new opportunities to thrive and prosper', which the author implies is unlike how things had previously been.

Use evidence from the interpretations to support your points.

Explain what the interpretation is trying to say.

Here's one more Sample Answer to help you

This sample answer will give you an idea of how to explain why the interpretations you've been given are different. It uses the same two interpretations as above.

Give one reason why these interpretations give different opinions on what Nazi Party offered the German people. [4 marks]

Give a clear reason in your first sentence.

Interpretations 1 and 2 may have different opinions about what the Nazi Party offered the German people because they focus on different aspects of the party. Interpretation 1 focuses on the 'collection of ideas' behind the Nazi Party — it's emphasising the lack of originality in Nazi ideology. However, Interpretation 2 looks at the new opportunities the Nazis seemed to offer. It doesn't examine ideology, but instead considers how the party seemed to provide new ways for Germans to 'prosper' in society.

Discuss both interpretations.

Use evidence from the text, then explain what it shows.

Explain how looking at different aspects of the party could have affected the authors' views.

After analysing those sauces, my stomach's rumbling...

Although you're evaluating sources and interpretations, the same basic rules apply. If you're asked to explain something, use evidence. If you're asked how far you agree, give a clear opinion.

English Society and Government in 1558

In 1558, England had been governed by Tudor monarchs for more than seventy years. The country had well-organised systems of central and local government, but there were some major divisions in society.

Queen Elizabeth I was from the House of Tudor

The Tudor family had ruled England since Henry VII became king in 1485. Here's their family tree:

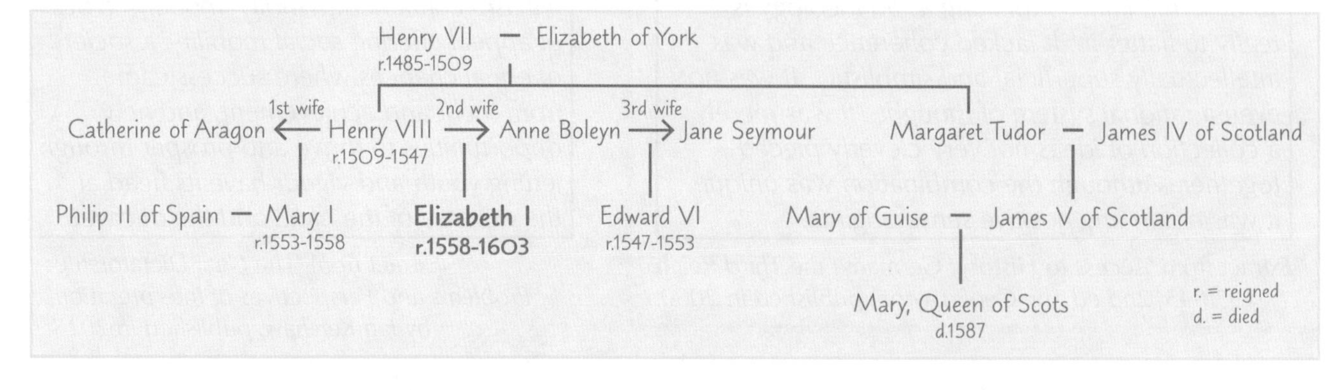

Elizabeth ruled with the Support of the Privy Council

1) Elizabeth was the most powerful figure in Elizabethan England. Everyone was expected to be loyal to the Queen and obey her.
2) The privy council was a group of around twenty of the Queen's most trusted counsellors. They advised her on all aspects of government and ensured her wishes were carried out. They were expected to obey her orders even if they disagreed with her.
3) Parliament was made up of members of the nobility and the gentry. The Queen needed Parliament's consent to pass new laws or raise taxes. Parliament only met when the Queen summoned it, and Elizabeth tried to avoid using it — she only called Parliament 13 times during her 44-year reign.
4) The Queen relied on members of the nobility and gentry to enforce law and order throughout the country. Local government posts like Justice of the Peace and sheriff were unpaid, but many men volunteered in order to increase their local power and influence. Justices of the Peace were particularly important — they enforced the law, provided for the poor and ensured roads and bridges were maintained.

Comment and Analysis

Elizabeth used patronage to ensure the support of the nobility and gentry. This often involved handing out titles and offices that gave the holder a source of income. Elizabeth distributed patronage widely to ensure that no-one felt left out — this helped to ensure political stability.

There were Social and Economic Divisions

1) England's population had been rising steadily since around 1500. Most people lived and worked in rural areas, but towns and cities were growing rapidly. London was by far the largest and most important city.
2) The economy was dominated by agriculture, but farming practices were changing (see p.107). The export of woollen cloth to Europe was very important to the economy, but merchants were also starting to explore trade with the Americas and Asia (see p.109-110).
3) Elizabethan society was dominated by a small, land-owning aristocracy of nobility and gentry. There was also a growing number of wealthy men who earned their living as lawyers or merchants.
4) There was great inequality, and the divide between rich and poor was growing. Poverty became a major problem in Elizabethan England (see p.107-108).

The gentry were part of the social elite in Elizabethan England, below the level of the nobility. Members of the gentry were people who owned land and lived off the income it provided. They didn't have to do other work to survive.

Elizabeth was very powerful, but she didn't rule alone...

To really ace the exam, you need to understand the key features of Elizabethan society and government. Make sure you know the role of the Queen, the privy council and Parliament.

The Challenges of a Female Monarch

Elizabeth I had a rocky start in life and faced some pretty serious problems when she first became queen.

Elizabeth I was Cautious, Intelligent and Powerful

© Mary Evans / Iberfoto

1) Elizabeth was Henry VIII's second child, the daughter of his second wife, Anne Boleyn. As a child, she was third in line to the throne (behind Edward VI and Mary I), so no-one really expected her to become queen.
2) Elizabeth had a difficult upbringing and sometimes feared for her life. In 1554, she was accused of conspiring against her half-sister, Queen Mary I, and placed under house arrest for almost a year.
3) Elizabeth was very cautious and only trusted a few close advisers. She could also be indecisive — she was reluctant to make decisions without carefully considering their possible consequences.
4) She was intelligent, confident and very well educated. Despite having had little training in how to govern, she became a powerful and effective leader.

Elizabeth faced many Difficulties when she became queen

She had been declared Illegitimate

1) In 1533, Henry VIII had divorced his first wife, Catherine of Aragon, and married Anne Boleyn. Divorce was forbidden in the Catholic Church, so many Catholics believed Henry's marriage to Anne was not valid and their daughter, Elizabeth, was illegitimate.
2) When Henry's marriage to Anne Boleyn was dissolved and Anne was executed in 1536, Henry declared Elizabeth illegitimate. Although Henry later changed his mind about this, some Protestants still questioned Elizabeth's legitimacy.

Comment and Analysis

The issue of Elizabeth's legitimacy weakened her claim to the throne and allowed others, especially Mary, Queen of Scots (see p.96), to claim that they had more right to rule.

People thought it was Unnatural for a Woman to be in charge

1) In the 16th century, most people believed the monarch should be a man. They thought that rule by a woman was unnatural. The violence and chaos of Mary I's reign had reinforced people's belief that women could not rule successfully.
2) Most people expected Elizabeth to act as a figurehead, without any real power. They thought she should let her male counsellors take control or find a husband to govern for her.
3) Elizabeth was determined to rule in her own right and refused to let her counsellors take over.

She was expected to Marry and produce an Heir

1) Because people believed women couldn't rule effectively, there was pressure for Elizabeth to find a husband who could rule for her.
2) There were also concerns about the succession. If Elizabeth died without an heir, there would be a risk of civil war, with different groups competing for the throne. To prevent this, Elizabeth was expected to marry and produce an heir as quickly as possible.
3) Elizabeth was reluctant to marry — women had to obey their husbands, so she would lose her power and freedom if she married. Because Elizabeth never married, she became known as the 'Virgin Queen'.

Comment and Analysis

Choosing a husband could create serious political problems. If Elizabeth chose a member of the English nobility, this would create anger and resentment among those who weren't chosen. But if she married a European prince or king, this could give a foreign country too much control over England.

It's not easy being queen...

Jot down three major difficulties that Elizabeth faced when she became queen. Write a sentence or two to explain why each of them was a problem.

REVISION TASK

Challenges at Home and From Abroad

As if the difficulties of being a female ruler weren't enough, Elizabeth also had other problems to deal with when she became queen. The economy was weak and there was a serious threat of a French invasion.

The English Economy was Weak

1) Under King Edward VI, huge sums of money had been spent on wars in Scotland. Queen Mary I had also spent too much money. As a result, Elizabeth inherited enormous debts when she became queen.
2) Mary I had sold off large amounts of land owned by the Crown to cover her debts. Although this had raised money in the short term, in the longer term it reduced the monarch's income from rent.
3) The taxation system was old-fashioned and ineffective. While ordinary people faced high taxes, it had become very common for members of the nobility and gentry to pay less tax than they owed.
4) England was suffering high levels of inflation. This meant that prices were rising, while wages stayed the same or fell. The poor (see p.107) and those living in urban areas were hit hardest by inflation.

Comment and Analysis

Elizabeth was reluctant to reform the tax system and raise taxes because she feared it would upset the nobility and gentry who supported her government.

Elizabeth quickly Ended the War with France...

1) In 1557, Mary I took England to war with France. She did this to support her husband, Philip II of Spain, who was already fighting the French.
2) The war was not a success. In January 1558, the French conquered Calais, England's last remaining territory on the European mainland. This made it more difficult for the English to control the Channel, and increased the risk of a French invasion.
3) When Elizabeth became queen in November 1558, she wanted to end the war with France as quickly as possible. Peace was agreed in 1559.

Comment and Analysis

Throughout her reign, Elizabeth tried to avoid foreign wars — a policy partly influenced by England's financial weakness. She feared that raising taxes to pay for a war would be unpopular and might fuel opposition to her rule.

...but there was still a French Threat in Scotland

1) When Elizabeth became queen, Scotland was controlled by France's Catholic royal family and there were many French troops in the country. However, French rule was unpopular with many Scots.
2) In 1558 Mary, Queen of Scots (p.96) married the heir to the French throne. As Catholics, the French royal family disliked Elizabeth (a Protestant), and wanted England to be ruled by a Catholic. Mary's marriage increased the risk that the French might invade from Scotland to try and put her on the English throne.
3) In the late 1550s, Scottish Protestants, led by the preacher John Knox, rebelled against French rule. They appealed to England for support, and in 1560 English troops and ships were sent to help them.
4) The French were defeated and forced to leave Scotland. The departure of the French, combined with the death of Mary's French husband in 1560, greatly reduced the threat of invasion.

Comment and Analysis

There were many Catholics in England who wanted to be ruled by a Catholic monarch. If the French invaded, there was a risk that the Catholics would betray Queen Elizabeth (a Protestant) and support the French.

The French Wars of Religion began in 1562 and continued until 1598. This long period of civil war between Catholics and Protestants weakened France and largely removed the threat of a French invasion for the rest of the 16th century.

Foreign wars — a luxury Elizabeth couldn't afford...

Include plenty of specific information in your answers. For example, don't just say that Elizabeth had lots of problems at the start of her reign, explain the different challenges she faced.

Religious Divisions in 1558

By 1558, 30 years of dizzying religious change had created deep divisions between Catholics and Protestants.

The Protestant Reformation created religious divisions

The Protestant Reformation began in Germany in the early 16th century and gradually spread across Europe. Reformers challenged many Catholic beliefs and practices.

- The Protestant reformers believed Christians were saved by faith, not by good deeds.
- They questioned the authority of the Pope.
- They translated the Bible from Latin into languages that ordinary people could understand.
- They thought churches should be plain and simple, unlike highly decorated Catholic churches.

There had been constant Religious Changes since the 1530s

Henry VIII Broke Away from the Roman Catholic Church

1) Until the 1530s, England was a Catholic country, and most people were Catholics.
2) In the early 1530s, Henry VIII divorced his first wife, Catherine of Aragon. The Pope refused to accept the divorce, and so Henry broke away from the Roman Catholic Church. He rejected the Pope's authority and made himself head of the Church of England.
3) Henry did not support the Protestant Reformation. He didn't try to reform the English Church and make it Protestant, so Catholic beliefs and practices remained largely unchanged.

Edward VI tried to make England More Protestant

1) Edward VI was a strong supporter of Protestantism and tried to reform the English Church.
2) He made churches and church services simpler. Statues and decorations were removed from churches and priests weren't allowed to wear their elaborate Catholic vestments. A new, Protestant prayer book was issued, and church services were held in English, not Latin.

Vestments are the robes that priests wear during church services.

Mary I Restored Catholicism and Persecuted Protestants

1) Queen Mary I was a devout Catholic. She restored the Pope as head of the English Church, removed Edward's Protestant reforms and brought back Catholic beliefs and practices.
2) Under Mary, Protestants were harshly persecuted. More than 280 people were executed for their beliefs, and hundreds more (known as Marian exiles) fled to Protestant countries in Europe.

Elizabeth I wanted Religious Stability

1) Elizabeth I had been raised as a Protestant. Although she hid her beliefs during Mary's reign to avoid being imprisoned, she was deeply religious and committed to Protestantism.
2) Elizabeth had seen the turmoil caused by Edward VI's extreme Protestant reforms and the violence of Mary I's Catholic restoration. She wanted to end the constant religious changes of the last 30 years by creating a stable and lasting religious settlement.

All these religious changes are making my head spin...

These religious divisions can be pretty confusing, so be careful not to get in a muddle. Remember that Elizabeth was a Protestant, and she faced opposition from many Catholics.

The Religious Settlement of 1559

After the turmoil of her predecessors' reigns, Elizabeth was determined to bring religious stability to England. In 1559, she passed her religious 'settlement', a clever compromise between Protestant and Catholic beliefs.

The Act of Supremacy gave Elizabeth Control over the Church

1) Henry VIII and Edward VI had used the title Supreme Head of the Church of England. In her Act of Supremacy (passed in 1559), Elizabeth altered this title to make herself the Supreme Governor of the English Church.
2) The Act of Supremacy required churchmen and people holding public office to swear the Oath of Supremacy. They had to recognise the Queen as Supreme Governor and promise to be loyal to her.
3) Most parish priests took the Oath. However, all but one of the Catholic bishops refused and lost their posts. They were replaced by Protestant bishops, some of whom had been Marian exiles (see p.93).

Comment and Analysis

The Act of Supremacy gave Elizabeth control of the English Church, without explicitly describing her as its 'Head'. This compromise satisfied those who believed a woman could not lead the Church.

The Act of Uniformity made Moderate Protestant Reforms

The Act of Uniformity and the Royal Injunctions, both passed in 1559, imposed moderate Protestant reforms on the English Church, but they also made some concessions to English Catholics:

Reforms

- Going to church was compulsory — there were fines for missing a church service.
- A new Book of Common Prayer was issued, which had to be used in all churches.
- All parishes had to have a copy of the Bible in English.

Concessions

- The wording of the communion service (an important Christian ceremony) was kept deliberately vague, so that it could be accepted by both Protestants and Catholics.
- Churches were allowed to keep some decorations, and priests had to wear certain Catholic vestments (robes).

Elizabeth wanted everyone in England to conform to her religious settlement. Royal commissioners were ordered to visit churches throughout the country to ensure that the Acts and Injunctions were being enforced.

Comment and Analysis

The Elizabethan religious settlement made England a Protestant country, but allowed some elements of Catholic belief and practice to continue. This clever 'middle way' was designed to satisfy the majority of the population, who held moderate religious beliefs and were willing to make some compromises for the sake of peace and stability.

The Church played an important role in English Society

1) Senior churchmen were involved in government — all bishops held a seat in the House of Lords, and the Archbishop of Canterbury was usually a member of the privy council.
2) Parish priests were often the most educated people in their communities, which made them respected and influential figures. As well as providing religious guidance, parish priests gave advice, helped to resolve disputes and played an important role in providing charitable support for the poor and elderly.
3) The Church helped promote national unity and obedience to the Queen. The Queen's coat of arms was often displayed churches, and church services included prayers for the Queen and her councillors.

Sometimes the 'middle way' is the only way...

Divide a piece of paper into two. Jot down the key features of the Act of Supremacy on one side and the Act of Uniformity and the Royal Injunctions on the other.

REVISION TASK

Challenges to the Religious Settlement

Elizabeth's religious settlement faced many challenges in the 1560s. Some were more serious than others.

The Puritans wanted to make the English Church More Protestant

1) The Puritans were extreme Protestants. For them, Elizabeth's religious settlement was only a first step, and they wanted her to make further reforms to remove all traces of Catholicism from the English Church.
2) Many Puritans had been Marian exiles. While in exile in Protestant parts of Europe, some had come into contact with the teachings of leading reformers like Martin Luther and John Calvin.
3) The Vestment Controversy of the 1560s was a serious Puritan challenge to the religious settlement. Puritan priests refused to wear the surplice, a white vestment used by Catholics, which the Royal Injunctions had made compulsory.
4) Elizabeth tolerated this at first, but in 1565 she ordered the Archbishop of Canterbury to ensure that all priests wore the surplice. Those Puritans who still refused lost their jobs or were imprisoned.

Many of the Protestant bishops appointed from 1559 supported the Puritans and were in favour of further reforms. However, the Archbishop of Canterbury, Matthew Parker, was a moderate who helped Elizabeth to uphold the 'middle way' of the religious settlement.

Many members of the Nobility continued to practise Catholicism

1) A large proportion of the nobility were still Catholic. The compromises in the religious settlement won some of them around, but others refused to attend church services — they were known as recusants.
2) The Catholic nobility was influential in areas outside the south-east, especially Lancashire. They used their strong local power bases to protect Catholics and maintain their traditional religious practices.
3) These Catholic nobles posed a potential threat to the religious settlement — there was a risk that they might try to overthrow Elizabeth and restore Catholicism.
4) To minimize this threat, Elizabeth did not force the Catholic nobility to attend church services. As long as they didn't make a public show of their beliefs, they were allowed to continue practising Catholicism.

The threat posed by the Catholic nobility became more serious when Mary, Queen of Scots, (a Catholic claimant to the English throne) arrived in England in 1568 (p.96).

France and Spain were Distracted by Domestic Difficulties

1) There was a risk that the Catholic rulers of France or Spain might try to reverse the religious settlement and replace Elizabeth with a Catholic monarch. However, neither country was really in a position to challenge the religious settlement during the 1560s.
2) The threat of a French invasion was serious in the first years of Elizabeth's reign, but faded with the start of the Wars of Religion in 1562 (see p.92).
3) In the 1560s, Spain was facing a growing revolt in the Netherlands. To prevent an alliance forming between England and the Protestant Netherlands, Spain tried to stay on good terms with Elizabeth and avoided challenging her religious settlement.

Comment and Analysis

The Catholic aspects of the settlement encouraged Catholic countries and the Pope to think that Elizabeth might eventually return to Catholicism. This helped to reduce the threat of a foreign challenge during the early years of the settlement.

The Papacy Lacked Military Support

1) The Pope had the power to excommunicate Elizabeth (expel her from the Catholic Church). This might encourage Catholic countries to invade England. It could also encourage rebellion at home by releasing Elizabeth's Catholic subjects from their duty of loyalty to her.
2) However, neither France nor Spain had the military resources to invade England, and there was no clear support for a revolt against Elizabeth at home, so the Pope didn't take any action against her in the 1560s.

Despite the settlement, things took a while to settle down...

Do you agree that foreign opposition was the most serious threat to the Elizabethan religious settlement in the 1560s? Explain your answer. [16]

Mary, Queen of Scots

Even though Elizabeth and Mary, Queen of Scots, were cousins, Elizabeth wasn't too pleased when Mary arrived in England for an unexpected visit in 1568. In fact, she was so unimpressed, she put Mary in prison...

Mary, Queen of Scots, had a Strong Claim to the English Throne

1) Mary was the only child of James V of Scotland. She was related to the Tudors through her grandmother, Margaret Tudor. Margaret was Henry VIII's sister, the wife of James IV and mother of James V (see p.90).
2) As a granddaughter of Margaret Tudor, Mary had a strong claim to the English throne. Because Mary was a Catholic, her claim was supported by many English Catholics.
3) Mary became queen of Scotland in 1542 when she was just six days old. Her mother acted as regent (she ruled on Mary's behalf), while Mary was raised in France.
4) In 1558, when Mary was 15 years old, she married the heir to the French throne. However, her husband died suddenly in 1560, and Mary returned to Scotland.

Comment and Analysis

Mary wanted to be named as heir to the English throne, but Elizabeth was unwilling to do this. She feared that making Mary her heir would encourage Catholic plots, both at home and abroad, to overthrow her and make Mary queen.

Mary Fled to England in 1568

1) In 1565 Mary married the Scottish nobleman Lord Darnley. The marriage was not a happy one. Darnley hated Mary's personal secretary, David Rizzio, and became convinced that the two were having an affair. In 1566 a group of Scottish nobles, accompanied by Darnley, stabbed Rizzio to death.
2) In 1567, Darnley was murdered. Many people believed that Mary and her close friend, the Earl of Bothwell, were behind the murder. Their suspicions seemed to be confirmed when Mary married Bothwell a few months later.
3) This marriage was unpopular with the Scottish nobles, who rebelled against Mary. They imprisoned her and forced her to abdicate (give up the throne) in favour of her one-year-old son, James. In 1568, Mary escaped from prison and raised an army. Her forces were defeated in battle and she fled south to England.

Some people (including Elizabeth) thought that the Scottish nobles had no right to overthrow Mary. As a result, they didn't accept her abdication, and still viewed her as the legitimate queen of Scotland.

Mary was Imprisoned, but still posed a Threat

1) Mary hoped that Elizabeth would help her regain control of Scotland. Elizabeth was not willing to do this — Mary's claim to the English throne meant that there would be a constant threat of invasion from the north if Mary regained power in Scotland.
2) Instead, Elizabeth had Mary imprisoned and set up an inquiry to investigate whether she had been involved in Darnley's murder.
3) Elizabeth didn't want the inquiry to find Mary guilty. A guilty verdict would lend support to the actions of the Scottish nobles, who had overthrown Mary, their legitimate queen.
4) However, Elizabeth didn't want a not-guilty verdict either, because this would force her to release Mary. Once free, Mary might use her claim to the English throne to try and overthrow Elizabeth.
5) In the end, the inquiry didn't reach a verdict — this enabled Elizabeth to keep Mary in captivity. Elizabeth hoped that imprisoning Mary would prevent her becoming the centre of Catholic plots, but Mary's presence caused problems for Elizabeth throughout the next 20 years (see p.97-99).

The so-called 'Casket Letters' were presented to the inquiry. They included several letters apparently written by Mary to Bothwell, which implicated the pair in Darnley's murder. Mary's supporters insisted that the letters were forgeries, but most members of the inquiry believed they were genuine.

Elizabeth really wasn't a fan of uninvited guests...

Why was Mary, Queen of Scots, a threat to Queen Elizabeth I? Explain your answer. [12]

The Revolt of the Northern Earls, 1569-1570

Mary, Queen of Scots, had barely been in England five minutes when she began causing trouble for Elizabeth.

The Northern Earls were unhappy for Several Reasons

1) Many northern nobles were still committed Catholics. They wanted to see the restoration of Catholicism in England under a Catholic monarch. The arrival of Mary, Queen of Scots, in 1568 (see p.96) gave them hope that Elizabeth could be replaced with Mary.
2) Elizabeth had confiscated large areas of land from the Earl of Northumberland and shared them between Northumberland's main rival in the north and a southern Protestant. Northumberland was also angry that Elizabeth had claimed all the profits from copper mines discovered on his estates.
3) Elizabeth had reduced the power of the northern nobles and increased her control in the north. In part, she did this through the Council of the North, which helped to govern the region. Under Elizabeth, the Council was controlled by southern Protestants. The northern nobles deeply resented this.
4) The northern nobles blamed Elizabeth's advisors for these policies. They believed that some privy councillors, especially William Cecil, had become too powerful. They wanted to remove these 'evil counsellors' and replace them with men who would be more sympathetic to their interests.

The Revolt of the Northern Earls broke out in November 1569

1) In 1569, the Duke of Norfolk (the wealthiest landowner in England) hatched a plan to marry Mary, Queen of Scots, and have her recognised as Elizabeth's heir. This plan was supported by Catholic nobles, including the Earls of Northumberland and Westmorland, because it meant that Elizabeth would be succeeded by a Catholic queen.
2) When the plan was uncovered, the Earls feared they would be executed for their involvement. In a desperate attempt to escape punishment, they rebelled and tried to overthrow Elizabeth.
3) In November 1569, the Earls captured Durham, where they celebrated Catholic Mass in the cathedral. They then marched south, probably making for Tutbury in Derbyshire, where Mary was imprisoned.
4) Before the rebels reached Tutbury, a large royal army forced them to retreat. Many of their troops deserted, and the two Earls fled to Scotland. Elizabeth showed the rebels little mercy. Westmorland fled abroad, but Northumberland was executed, as were at least 400 rebel troops.

The revolt was a Serious Threat to Elizabeth's rule

1) The Revolt of the Northern Earls was the most serious rebellion of Elizabeth's reign. It posed a major threat to Elizabeth's rule and showed the danger that Mary, Queen of Scots, represented as a rallying point for English Catholics.
2) News of the rebellion created widespread fear among English Protestants about Catholic plots and revenge. These fears were fuelled by memories of the harsh persecution of Protestants during the reign of Queen Mary I.
3) In 1570, Pope Pius V excommunicated Elizabeth. This was supposed to strengthen the revolt, but news of it didn't arrive until after the rebels had fled. But the excommunication did make the Catholic threat seem more serious, because it meant that Catholics no longer had to obey the Queen and were encouraged to overthrow her.

There was little support for the revolt among the rest of the Catholic nobility and ordinary people — when faced with a choice between Elizabeth and their religion, most Catholics chose to support the Queen. 1569-70 was the last time English Catholics tried to remove Elizabeth by force.

Comment and Analysis

The Revolt of the Northern Earls and the papal excommunication changed Elizabeth's attitude towards Catholics, who were now seen as potential traitors. From 1570, Elizabeth became less tolerant of recusancy and took increasingly harsh measures against English Catholics.

Those Northern Earls were Revolting...

As well as knowing what happened in Elizabethan England, you also need to know why things happened — so be sure to learn what caused events like the Revolt of the Northern Earls.

Catholic Plots at Home

During the 1570s and 1580s, there were several Catholic plots to assassinate Elizabeth and replace her with Mary. The plots involved European conspirators and were supported by France, Spain and the Pope.

The Ridolfi Plot aimed to put Mary on the English Throne

1) Roberto di Ridolfi was an Italian banker who had played a small part in the Revolt of the Northern Earls. In 1571 he used his Catholic contacts in England and Europe to develop a plot to overthrow Elizabeth.
2) Ridolfi planned to assassinate Elizabeth, then marry Mary to the Duke of Norfolk and make her queen. He was supported by the Pope, and by King Philip II, who agreed to provide troops for a Spanish invasion.
3) The plot failed, largely because Elizabeth's allies passed the names of the main conspirators to her. They also intercepted letters sent by Mary, which implicated her and Norfolk in the plot.
4) Norfolk was arrested and executed. Mary was not punished, although her supervision was made tighter.

Walsingham uncovered the Throckmorton Plot in 1583

1) The Throckmorton Plot of 1583 aimed to assassinate Elizabeth and replace her with Mary. The conspirators planned for an invasion of England by French troops, financed by Philip II of Spain and the Pope.
2) A leading figure in the plot was Francis Throckmorton, a young Catholic man who carried messages between Mary and Catholic conspirators abroad. The plot was uncovered by Walsingham, who placed Throckmorton under surveillance for several months.
3) In response to the Throckmorton Plot, Elizabeth's closest advisors drafted the Bond of Association, which aimed to prevent any more such plots. The Bond, which was signed by the English nobility and gentry, required the signatories to execute anyone who attempted to overthrow the Queen.

Francis Walsingham was Elizabeth's principal secretary and spymaster. He established a large spy network in England and Europe. Walsingham intercepted the letters of Catholic conspirators and worked with an expert cryptographer to decode them. He also used double agents to infiltrate Catholic networks.

The Catholic Plots posed a Real Threat to Elizabeth...

1) Mary's presence in England and her strong claim to the throne made the plots seem credible and meant that they posed a real threat to Elizabeth's rule. Many people were afraid that they would be successful.
2) As the head of the Catholic Church, the Pope could rally support for the plots. For some Catholics, obedience to the Pope was more important than obedience to Elizabeth.
3) Foreign powers, especially France and Spain, were involved in the plots, so there was a danger they would lead to a foreign invasion.

...but they had some Significant Weaknesses

1) Elizabeth was a popular ruler and the conspirators lacked public support. As the failure of the Revolt of the Northern Earls (see p.97) had shown, there was little appetite in England for a Catholic revolution.
2) Philip II was reluctant to destroy his alliance with Elizabeth. As a result, his support for the Catholic plots was half-hearted — although he promised to help the conspirators, he rarely followed through on his promises.
3) Elizabeth's informants, and later Walsingham's highly efficient spy network, ensured that the plots were uncovered before they were fully developed.

Don't lose the plot, just learn this page...

Read this page through once more, then cover it up and scribble down the main features of the Ridolfi and Throckmorton Plots. How serious a threat did these plots pose to Elizabeth's rule?

Catholic Plots at Home

In 1586, Walsingham used his spy network to prove that Mary had supported the Babington Plot. His evidence persuaded Elizabeth to put Mary on trial and execute her for treason.

Walsingham knew about Every Stage of the 1586 Babington Plot

1) The Babington Plot was another conspiracy involving France and Spain. Again, the conspirators planned to assassinate Elizabeth and give the English throne to Mary, this time with the support of a joint Franco-Spanish invasion force.
2) Anthony Babington was one of the key conspirators. He was responsible for sending information to Mary from her supporters in England and Europe, and passing back her replies.

Through his spy network, Walsingham followed every stage of the plot. Using a double agent, he managed to secretly intercept all letters sent to and from Mary, and have them decoded. One of Mary's letters approved plans to assassinate the Queen and free Mary from prison.

3) By August 1586, Walsingham had all the evidence he needed to break the plot. Babington and the other conspirators were arrested, tried and executed for treason.

The Babington Plot led to the Execution of Mary, Queen of Scots

1) Mary had been implicated in Catholic plots before, but Elizabeth had always been reluctant to take action against her. The evidence gathered by Walsingham finally persuaded her to put Mary on trial.
2) In October 1586, Mary was found guilty of treason and sentenced to death.
3) After hesitating for several months, Elizabeth eventually signed Mary's death warrant. The execution took place on 8th February 1587.

Comment and Analysis

Because Mary was queen of Scotland, Elizabeth was very reluctant to execute her. Elizabeth believed in the Divine Right — that rulers were sent by God to govern their country. Therefore, she felt she had no right to execute a legitimate monarch. She also feared that executing Mary would undermine her own claim to rule by Divine Right and might fuel more plots against her.

Mary's execution Reduced the Threat from Catholics at Home...

The execution of Mary, Queen of Scots, removed the long-standing Catholic threat to Elizabeth at home. English Catholics now had no-one to rally around, and they lost hope of ever overthrowing Elizabeth and reversing the religious settlement. There were no more major Catholic plots during Elizabeth's reign.

...but it Increased the Threat from Abroad

1) Mary's execution inflamed Catholic opposition abroad and increased the threat of a foreign invasion.
2) In 1587, relations with Spain were at a low point — the two countries were at war over the Netherlands, and King Philip II had been preparing for an attack on England since 1585 (see p.101-103). Mary's execution made the situation worse. Philip was now even more determined to invade.
3) There was also a danger that Mary's son, James VI of Scotland might seek revenge for his mother's death. There were fears that he would form an alliance with other Catholic powers in Europe in order to invade England.

The Babington Plot wasn't very well executed...

EXAM QUESTION

Why did Queen Elizabeth have Mary, Queen of Scots, executed in 1587? Explain your answer. [12]

Relations with Spain

England and Spain had tried to stay on good terms, but the rivalry between them led to growing tensions.

England and Spain were Political and Religious Rivals

1) King Philip II of Spain had been married to Queen Mary I of England, and the two countries had fought together against France in the 1550s. The war with France ended in 1559 (see p.92), but Elizabeth and Philip tried to maintain good relations with each other.
2) Spain was a great imperial power. In Europe, Philip ruled Spain, the Netherlands and parts of Italy. He also had a large empire in North and South America. In 1581, Philip became king of Portugal. This gave him control of the important Atlantic port of Lisbon, as well as Portugal's overseas empire. By the 1570s, England was starting to have ambitions for an empire of its own, and hoped to become an imperial power to rival Spain (see p.109-111).
3) Philip was a very devout Catholic and disliked the Elizabethan religious settlement of 1559. He became involved in several Catholic plots against Elizabeth in the 1570s and 1580s, although his involvement in these plots was mostly reluctant and half-hearted (see p.98).

Comment and Analysis

Spain's military and naval forces were much greater than England's, so Elizabeth was always reluctant to do anything that might destroy her alliance with Philip and lead to war with Spain.

There was Commercial Rivalry in the Spanish Netherlands...

English exports to Europe were vital to the English economy. Many English goods reached the European market via Dutch ports, especially Antwerp (which was in the Netherlands in the 16th century). Because Spain ruled the Netherlands, Philip could limit English access to these vital Dutch ports.

In 1568, Spanish ships laden with gold bullion took refuge in English ports to escape bad weather. Elizabeth seized the gold for herself, which enraged Philip. In response, Philip seized English ships in Antwerp and banned English trade with the Netherlands for a time. This damaged England's economy and caused much hardship for English people.

...and in the New World

1) Trade with Spain's colonies in North and South America was very profitable, but foreigners weren't allowed to trade with them unless they had a licence. Very few Englishmen were granted licences.
2) Elizabeth encouraged privateers (men who sailed their own vessels) to trade illegally with Spanish colonies, raid Spanish ships and attack the treasure fleets carrying gold and silver from the Americas to Spain. Because the privateers were supposedly independent, Elizabeth could deny any responsibility for their activities. This helped to prevent open conflict with Philip.
3) Elizabeth received a share of the privateers' profits. Given England's financial weakness (see p.92), this was a very important source of income for her. The treasure she received from Drake in 1580 was worth more than all the rest of her income for that year put together.

Francis Drake was a leading privateer. He was involved in several expeditions in the New World in the late 1560s and 1570s. Between 1577 and 1580 Drake sailed around the world (see p.110). He carried out a number of raids on Spanish settlements and ships, returning with huge amounts of treasure.

Comment and Analysis

The Ridolfi Plot of 1571 (see p.98) damaged Elizabeth's trust in Philip and made her more willing to support the activities of English privateers.

The Americas — a whole New World of commercial rivalry...

England's relationship with Spain was a major headache for Elizabeth throughout her reign. Make sure you understand how and why the relationship changed over time.

War with Spain, 1585-1588

By the 1580s, the tension between England and Spain had reached boiling point. Elizabeth and Philip were still reluctant to confront one another, but in 1585 they finally went to war over the Netherlands.

Elizabeth's Support for the Dutch Rebels led to War with Spain

1) In 1581, Protestant rebels in the Netherlands declared independence from Spain and established a Dutch republic. Elizabeth gave limited financial help to the rebels, but she was reluctant to provoke Philip by getting directly involved.
2) In 1584 the rebel leader, William the Silent, was assassinated, and the Dutch revolt was in danger of being defeated. Elizabeth decided to give direct assistance to the rebels — in 1585 she signed the Treaty of Nonsuch, which placed the Netherlands under her protection and promised military assistance.
3) Several factors influenced Elizabeth's decision to sign the Treaty of Nonsuch:

Religious

Elizabeth wanted to protect Dutch Protestantism and prevent Philip forcing Catholicism on the Netherlands.

Commercial

The Netherlands' ports were essential entry points into Europe for most English exports.

Military

If the rebels were defeated, Philip might use the Netherlands as a base for an invasion of England.

Strategic

In 1584, Spain was seeking control of the French crown. If the Dutch rebels were also defeated, then Spain would control almost the entire Channel and Atlantic coasts of Europe.

Comment and Analysis

Because of her belief in the Divine Right, Elizabeth didn't want to remove Philip as ruler of the Netherlands. She just wanted to ensure freedom of worship for Dutch Protestants and protect England's military, commercial and strategic interests.

Dudley's campaigns in the Netherlands were Unsuccessful

1) Robert Dudley, Earl of Leicester, was appointed to lead the military expedition to the Netherlands. When he arrived, he accepted the position of Governor-General. This was a serious mistake — it suggested that Elizabeth had taken control of the Netherlands for herself, which risked provoking Philip even further. Elizabeth forced Dudley to resign the position immediately.
2) Dudley's campaigns of 1586-1587 were unsuccessful. He suffered several heavy defeats at the hands of the Spanish general, the Duke of Parma, and had no clear military successes. He resigned his post in 1587 and returned to England.
3) There were several reasons for the failure of the English campaigns in the Netherlands:
   - Dudley wasn't a talented general.
   - His officers were bitterly divided over questions of strategy.
   - Dudley had a very small army compared to the number of Spanish troops.
   - The English army was poorly equipped.
   - Elizabeth didn't provide sufficient funds to pay the English troops.
4) English naval support for the Dutch rebels was more effective — a fleet of English ships patrolled the Dutch coastline, preventing the Spanish from landing some of their forces by sea.

England and Spain — reluctant enemies...

'Commercial rivalry was the most important reason for the outbreak of war with Spain in 1585.' Do you agree with this statement? Explain your answer. [16]

Drake's Raid on Cadiz, 1587

In 1587, Francis Drake attacked the Spanish port of Cadiz. The attack, which became known as 'the singeing of the King of Spain's beard', was a major setback in Spain's preparations for the Armada.

Drake was sent to Disrupt Spanish Preparations for the Armada

- Philip saw the 1585 Treaty of Nonsuch as a declaration of war on Spain. In response, he began building a huge fleet (an Armada) that he planned to use to invade England.
- Elizabeth was aware of Philip's plans. In 1587, she sent Francis Drake, one of her most successful privateers (see p.100), to spy on Spanish preparations and attack their ships and supplies.

Drake Attacked the Spanish port of Cadiz in 1587

1) Most of the new ships for the Armada were being built in the Portuguese port of Lisbon. This deep water port was protected by strong fortifications, and Drake knew he couldn't attack it with any hope of success.
2) Instead, Drake decided to attack the port of Cadiz, which wasn't well defended. Fewer naval ships were anchored there, but the port was the centre for a large number of naval supplies, which Drake intended to seize or destroy.
3) In April 1587, Drake sailed into Cadiz harbour and began to attack the ships anchored there. He destroyed around 30 ships and seized many tonnes of supplies, including food and weapons.

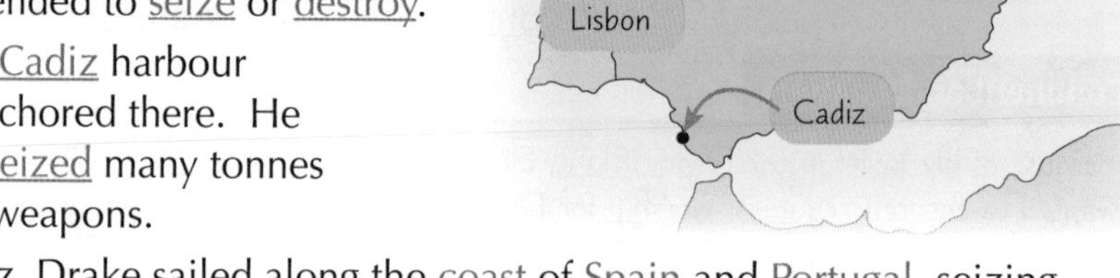

4) After his successful raid on Cadiz, Drake sailed along the coast of Spain and Portugal, seizing Spanish ships and destroying supplies which were being sent to Lisbon for the Armada.
5) Drake also captured the San Filipe, a Spanish ship returning from the Americas laden with gold, spices and silk. Its valuable cargo easily covered the cost of Drake's expedition, and enabled Elizabeth to improve England's defences.

The raid on Cadiz was a Serious Setback for the Spanish Armada

1) The raid on Cadiz had a major impact on Philip's plans to invade England, delaying the Armada by more than a year.
2) Obtaining fresh supplies and weapons was very expensive and seriously strained Spain's finances.
3) During his raids, Drake captured more than 1000 tons of planks made from seasoned wood, which were needed to make the barrels used to carry food and water. As a result, the Spanish had to make their barrels from unseasoned wood, which couldn't preserve food and water very well.
4) This caused supply problems for the Armada and affected the morale of Spanish troops and sailors. Fresh water supplies were lost and many tons of food rotted as the fleet sailed to England in 1588.

Comment and Analysis

Drake described his raid on Cadiz as 'singeing the King of Spain's beard'. He meant that he had inflicted temporary damage on King Philip's Armada, but hadn't destroyed it entirely — it would 'grow back' in time.

I've always thought facial hair was a fire hazard...

The 'singeing of the King of Spain's beard' might sound silly, but it's a really handy phrase — it tells you a lot about the impact of Drake's raid on Philip's preparations for the Armada.

The Spanish Armada, 1588

The Spanish Armada was launched in 1588, but right from the start, things didn't go according to plan...

The Armada Planned to meet the Duke of Parma at Dunkirk

1) By the spring of 1588, the Spanish Armada was complete and Philip was ready to launch his 'Enterprise of England'. The Armada was a huge fleet of around 130 ships, manned by approximately 8000 sailors and carrying an estimated 18,000 soldiers.
2) Philip appointed the Duke of Medina Sidonia to lead the Armada. Philip respected the Duke's high social status and trusted him to obey instructions. However, the Duke had little military or naval experience, and he tried unsuccessfully to turn down the command.
3) The Spanish had thousands more soldiers stationed in the Netherlands under the leadership of the Duke of Parma. Philip's plan was for the Armada to meet Parma's army at Dunkirk. The combined forces would then sail across the Channel to England under the protection of the Armada's warships.

The Armada reached the English Channel in July 1588

1) The Armada set out in May 1588, but was delayed for several weeks by bad weather in the Bay of Biscay and by the attempts of an English fleet to intercept it.
2) In July the Spanish fleet was sighted off Cornwall and beacons (signal fires) were lit along the south coast to send the news to Elizabeth in London. English ships set sail from Plymouth to meet the Armada.

3) The Armada sailed up the Channel in a crescent formation. This was an effective defensive strategy, which used the large, armed galleons to protect the weaker supply and troop ships.
4) The English navy carried out a few minor raids, but was unable to inflict much damage. Only two Spanish ships were lost, and these were both destroyed by accident.

The English Attacked the Spanish at Calais and Gravelines

1) Having sailed up the Channel, Medina Sidonia anchored at Calais to wait for Parma's troops. However, Parma and his men were being blockaded by Dutch ships and weren't able to reach the coast in time.
2) In the middle of the night, the English sent eight fireships (ships loaded with flammable materials and set on fire) among the anchored Spanish ships. This caused panic among the Spanish sailors, who cut their anchor cables, broke their defensive formation and headed for the open sea.
3) The Spanish ships regrouped at Gravelines, but the weather made it impossible for them to return to their defensive position at Calais. The English moved in, and the following battle lasted for many hours. Five Spanish ships were sunk, and the rest of the fleet was forced to sail away from the French coast and into the North Sea.
4) An English fleet followed the Spanish as far north as Scotland to make sure they did not regroup and return to collect Parma's army.

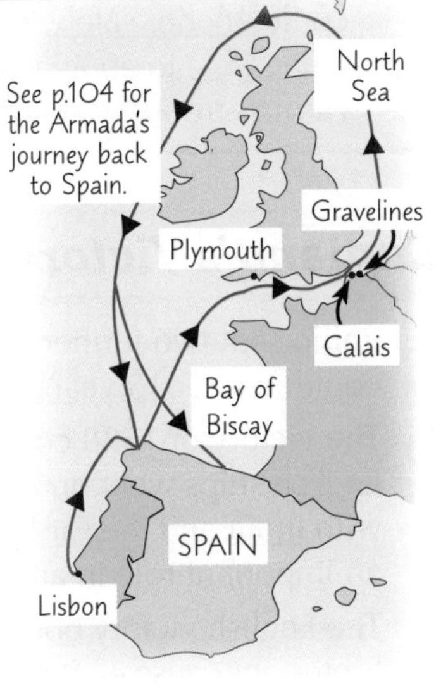

See p.104 for the Armada's journey back to Spain.

So much for King Philip's cunning plan...

Have another read of the last three pages, then cover them up and jot down a timeline of the Spanish Armada. Include all the key events from the Treaty of Nonsuch to the Battle of Gravelines.

REVISION TASK

The Spanish Armada, 1588

The English navy had defeated the Armada, and the Spanish ships now faced a dangerous journey home.

The Armada's Journey back to Spain was a Disaster

1) Medina Sidonia decided to call off the attack on England and return to Spain by sailing round Scotland and Ireland. The Spanish sailors were unfamiliar with this very dangerous route, and they encountered several powerful Atlantic storms.
2) Many ships sank or were wrecked on the Scottish and Irish coasts, where the local inhabitants showed the survivors little mercy. Those ships that completed the journey ran short of supplies, and many men died of starvation and disease. In all, less than half the fleet and fewer than 10,000 men made it back to Spain.

Several Factors contributed to the Defeat of the Armada

English Strengths

- The English had improved their ship building, giving them several technological advantages. Spain relied on large ships which were heavy and difficult to handle, whereas the English built long, narrow ships which were faster and easier to handle. English cannons could also be reloaded much more quickly than Spanish ones.
- English tactics were more effective. Spanish ships aimed to come alongside their opponents, board their vessels and overcome the enemy in hand-to-hand fighting. The Spanish couldn't use this tactic against the English, who used their greater manoeuvrability to stay out of range. Instead of boarding the Spanish ships, the English fired broadsides (massive barrages of cannonballs) which could sink them.

Spanish Weaknesses

- Most of Spain's men lacked experience of naval warfare, whereas the English fleet was manned by experienced sailors.
- The Spanish plan to meet the Duke of Parma at Dunkirk was seriously flawed. Spain didn't control a deep water port where the Armada could anchor safely, so the ships were extremely vulnerable to an attack while it waited for Parma's troops to escape the Dutch blockade.

Luck

- The death of Spain's leading admiral, Santa Cruz, in February 1588, led to the appointment of the inexperienced Duke of Medina Sidonia to lead the Armada.
- The weather made it impossible for the Spanish fleet to return to the Channel after the battle of Gravelines, forcing it to travel into the dangerous waters off the Scottish and Irish coasts.

England's Victory Removed the threat of a Spanish Invasion

1) Philip sent two further Armadas in the 1590s, but they were both unsuccessful. Although war with Spain continued for 15 years, the Armada of 1588 was the last serious Spanish threat to Elizabeth's throne.
2) The victory of 1588 contributed to England's development as a strong naval power to rival Spain. English ships went on many voyages of discovery and established valuable trade routes, especially with India and the Far East (see p.110). By the end of Elizabeth's reign, the navy was also playing an important role in attempts to set up an English colony in North America (see p.111).
3) The English victory boosted Elizabeth's popularity and strengthened the Protestant cause — it was seen as a sign that God favoured Protestantism.

The defeat of the Armada — a great English victory...

'Luck was the main reason why England managed to defeat the Spanish Armada.' Explain whether you agree or disagree with this statement. [16]

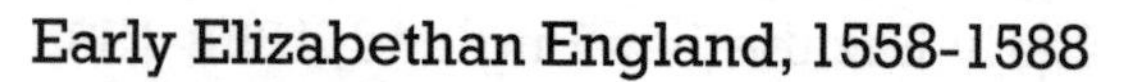

Education

During Elizabeth's reign, people increasingly began to recognise the importance of education. Many new schools were set up and more people than ever learned how to read and write.

Children received a Basic Education at Home

1) Children received their early education at home. Most parents probably taught their children how to behave correctly and gave them a basic religious education. From the age of six, all children had to go to Sunday school, where they learnt things like the Lord's Prayer, the 10 Commandments and the Creed (a basic statement of the Christian faith).
2) From a young age, boys were trained in simple work skills, while girls helped their mothers with household activities.
3) Some children from noble households were taught at home by a private tutor. Others were sent to live with another noble family and educated there.

This kind of education was intended to teach children how to behave in noble society and give them the skills to be successful at court.

Petty Schools taught Reading, Writing and Maths

1) Petty schools were small, local schools that provided a basic education. Many petty schools were run by the local parish priest. Others were attached to grammar schools, or were set up by private individuals.
2) The schools taught basic reading and writing, and sometimes a little maths. There wasn't a set curriculum, although lessons usually had a strong religious focus. The schools didn't usually have any books — instead the main teaching aid was the hornbook, a wooden board showing the alphabet and the Lord's Prayer.
3) Most pupils were boys, although some petty schools admitted a few girls. There was no fixed age for pupils to start school, but they usually started at about six and stayed until they could read and write.

Only a small minority of children in Elizabethan England went to school, but the number was growing. Education was increasingly important for many careers, including trade and government administration.

There was a Big Increase in the number of Grammar Schools

1) Grammar schools had existed for centuries, but there was a big expansion during Elizabeth's reign, with the foundation of around 100 new grammar schools.
2) It was very rare for girls to go to grammar school — most pupils were boys from the upper and middle classes. Some schools offered free places to bright boys from poorer backgrounds, but few poor boys were able to attend because their parents needed them to work at home.
3) Children usually started grammar school around the age of seven. Lessons focused mainly on Latin and classical literature (literature from Ancient Greece and Rome), and a few schools also taught Greek.

There was no state education system at this time. Instead, most schools were set up by wealthy individuals.

The number of University Students was Increasing

1) When they left grammar school, some boys went on to study at one of the two English universities, Oxford and Cambridge. The growing prosperity of the upper and middle classes meant that the number of university students increased during Elizabeth's reign.
2) University courses were conducted almost entirely in Latin. Students studied advanced written and spoken Latin, before moving on to study arithmetic, music, Greek, astronomy, geometry and philosophy. After completing an undergraduate degree, students might specialise in law, theology or medicine.

Comment and Analysis

The printing press had been introduced to England in the late 15th century. As printing spread, it encouraged increased literacy levels because it made books much cheaper and more widely available.

Those Elizabethans really loved their Latin...

Write down these headings: Home, Petty School, Grammar School, University. Under each heading, jot down the main things pupils were taught in that place.

REVISION TASK

Sports, Pastimes and the Theatre

Some Elizabethan pastimes, including tennis, fencing, football and the theatre, are still popular today.

Hunting and Sports were an Important part of Court Life

The royal court was a large group of people who surrounded the Queen at all times. Over 1000 people attended the court, including Elizabeth's personal servants, members of the privy council, nobles, ambassadors and other foreign visitors. The Queen's favourite sports became an important part of court life.

- Elizabeth and her courtiers often hunted deer and other wild animals. As well as being a form of entertainment, hunting was an important source of food for the court.
- The Queen was skilled at hawking, spending many hours with her trained falcons as they hunted. Training falcons was an expensive process, which only the rich could afford.
- Elizabeth's courtiers and other noblemen were expected to be skilled at fencing — they practised from a young age. Tennis and bowls were also becoming increasingly popular. These sports required expensive equipment, so they were only played by the rich.

Ordinary people had Little Time for Leisure Activities

1) Most people worked six days a week and went to church on Sundays, so they had little leisure time. However, there were several festival days in the calendar, including Midsummer's day and Ascension day. On these days, people were free to enjoy sports, feasting and other pastimes.
2) Football was a popular sport, often played between two villages. An unlimited number of players could participate, and there were few rules. As a result, games often descended into long and violent fights.
3) Blood sports like cockfighting and bull- or bear-baiting were also very popular. People would gamble on the outcome of the fights.

The Theatre became Very Popular later in Elizabeth's reign

A performance at London's Globe Theatre, which was built in 1599.

1) There were no permanent theatres in England at the start of Elizabeth's reign. Instead, companies of actors travelled around, performing in village squares or the courtyards of inns.
2) The first theatres were built in London in the 1570s. They included The Theatre and The Curtain. They were usually round, open-air buildings with a raised stage that stretched out into the audience.
3) The theatre appealed to both rich and poor. Poorer audience members, known as groundlings, stood around the stage, while richer people sat under cover around the theatre's walls.
4) Elizabeth enjoyed plays and often had them performed at court. She supported her favourite performers and even set up an acting company, The Queen's Men.

Comment and Analysis

The London authorities and the Puritans opposed the theatre because they saw it as a source of crime and immorality. As a result, many theatres were built just outside the City of London in Southwark.

Support from the elite was essential to the development of Elizabethan theatre — acting companies relied on members of the elite to fund or promote their performances and protect them from opponents of the theatre. Two of the most important Elizabethan companies, The Admiral's Men and The Lord Chamberlain's Men (William Shakespeare's company), were supported by members of the privy council.

I'm not sure I like the sound of Elizabethan football...

Remember that there were social distinctions in leisure activities — the rich and the poor mostly enjoyed different pastimes and even at the theatre the two groups didn't mix.

Poverty

The growing number of people living in poverty was a major problem in Elizabethan society.

Population Growth led to Rising Prices

1) In the 16th century, England's birth rate rose and the death rate fell. This led to huge population growth — during Elizabeth's reign, the English population grew from around 3 million people to over 4 million.
2) Food production didn't keep pace with the growth in population. As a result, food prices rose and sometimes there were food shortages.
3) England also suffered several poor harvests in the 1550s and 1560s. This led to food shortages and made the problem of rising food prices even worse, causing serious hardship for the poor.
4) Prices for food and other goods rose much more quickly than wages. Standards of living fell for many workers as they struggled to afford the necessities — many were forced into poverty.
5) Because of the rapid population growth, there was growing competition for land, and so rents increased. This trend was made worse by changes in farming practices.

In 1563, the government passed the Statute of Artificers, which set a maximum daily wage for skilled workers (e.g. butchers and carpenters). This made things even more difficult for workers, because it prevented wages from rising to match price increases.

Comment and Analysis

Henry VIII's financial problems were still having a knock-on effect early in Elizabeth's reign. Henry VIII had debased the coinage — he issued coins that were not pure gold and silver, but had cheaper metals mixed in. Businessmen believed that the coinage was worth less than before, so they put their prices up. Elizabeth's government began to tackle this problem in 1560, but it still contributed to rising prices at the start of her reign.

Developments in Agriculture left many people Unemployed

1) Traditional farming methods involved many farmers renting strips of land in large open fields. This was subsistence-level farming — each farmer only grew enough crops to supply himself and his family.
2) This kind of farming was very inefficient, and in the 16th century landowners began changing their farming techniques to try and make more money from their land. Instead of sharing open fields among many farmers, they enclosed these fields to create a few large farms.
3) These new, enclosed farms required fewer labourers, so farmers who rented land were evicted, leaving them unemployed and homeless.
4) Exporting wool to Europe was more profitable than selling grain, so many landowners stopped growing grain and began sheep farming. This fall in grain production contributed to rising food prices. It also meant that the country was more likely to suffer food shortages when there was a bad harvest.

Comment and Analysis

These enclosures of farm land forced many people to leave their villages and migrate to towns or cities in search of work. The government viewed these migrant workers as 'vagabonds'. They feared that the growth of vagabondage would encourage riots and rebellions.

Religious Changes meant there was Less Support for the Poor

1) Between 1536 and 1541, Henry VIII had closed down England's monasteries and sold off most of their land (this was called the 'dissolution of the monasteries').
2) The monasteries had performed important social functions, including providing support for many poor, ill and disabled people. The dissolution of the monasteries removed a valuable source of assistance for people in times of need.

The enclosures closed the door to many farm labourers...

Do you agree that population growth was the main reason for rising levels of poverty in Elizabethan England? Explain your answer. [16]

Poverty

Elizabeth's government introduced a series of Poor Laws to try and tackle the problem of poverty.

The Government became More Involved in Poor Relief

1) Traditionally, the main source of support for the poor was charity — rich people made donations to hospitals, monasteries and other organisations that helped the poor. However, during Elizabeth's reign the problem of poverty became so bad that these charitable donations by individuals were no longer enough.
2) People began to realise that society as a whole would have to take responsibility for helping the poor, and so the government began to take action to tackle the problem of poverty.

Comment and Analysis

The government feared that the rising poverty levels were a serious threat to law and order. As poverty levels rose, crime rates had also increased, and the government feared that the poor might rise up in rebellion if the problem of poverty wasn't tackled.

People believed the Poor could be split into Three Categories

The Helpless Poor

Those who were unable to support themselves — including young orphans and the elderly, sick or disabled.

The Deserving Poor

People who wanted to work, but weren't able to find a job in their home town or village.

The Undeserving Poor

Beggars, criminals and people who refused to work. Also migrant workers ('vagabonds') who left their homes and travelled around looking for work.

The Poor Laws gave Help to the Helpless and Deserving Poor

1) Because voluntary donations were no longer sufficient to fund poor relief, the government began to introduce taxes to raise money for the poor.
2) The 1563 Poor Law gave magistrates the power to raise local funds for poor relief and introduced fines for people who refused to pay. However, each person was still free to decide how much they would contribute.
3) Another Poor Law in 1572 gave local officials the power to decide how much people should pay. By the end of the century there was a national system of taxation to pay for poor relief.
4) These taxes were used to provide hospitals and housing for the elderly, sick and disabled. Poor children were given apprenticeships, which usually lasted at least seven years, and local authorities were expected to provide work for the deserving poor. The Poor Law of 1576 said that poor people could be sent to prison if they refused to take work.

The Undeserving Poor were treated Harshly

Under the 1563 Poor Law, the undeserving poor could be publicly whipped. In 1572 the punishment was made even harsher — they faced whipping and having a hole bored through their right ear. Repeat offenders could be imprisoned or might even face execution.

Comment and Analysis

The undeserving poor were treated so harshly because they were seen as a serious threat to society. Many people believed that poor criminals and vagabonds had encouraged the Revolt of the Northern Earls in 1569 (see p.97). The harsh punishments for the undeserving poor introduced in 1572 were probably a direct response to the Revolt.

The Poor Laws helped some, but punished others...

EXAM QUESTION

Write a brief description of two features of government policies towards the poor in early Elizabethan England. [4]

Exploration and Discovery

Elizabeth's reign was an exciting time to be a sailor. Developments in navigation and ship-building were finally opening up the oceans and enabling explorers to discover the world beyond Europe.

The English were Slow to take an interest in Exploration

1) The Portuguese and Spanish were the first to explore the world beyond Europe. In the 1400s, their fleets began to set out on voyages of discovery to Africa, the Americas and Asia. By the time Elizabeth became queen in 1558, both Portugal and Spain had established many colonies in the Americas.
2) However, it was only from the 1560s that English sailors began to take an interest in global exploration and set out on their own voyages of discovery.

New Technology made Longer Journeys possible

1) Until the 15th century, most European sailors relied on coastal features to navigate. This made it impossible for them to cross oceans, where they could be out of sight of land for weeks at a time.
2) As the Portuguese and Spanish began to explore the oceans, they developed more advanced navigational techniques. They learnt how to navigate by the position of the stars or the Sun using a special instrument called a sea astrolabe.
3) During Elizabeth's reign, English sailors began to learn these techniques. In 1561, a key Spanish book, 'The Art of Navigation' by Martin Cortés, was translated into English. This gave English sailors detailed information about how to navigate across the Atlantic using a sea astrolabe.
4) Other innovations helped English sailors to navigate more accurately. From the 1570s, they began using the log and line, which helped them to estimate their speed with more accuracy. In the 1590s, English navigator John Davis invented the backstaff, which was easier to use and more accurate than the sea astrolabe. There were also improvements in map-making, which made maps and naval charts more detailed and reliable.

Improvements in ship-building also encouraged exploration. From the 1570s, the English began to build larger, longer ships. These new ships were better-suited to long ocean voyages because they were faster, more stable and easier to navigate. They could also carry larger cargoes, which made their journeys more profitable.

Rivalry with Spain encouraged Exploration

1) In the 1550s, English international trade was dominated by exports of woollen cloth to Europe. Most exports were traded through Antwerp, which was controlled by the Spanish. As tensions between England and Spain rose (see p.100), it became increasingly difficult for English merchants to trade freely through Antwerp.
2) This encouraged English merchants make their international trade more varied. Some looked for new routes into Europe, trading with German towns or through the Baltic. Others began to look further afield, especially to the Americas and Asia (see p.110).
3) As the commercial and political rivalry between England and Spain grew, Elizabeth realised that England needed to compete with Spain globally, not just within Europe. She encouraged English merchants to get involved in long-distance trade and privateering (see p.110), and to explore opportunities to establish English colonies in the Americas (see p.111).

Elizabeth encouraged the development of England's international trade by granting some merchants monopolies, which gave them exclusive rights to trade in a particular part of the world. E.g. in 1577 she gave a group of English merchants called the Spanish Company a monopoly on English trade with Spain's colonies, and in 1600 she gave the East India Company a monopoly on trade with Asia (see p.110).

No sat-nav? I'd have been lost in Elizabethan England...

Navigating by the Sun and stars might not sound very advanced compared to modern technology, but don't forget that for the Elizabethans these techniques were at the cutting-edge.

Exploration and Discovery

English sailors weren't that interested in voyages of discovery at first, but once they recognised the economic opportunities on offer in the Americas and Asia, there was no stopping them.

Explorers were Attracted by Economic Opportunities

1) Spanish trade with its colonies in the Americas was highly profitable — their treasure ships returned to Europe full of silver and gold. The wealth of the region attracted English sailors who hoped to get rich by trading illegally with Spain's colonies and raiding Spanish settlements and treasure ships. Some also hoped to profit by establishing English colonies in the region.
2) English merchants were also keen to develop trade with Asia. Traditionally, trade in Asian luxuries like silk and spices was dominated by merchants from Venice, who kept prices very high.
3) From the 1570s, English explorers began to look for new routes to Asia which would enable them to bypass these Venetian middlemen. Some tried to find the so-called North West passage around the top of North America, while others sailed through the Mediterranean and then went overland to India. In 1591, James Lancaster sailed to India around the Cape of Good Hope (the southern tip of Africa).
4) Following Lancaster's success, the East India Company was set up in 1600 to trade with Asia. It sponsored successful trading expeditions to the region in 1601 and 1604.

Francis Drake sailed Around the World

1) Between 1577 and 1580, Francis Drake (see p.100) sailed all the way around the world. This was only the second global circumnavigation (journey around the world) and the first by an English sailor.
2) Drake probably wasn't trying to sail around the world. It seems that he was sent by Queen Elizabeth to explore the coast of South America, looking for opportunities for English colonisation and trade. He almost certainly planned to make money on the expedition by raiding Spanish colonies and treasure ships.

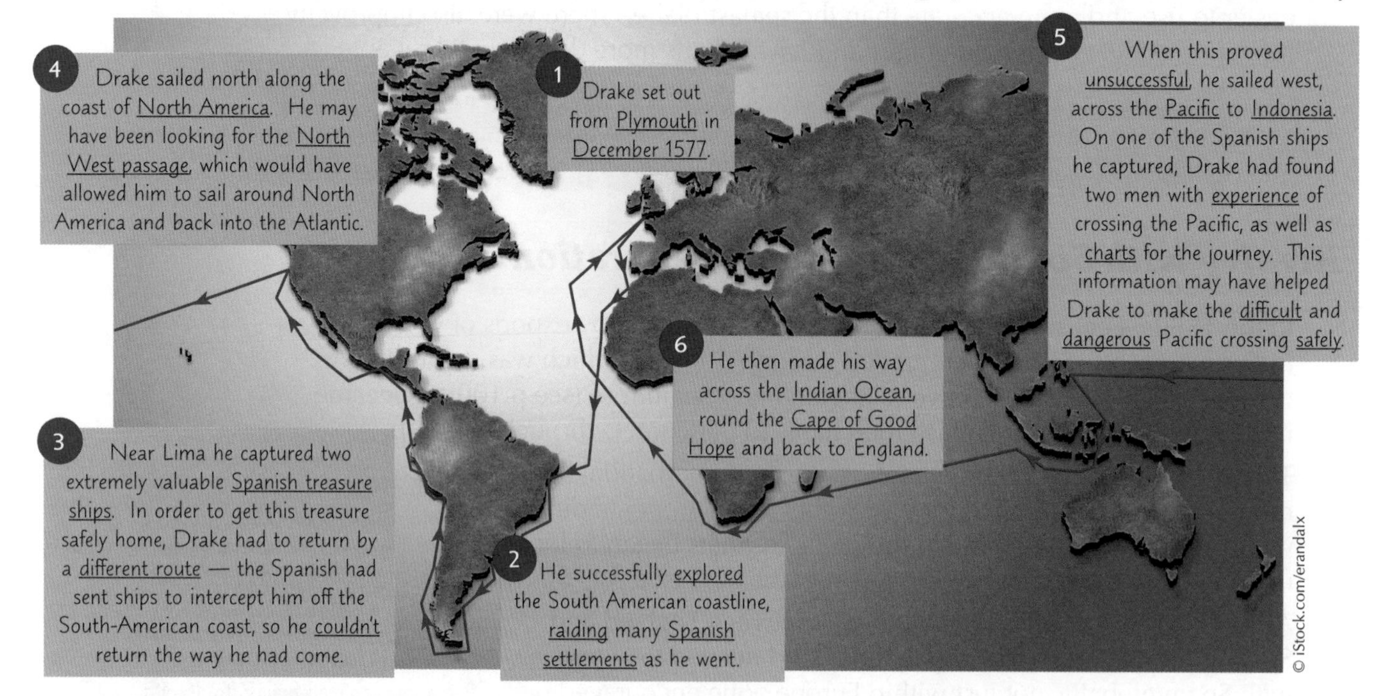

3) On his return to England, Drake was knighted by Queen Elizabeth aboard his ship, the Golden Hind. This royal recognition and the vast wealth that Drake brought back from the journey encouraged more English sailors to set out on long-distance journeys.

Circumnavigation — taking the roundabout route...

Why did English sailors get more involved in global exploration during Elizabeth's reign? Explain your answer. [12]

Raleigh and Virginia

In the 1580s, England tried to challenge Spain's dominance as an imperial power by establishing a colony in North America. But creating a permanent settlement turned out to be pretty tricky...

Walter Raleigh received Permission to Explore and Colonise

1) By the early 1580s, England had claimed some territory in North America, but hadn't managed to establish a successful colony yet. During his journey around the world, Drake had claimed New Albion (in California) for England.
2) The English also claimed Newfoundland in eastern Canada. In 1583, Sir Humphrey Gilbert set out to establish a colony in Newfoundland, but the expedition failed.
3) After Gilbert's failure, Elizabeth gave Walter Raleigh permission to explore and colonise unclaimed territories. She wanted Raleigh to establish a colony on the Atlantic coast of North America.

Comment and Analysis

An English colony would challenge Spain's dominance in the Americas and could be used as a base for attacking Spanish treasure ships. It was also hoped that the colony would provide opportunities for trade and be a source of raw materials that might be useful in future wars with Spain.

Raleigh's attempts to Colonise Virginia were Unsuccessful

1) In 1584, Raleigh sent a fact-finding mission to North America. The fleet landed on Roanoke Island, explored the area and returned to England with two Native Americans. They gave a glowing report of the region, which encouraged Raleigh to organise a second expedition.

Raleigh named his colony Virginia after Elizabeth, who was known as the 'Virgin Queen'.

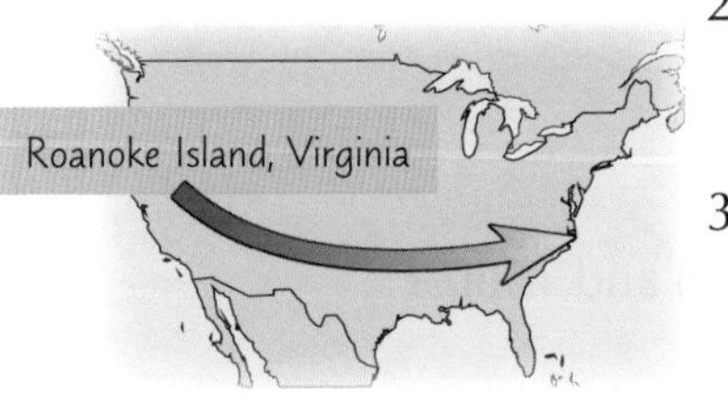
Roanoke Island, Virginia

2) The next year, Raleigh sent five ships to Virginia, led by Sir Richard Grenville. 108 settlers (known as planters) tried to establish a permanent colony on Roanoke, while Grenville went back to England for supplies.
3) When Francis Drake visited Roanoke in 1586, Grenville still hadn't returned and the planters were running low on supplies. Most of the planters decided to return to England with Drake, although a small group of men were left to maintain the colony.
4) A third expedition reached Roanoke in 1587 and found it deserted — it's thought that the men who stayed behind in 1586 were killed by local people. Around 100 planters settled on the island and began to build a colony. They were expecting supplies from England in 1588, but the fleet was delayed by the Spanish Armada (see p.103-104).
5) When the supply ships finally reached Roanoke in 1590, all the planters had disappeared. They were never found, and Roanoke soon became known as the 'Lost Colony'.

Several Factors led to the Failure of the Roanoke Colony

Bad Timing

If the supply ships hadn't been delayed by the Armada, the Roanoke colony might have survived.

Lack of Supplies

The planters didn't take enough supplies with them and found it difficult to grow food on Roanoke. This made them more vulnerable to problems like the delay of the supply ships in 1588.

Poor Planning

Establishing a colony thousands of miles from England was a major challenge, which required detailed planning and organisation. However, initial exploration of Roanoke was inadequate and the whole project was poorly organised. This was largely because Raleigh's funds were too limited.

As Raleigh learned, if you fail to plan, you plan to fail...

Make a timeline of Raleigh's attempts to colonise Virginia. Include all the expeditions to Roanoke Island between 1584 and 1590, and the key events of each expedition.

Revision Summary

That's the Elizabethans all done and dusted — time to test your knowledge with a quick revision summary.

- Try these questions and tick off each one when you get it right.
- When you've done all the questions for a topic and are completely happy with it, tick off the topic.

Queen, Government and Religion, 1558-1569 (p.90-96)

1) Who were Queen Elizabeth I's parents?
2) What was the role of the privy council?
3) Describe Queen Elizabeth's character.
4) Give three reasons why the threat of invasion by the French had lessened by 1562.
5) Write down four key beliefs of the Protestant reformers.
6) Name the two Acts of the Elizabethan religious settlement.
7) Why did the Puritans oppose the religious settlement?
8) Explain what the word 'recusant' means.
9) Why did Mary, Queen of Scots, have a strong claim to the English throne?
10) What were the 'Casket Letters'?

Challenges at Home and Abroad, 1569-1588 (p.97-104)

11) Give three reasons for the 1569 Revolt of the Northern Earls.
12) Name three Catholic plots against Queen Elizabeth.
13) Who was Francis Walsingham?
14) Why was Queen Elizabeth reluctant to execute Mary, Queen of Scots?
15) Why were there growing tensions between England and Spain in the 1570s and 1580s?
16) Give four reasons why Dudley's campaign in the Netherlands failed.
17) Why did Francis Drake sail to Spain in 1587?
18) Explain what the phrase 'the singeing of the King of Spain's beard' means.
19) Who led the Spanish Armada?
20) How did the English attack the Armada at Calais?
21) Write down four reasons why the English navy defeated the Spanish Armada.

Elizabethan Society in the Age of Exploration, 1558-1588 (p.105-111)

22) What was a petty school?
23) Give three subjects students studied at university.
24) Name three pastimes that were popular at Elizabeth's court.
25) Name two theatres that were built in London during Elizabeth's reign.
26) Why was the problem of poverty growing in Elizabethan England?
27) What were the three categories of poor people in Elizabethan England?
28) Give two measures that were introduced by the 1563 Poor Law.
29) How did new technology encourage global exploration?
30) Explain why Francis Drake sailed across the Pacific.
31) Who organised the attempted colonisation of Virginia in the 1580s?
32) Why is Roanoke Island known as the 'Lost Colony'?

The War Ends

World War I lasted from 1914-1918. Fighting ended with the armistice on November 11th 1918. By this time, Germany was experiencing widespread unrest, which eventually resulted in a revolution.

The war was Devastating for Germany

1) Near the war's end, German people were suffering severe hardship.
2) The Allies had set up naval blockades which prevented imports of food and essential goods. By 1918, many people faced starvation.
3) Public opinion turned against Kaiser Wilhelm II, who ruled the German Empire like a king. Many Germans wanted a democracy and an end to the war — there was widespread unrest.

- In November 1918 some members of the German navy rebelled and refused to board their ships.
- In Hanover, German troops refused to control rioters.
- A Jewish communist called Kurt Eisner encouraged a general uprising, which sparked mass strikes in Munich.

A British cartoon from 1917. German civilians queue for food as an over-fed official walks past them. The cartoonist is highlighting the difference between the lifestyle of Germany's rich officers and that of the rest of its struggling population.

Social Unrest turned into Revolution

1) By November 1918, the situation in Germany verged on civil war. A huge public protest was held in Berlin, and members of the SPD (Social Democratic Party) called for the Kaiser's resignation.
2) Kaiser Wilhelm abdicated (resigned) on 9th November 1918. On the same day, two different socialist parties — the Social Democratic Party and the Independent Social Democratic Party (USPD) — declared a republic.
3) On November 10th, all the state leaders that had been appointed by the monarchy left their posts. New revolutionary state governments took over instead. The monarchy had been abolished and Germany had the chance to become a democracy.

A republic is a country ruled without a monarch (king or queen) — power is held by the people via elected representatives.

Germany was made up of 18 states, and each had its own government. The national government decided national affairs, and state governments dealt with more local affairs.

The signing of the armistice

- On 11th November 1918, a ceasefire to end the First World War was agreed. The Allies (Britain, France and the USA) signed an armistice (truce) with Germany.
- The new republic was under pressure to sign. The government didn't think Germany could continue fighting — its people were starving and military morale was low.
- The armistice wasn't supported by some right-wing Germans, who saw the truce as a betrayal. They believed Germany could still win the war.

The Socialists set up a Temporary Government

1) After the abdication of the Kaiser, Germany was disorganised. Different political parties claimed control over different towns.
2) A temporary national government was established, consisting of the SPD and the USPD. It was called the Council of People's Representatives.
3) It controlled Germany until January 1919, when elections were held for a new Reichstag (parliament) — see p.114.

Revolutions pop up in history over and over and over again...

EXAM QUESTION

Explain the reasons for the German Revolution in 1918.
Your answer could consider naval blockades and/or the monarchy. [12]

The Weimar Republic

The Weimar Republic was the first time Germany had ever been governed as a democracy. It was designed to give the German people a voice. However, there were major flaws in its constitution that made it weak.

The Weimar Republic was formed

1) The Council of People's Representatives organised elections in January 1919 to create a new parliament. Germany was now a democracy — the people would say how the country was run.
2) Friedrich Ebert became the first President, with Philip Scheidemann as Chancellor. Ebert was leader of the SPD, a moderate party of socialists.
3) In February 1919, the members of the new Reichstag (parliament) met at Weimar to create a new constitution for Germany. Historians call this period of Germany's history the Weimar Republic.

The constitution decided how the government would be organised, and established its main principles.

The Weimar Constitution made Germany More Democratic...

The new constitution reorganised the German system of government.

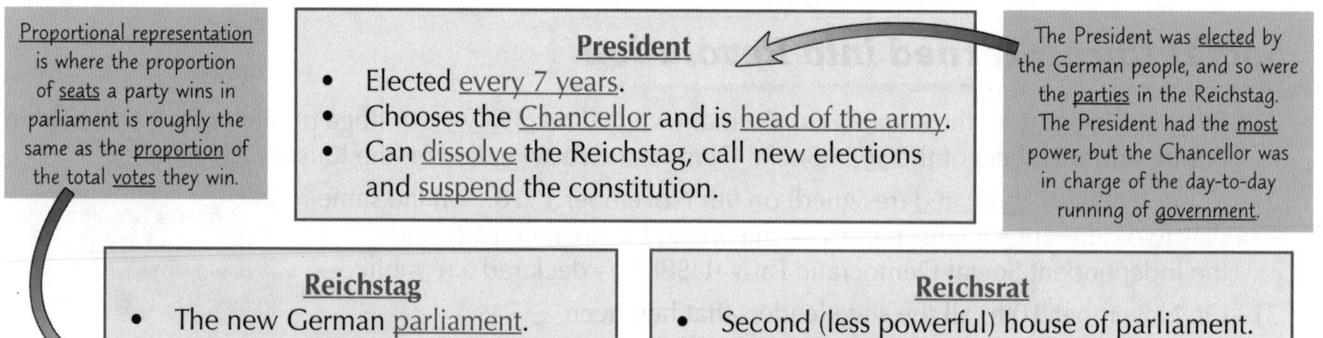

1) The new constitution was designed to be as fair as possible. Even very small political parties were given seats in the Reichstag if they got 0.4% of the vote or above.
2) The constitution allowed women to vote for the first time, and lowered the voting age to 20 — more Germans could vote and the German public had greater power.

...but the Consitution had Weaknesses

Even though the new constitution was more democratic, it didn't prove to be very efficient.

1) Proportional representation meant that even parties with a very small number of votes were guaranteed to get into the Reichstag. This meant it was difficult to make decisions because there were so many parties, and they all had different points of view.
2) When a decision couldn't be reached, the President could suspend the constitution and pass laws without the Reichstag's consent.
3) This power was only supposed to be used in an emergency, but became a useful way of getting around disagreements that took place in the Reichstag. This meant it undermined the new democracy.

The President's ability to force through his own decision was known as 'Article 48'.

The Weimar Republic was vulnerable from the beginning...

When you're writing an answer in the exam, make sure you develop the points you make. For example, don't just say that Weimar Republic was weak — explain why it was weak.

Early Unpopularity

The Treaty of Versailles was signed in June 1919. The treaty was very unpopular in Germany and many Germans resented the new government for accepting its terms — not exactly a great start for the Republic.

Ebert signed the Treaty of Versailles

1) After the armistice, a peace treaty called the Treaty of Versailles was imposed on Germany.
2) The terms of the treaty were mostly decided by the Allied leaders — David Lloyd George (Britain), Georges Clemenceau (France) and Woodrow Wilson (USA).

Comment and Analysis

As a result, the Weimar Republic became associated with the pain and humiliation caused by the Treaty of Versailles.

The new German government wasn't invited to the peace conference in 1919 and had no say in the Versailles Treaty. At first, Ebert refused to sign the treaty, but in the end he had little choice — Germany was too weak to risk restarting the conflict. In June 1919, he accepted its terms and signed.

The Terms of the Versailles Treaty were Severe

1) Article 231 of the treaty said Germany had to take the blame for the war — the War-Guilt Clause. → Many Germans didn't agree with this, and were humiliated by having to accept total blame.
2) Germany's armed forces were reduced to 100,000 men. They weren't allowed any armoured vehicles, aircraft or submarines, and could only have 6 warships. → This made Germans feel vulnerable.
3) Germany was forced to pay £6600 million in reparations — payments for the damage caused by German forces in the war. The amount was decided in 1921 but was changed later. → The heavy reparations seemed unfair to Germans and would cause lasting damage to Germany's economy.
4) Germany lost its empire — areas around the world that used to belong to Germany were now called mandates. They were put under the control of countries on the winning side of the war by the League of Nations — an organisation which aimed to settle international disputes peacefully. → People opposed the losses in territory, especially when people in German colonies were forced to become part of a new nation.
5) The German military was banned from the Rhineland — an area of Germany on its western border with France. This left Germany open to attack from the west.

Germany Felt Betrayed by the Weimar Republic

The Treaty of Versailles caused resentment towards the Weimar Republic.

1) Germans called the treaty a 'Diktat' (a treaty forced upon Germany), and many blamed Ebert for accepting its terms.
2) Some Germans believed the armistice was a mistake and that Germany could have won the war. They felt 'stabbed in the back' by the Weimar politicians, who brought the Treaty of Versailles upon Germany unnecessarily.

The Weimar politicians involved in signing the armistice became known as the 'November Criminals'.

Comment and Analysis

The Treaty of Versailles played an important part in the failure of the Weimar Republic. It harmed the Republic's popularity, and created economic and political unrest that hindered the government for years.

This German cartoon demonstrates Germany's feelings towards the Treaty of Versailles. The Allies are shown as demons, out for revenge.

Germans felt 'stabbed in the back' by the government...

REVISION TASK

Scribble down as much as you can remember about the terms of the Treaty of Versailles. Include how Germans felt about it and the consequences for the Weimar Republic.

Years of Unrest

The first four years of the Weimar Republic (1919-1923) were dominated by political, social and economic unrest. It created hardship for the German people, and fuelled criticism of Ebert's government.

There was Widespread Discontent in Germany

1) By 1919, thousands of Germans were poor and starving, and an influenza epidemic had killed thousands.
2) Many Germans denied they had lost the war and blamed the 'November Criminals' who had agreed to the armistice and the Treaty of Versailles.
3) Others who were blamed for losing the war included communists and Jews.
4) The government was seen as weak and ineffective — the Treaty of Versailles made living conditions worse.

Soon there were Riots and Rebellions

The government faced threats from left-wing and right-wing political groups.

The extreme left wanted a revolution...

- In January 1919, communists led by Karl Liebknecht and Rosa Luxemburg tried to take over Berlin. They took control of important buildings like newspaper headquarters, and 50,000 workers went on strike in support of the left-wing revolution. This became known as the Spartacist Revolt.
- Ebert asked for help from the right-wing Freikorps (ex-German soldiers) to stop the rebellion. Over 100 workers were killed. The Freikorps' use of violence caused a split on the Left between the Social Democratic Party and the communists.

The right also rebelled against the Weimar government...

- In March 1920, some of the Freikorps themselves took part in the Kapp Putsch ('Putsch' means revolt) — led by Wolfgang Kapp. They wanted to create a new right-wing government.
- The Friekorps marched into Berlin to overthrow the Weimar regime. But German workers opposed the putsch and staged a general strike. Berlin was paralysed and Kapp was forced to give up.
- Even after the putsch failed, threats to the government remained. In 1922, some former Freikorps members assassinated Walter Rathenau — he'd been Foreign Minister and was Jewish.

As Germany's economic problems got worse after the war, anti-Semitic (anti-Jewish) feelings increased.

In 1923 Germany Couldn't Pay its Reparations

1) By 1923, Germany could no longer meet the reparations payments set out by the Treaty of Versailles.
2) France and Belgium decided to take Germany's resources instead, so they occupied the Ruhr — the richest industrial part of Germany. This gave them access to Germany's iron and coal reserves. The occupation led to fury in Germany, and caused a huge strike in the Ruhr.
3) German industry was devastated again. Germany tried to solve her debt problem by printing more money, but this plunged the economy into hyperinflation.
4) In 1918, an egg cost ¼ of a Mark. By November 1923, it cost 80 million Marks.

Hyperinflation happens when production can't keep up with the amount of money in circulation, so the money keeps losing its value.

The consequences of hyperinflation

- Germany's currency became worthless. Nobody wanted to trade with Germany, so shortages of food and goods got worse.
- Bank savings also became worthless. The hardest hit were the middle classes.

By 1923, even basic necessities were hard to get hold of. The German people were undergoing immense hardship, which they'd now come to associate with the rise of the Weimar Republic.

Hyperinflation — sounds good for blowing up balloons...

To what extent do you agree that the crises and revolts in Germany between 1918 and 1923 were inevitable, given the circumstances of the Weimar Republic? [16]

Recovery

In 1923, Gustav Stresemann became Chancellor of the Weimar Republic. His domestic and international policies helped the German economy to recover, resulting in the 'Golden Years' of the Weimar Republic

Stresemann introduced a New Currency

1) Gustav Stresemann was Chancellor of the Weimar Republic between August and November 1923. He made important changes to help Germany to recover from its economic crisis.
2) In September 1923, he ended the strike in the Ruhr. This reduced tension between Germany, France and Belgium, and meant the government could stop compensation payments to strikers.
3) In November 1923, Stresemann replaced the German Mark with the Rentenmark to stabilise Germany's currency.
4) Stresemann created the 'great coalition' — a group of moderate, pro-democracy socialist parties in the Reichstag who agreed to work together. This allowed parliament to make decisions more quickly.

Stresemann wanted International Cooperation

In November 1923, Stresemann became Foreign Minister. He tried to cooperate more with other countries and build better international relationships. Germany's economy prospered as a result.

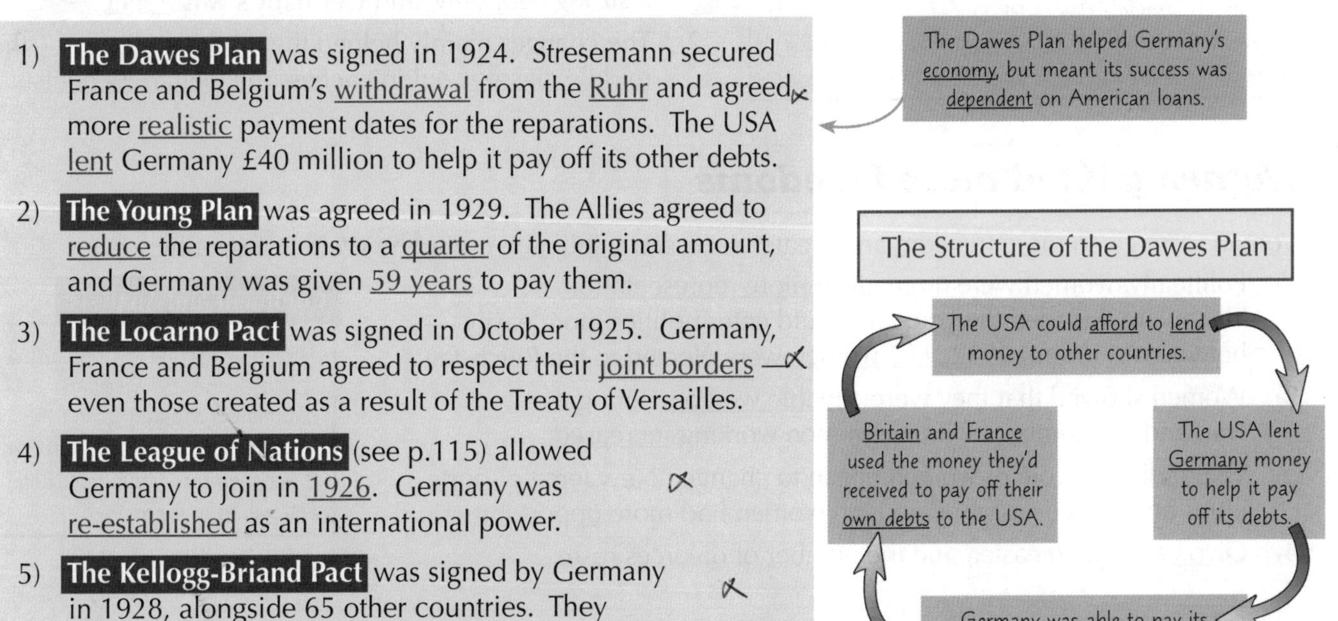

1) **The Dawes Plan** was signed in 1924. Stresemann secured France and Belgium's withdrawal from the Ruhr and agreed more realistic payment dates for the reparations. The USA lent Germany £40 million to help it pay off its other debts.
2) **The Young Plan** was agreed in 1929. The Allies agreed to reduce the reparations to a quarter of the original amount, and Germany was given 59 years to pay them.
3) **The Locarno Pact** was signed in October 1925. Germany, France and Belgium agreed to respect their joint borders — even those created as a result of the Treaty of Versailles.
4) **The League of Nations** (see p.115) allowed Germany to join in 1926. Germany was re-established as an international power.
5) **The Kellogg-Briand Pact** was signed by Germany in 1928, alongside 65 other countries. They promised not to use violence to settle disputes.

Germany had begun to Recover — but Depended on US Money

1) Life was beginning to look better for Germany thanks to the work of Stresemann.
2) But he died in October 1929, just before the disaster of the Wall Street Crash — a massive stock market crash in the USA which started a global economic depression.
3) The plans he had agreed would only work if the USA had enough money to keep lending to Germany — but after the crash, it didn't. Things were suddenly going to get worse again (see p.121).

Comment and Analysis

Germany's economic recovery helped restore faith in the Weimar Republic — there was strong support for pro-Weimar political parties in the 1928 elections.

No need to Strese, mann — it's all under control...

Don't forget to make sure that your spelling, punctuation and grammar are all accurate — you'll be marked on it in some questions in the exam. See p.136-137 for a few useful pointers.

Changes Under the Weimar Republic

Despite political, social and economic unrest, life did improve for some under the Weimar Republic.

Living standards Improved for the Working Classes

During the 'Golden Years', living standards improved in the Weimar Republic. This was a result of Germany's economic prosperity, but also of the reforms which took place throughout the 1920s.

What Improved	How It Improved
Unemployment	The unemployed were more protected. In 1927 the government introduced unemployment insurance. Workers could pay into the scheme and would receive cash benefits if they became unemployed.
Wages	The working classes became more prosperous. Wages for industrial workers rose quickly in the late 1920s.
Housing	The government launched mass housing projects. More than 2 million new homes were built between 1924 and 1931. This also provided extra employment.

Comment and Analysis

Not everyone benefited from higher standards of living. The middle classes felt ignored by the Weimar government and their resentment made it easier for the government's political opponents to gain support.

Despite these changes, some problems remained:

1) Higher living standards could only be maintained with a strong economy, and Germany's was fragile.
2) The changes mainly helped the working classes — the middle classes couldn't access the welfare benefits.

Women gained more Freedoms

Women were given more freedom and greater access to public life under the Weimar Republic.

1) Politically, women were more given more representation. They were awarded the vote and could enter politics more easily — between 1919 and 1932, 112 women were elected to the Reichstag.
2) Women showed that they were capable workers during the war, and the number of young women working increased.
3) The traditional role of women began to change. New female sports clubs and societies sprang up, and women had more opportunities.
4) Divorce became easier, and the number of divorces rose.

Comment and Analysis

These changes fuelled right-wing criticism — some German nationalists thought giving women more power and freedom threatened traditional family life and values in Germany.

The Weimar Republic had many Cultural Achievements

1) The Weimar Republic was a period of creativity and innovation in Germany. Freedom of expression generated new ideas. Artists began to question traditional forms and styles, especially ones that focused on authority and militarism.
2) There were advances in the arts — some developments were bold and new, like the drama of Bertholt Brecht. The Bauhaus School of design was highly influential, especially in fine arts and architecture.
3) There were also important changes in music, literature and cinema. German films were successful — e.g. 'Metropolis' directed by Fritz Lang.
4) The Weimar Republic encouraged new ways of critical thinking at places like Frankfurt University, and a cabaret culture developed in Berlin.

Not all Germans liked the rejection of traditional forms and values in Weimar culture. Some were afraid it symbolised a loss of German tradition.

It wasn't all doom and gloom...

'There were no great changes to German society under the Weimar Republic.' To what extent do you agree with this view? [16]

Early Stages of the Nazi Party

Hitler entered German politics around the time the Weimar Republic was formed. By the time the Nazi Party was founded in 1920, he was growing in influence and became an opponent of the Weimar government.

Adolf Hitler became the Voice of the German Workers' Party

Hitler began his political career in the German Workers' Party — a nationalist party led by Anton Drexler.

1) Hitler joined the German Workers' Party in January 1919, when he was still in the German army. He became known for his talent as a passionate and skilled speaker, and crowds gathered to hear him talk.
2) The German Workers' Party began to rely on him to get new party members, and in 1920 he was made chief of propaganda.
3) In 1920, the party was re-branded as the National Socialist German Workers' Party (the Nazi Party). In July 1921, Hitler became its leader.
4) The party was a nationalist party — it thought that the interests of Germans should be at the centre of government policy. It was anti-Semitic (anti-Jewish) and was opposed to the Weimar Republic. Above everything, it wanted to restore Germany's greatness.
5) This extract from one of Hitler's speeches shows his nationalist passion.

In 1919, the German Workers' Party had around 60 members. By the end of 1920, it had around 2000.

> 'For the murderers of our Fatherland who all the years through have betrayed and sold Germany, they are the same men who, as the November criminals, have plunged us into the depths of misfortune.
>
> We have the duty to speak since in the near future, when we have gained power, we shall have the further duty of taking [...] these traitors to their State and of hanging them on the gallows to which they belong.'
>
> *Extract from a speech made by Hitler in Munich in 1923.*

Hitler implies Germany is a victim that has been 'betrayed'.

He appears loyal to his country. He says it was Germany's 'duty' to get rid of 'traitors' like Weimar's 'November criminals'.

Hitler wanted revenge. This appealed to many who felt Germany had been treated unfairly.

The Nazi Party Developed its Identity

As the Nazi Party grew in popularity, it established an identity that appealed to as many people as possible.

1) In February 1920, the Nazi Party promoted its policies in the 'Twenty-Five Point Programme'.
2) The Programme stressed the superiority of the German people and promoted anti-Semitism.
3) The party wanted to raise pensions, and improve health and education — but only for Germans.
4) Rejecting the Treaty of Versailles and promoting German greatness gave the party a nationwide appeal.
5) In 1921, Hitler founded his own party militia called the SA ('storm troopers'). The SA were political thugs — they carried out violent anti-Semitic attacks and intimidated rival political groups. Many people were scared of them, but some Germans admired them.

Extract from the Twenty-Five Point Programme:

- The Treaty of Versailles should be abolished.
- All German-speakers should be united.
- Only Germans (people with German blood) can be classed as citizens. Jews cannot be citizens.
- Improved pensions and land reform.

Comment and Analysis

The Nazis took advantage of economic problems to provide Germans with useful scapegoats like the Jews. The SA gave the party a military feel, which made it seem organised and disciplined. It also gave many ex-soldiers a job and a purpose.

Hitler was charismatic and stood for German greatness...

When you're asked to infer something from a source in the exam, you'll need to pick out individual words or phrases used in the text and say what those words suggest.

The Munich Putsch

In 1922, a nationalist party overthrew the Italian government, inspiring Hitler to do the same in Germany.

Hitler tried to Overthrow the Government in the Munich Putsch

In 1923, the Weimar Republic was in crisis:

Hitler thought the time was right to attempt a putsch (revolt)...

- In 1923, things were going badly for the Weimar Republic — it seemed weak.
- Hyperinflation was at its peak and there were food riots.
- Many Germans were angry at the French and Belgian invasion of the Ruhr (see p.116). When the government stopped resistance by ending the strike there in 1923 (see p.117), discontent increased.

In November 1923, the Nazis marched on Munich...

- Hitler's soldiers occupied a beer hall in the Bavarian city of Munich where local government leaders were meeting. He announced that the revolution had begun.
- The next day Hitler marched into Munich supported by his stormtroopers. But news of the revolt had been leaked to the police, who were waiting for Hitler. The police fired on the rebels and the revolt quickly collapsed.

1) Hitler was imprisoned for his role in the Munich Putsch, but his trial gave him valuable publicity.
2) He wrote a book in prison called 'Mein Kampf' ('My Struggle') describing his beliefs and ambitions.
3) Mein Kampf was vital in spreading Nazi ideology — millions of Germans read it. It introduced Hitler's belief that the Aryan race (which included Germans) was superior to all other races, and that all Germans had a right to 'Lebensraum' (more space to live).

After the Munich Putsch Hitler Changed Tactics

1) By the mid-1920s, the German economy was starting to recover under Stresemann (see p.117). As a result, general support for the Nazis declined and overturning the government through a coup no longer seemed realistic.
2) The Nazi Party was banned after the Munich Putsch, along with the SA. Hitler was released from prison in December 1924 and the ban on the party was lifted in February 1925. Hitler re-established the Nazi Party with himself as supreme leader.
3) Hitler changed tactics — he now tried to gain control through the democratic system. This involved restructuring the Nazi Party so it could compete more successfully in national elections.

Comment and Analysis

The dip in support for the Nazi Party between 1924 and 1928 shows how important economic unrest was to Hitler's success. Nazi ideology thrived when Germany was struggling.

1. In 1926, Hitler held a conference with the Nazi leadership at Bamberg. He was worried that the party had become divided — some members wanted the party to go in a more socialist direction. He made it clear that the party would only follow his agenda.

2. The Nazi Party adopted a national framework and became more centralised. In 1926 Hitler appointed leaders called 'gauleiters' to run regional branches of the Nazi Party. Gauleiters were controlled by the party leadership in Munich, and supervised district and local branches of the party. This brought every level of the party under Hitler's control.

3. Nazi propaganda increased and was centrally controlled by the leadership in Munich. This made propaganda campaigns more efficient. In 1926 Hitler re-established the SA and began to use them for propaganda purposes.

4. The Nazi Party created new organisations for different social groups. In 1926 it founded the Hitler Youth to attract younger voters, and it also created societies for different professions, e.g. The National Socialist Teachers' League. These organisations made different sectors of society feel valued by the party.

The Nazis needed to putsch a bit harder...

Summarise the events of the Munich Putsch and list three reasons why it was important.

The Great Depression

The Wall Street Crash in 1929 caused the Great Depression, leading to a fall in support for the government.

The Wall Street Crash Ended economic Recovery

In October 1929 the Wall Street stock market in America crashed. It sparked an international economic crisis and meant the USA couldn't afford to prop up the German economy any longer.

1) Germany's economic recovery between 1924 and 1929 was built on unstable foundations. The biggest problem was that it was dependent on loans from the USA, which had been agreed in the Dawes Plan (see p.117).
2) After the Wall Street Crash, the USA couldn't afford to lend Germany money anymore. It suspended future payments and wanted some old loans to be repaid.

- Germany's economy collapsed without American aid. Industrial production went into decline — factories closed and banks went out of business.
- There was mass unemployment. In October 1929 1.6 million people were out of work, and by February 1932 there were over 6 million.

Brüning's policies Decreased Support for Weimar

In March 1930, the Weimar Republic appointed a new Chancellor, Heinrich Brüning, to deal with the crisis. He introduced tough economic policies to keep inflation from rising like it had done in 1923 (see p.116).

Brüning's economic policies weren't popular...

- Brüning increased the cost of imported food to help German agriculture, but this also raised food prices.
- Government salaries and pensions were reduced and taxes increased.
- Social services were cut back, and unemployment benefits were reduced.

As many Germans were struggling financially, the government seemed to be adding pressure by reducing support.

1) Everyday life in Germany seemed to be made worse by Brüning's policies.
2) They were designed to help the economy, but they also caused standards of living to fall — Brüning was nicknamed the 'Hunger Chancellor'.
3) By 1932, many different sectors of society were discontent with the Weimar government. High unemployment and reduced benefits also meant the government lost some backing from the working classes, who had always formed a large part of their support.

Comment and Analysis

Not all historians think that Brüning's policies made German society worse — some think the economic crisis was so severe that it would've taken years for any improvements to be seen.

The Government became Less Democratic

1) Brüning's economic policies were so unpopular that he had difficulty passing them in the Reichstag. He began to rely on 'Article 48' of the Weimar constitution (see p.114). Brüning asking President Hindenburg to suspend the constitution, so he could make decisions without parliamentary approval.
2) By 1932, Brüning was regularly bypassing parliament to force his economic measures through.

Comment and Analysis

Weimar no longer felt like a democracy and the German people felt neglected. They began to look towards alternative political parties like the Nazi Party and the Communist Party.

Germany's extremist parties became more attractive...

EXAM QUESTION

Explain why the Great Depression weakened support for the Weimar Republic. [12]
You could write about unemployment and/or Chancellor Brüning.

The Rise of the Nazis

The desperation caused by the economic Depression in Germany in the 1920s and 1930s meant that the German people were willing to consider any political party that promised something different.

The Nazis increased in Popularity during the Depression

Popular discontent with the Weimar government and economic instability meant that many Germans had lost faith in democracy. This created an opportunity for extremist parties to grow.

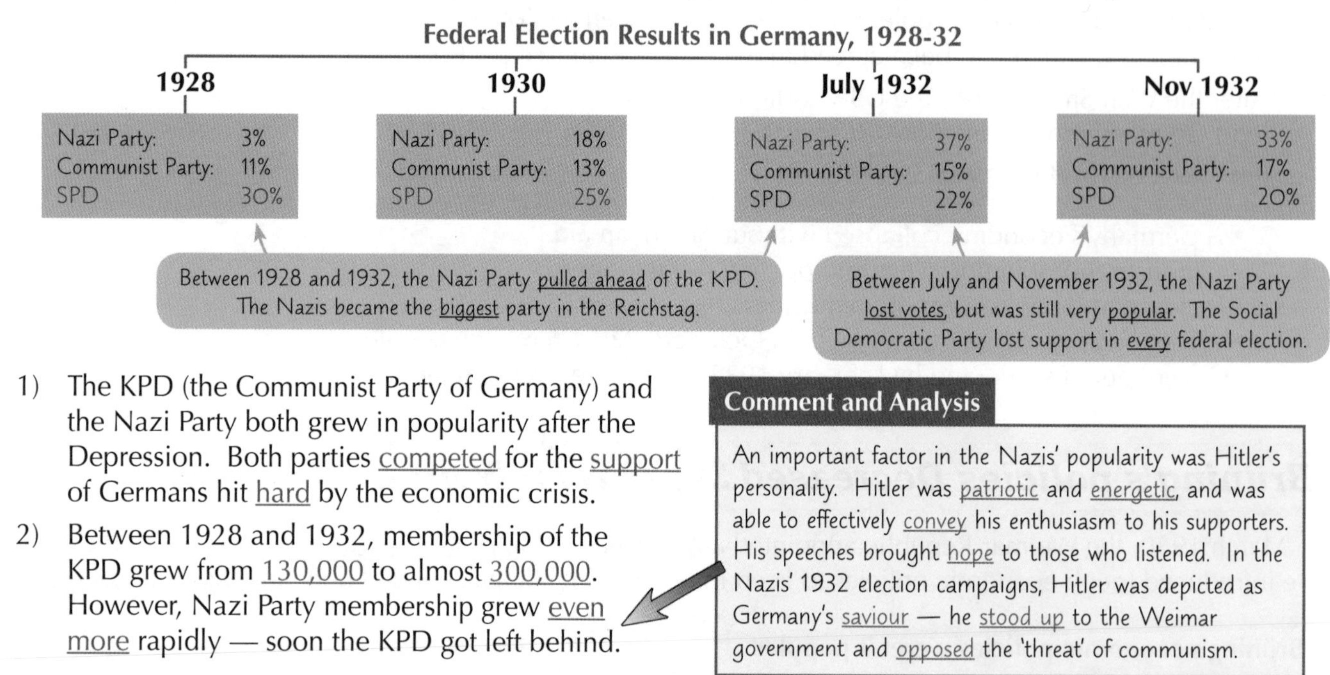

1) The KPD (the Communist Party of Germany) and the Nazi Party both grew in popularity after the Depression. Both parties competed for the support of Germans hit hard by the economic crisis.
2) Between 1928 and 1932, membership of the KPD grew from 130,000 to almost 300,000. However, Nazi Party membership grew even more rapidly — soon the KPD got left behind.

Comment and Analysis

An important factor in the Nazis' popularity was Hitler's personality. Hitler was patriotic and energetic, and was able to effectively convey his enthusiasm to his supporters. His speeches brought hope to those who listened. In the Nazis' 1932 election campaigns, Hitler was depicted as Germany's saviour — he stood up to the Weimar government and opposed the 'threat' of communism.

The Nazi Party Appealed to many Different Groups in Society

The Nazis promised a more prosperous and less humiliating future, which was very popular among the German people — by 1930, membership had grown to over 300,000.

1) After the onset of the Depression, the Nazi Party's popularity soared. Hitler's promise to make Germany great again appealed to the growing ranks of unemployed and young people who wanted a brighter future.
2) Some people also supported the Nazis' anti-communist and anti-Jewish views. Communists and Jews were useful scapegoats for Germany's economic problems and gave Germans someone to blame.
3) Some wealthy businessmen who had lost out in the Great Depression turned to the Nazi Party. They approved of the Nazis' anti-communist stance and wanted the economic prosperity Hitler had promised.

Comment and Analysis

After the Depression hit Germany, more Germans began to vote. Participation in elections increased by around 10% between 1928 and 1932. Many of these new voters were attracted by the changes the Nazi Party promised.

The Nazi Party was well organised...

- By the 1930s, the Nazi Party seemed strong and organised in comparison to the Weimar government. The SA held demonstrations, distributed propaganda and appeared more disciplined than they had been in the early 1920s. The Nazi Party became more respectable and this helped Hitler secure support from the middle classes.
- Propaganda was very efficient. It often focused on regional issues and targeted specific groups. This made individuals feel valued by the Party and stole votes from smaller parties.

The Nazis and Communists both gained in popularity...

Scribble down as many reasons as you can think of for the rise of the Communist Party and the Nazi Party between 1928 and 1932. Think about who supported each party and why.

Hitler Becomes Chancellor

As the Depression got worse, political instability grew. Several parties were competing for power in the elections of 1932 (see p.122). In 1933, the Nazis would emerge on top. Hitler's rise continued.

Hindenburg Refused to give the Nazis power

1) By April 1932, economic conditions had worsened. The country was desperate for a strong government.
2) President Hindenburg had to stand for re-election because his term of office had run out. He was a national hero, but Hitler decided to run against him. Despite claiming he'd win easily, Hindenburg didn't win a majority in the first election. In the second ballot he won 53%, beating Hitler's 36.8%.
3) In May 1932, Chancellor Brüning was dismissed and replaced by Franz von Papen.
4) In the elections of July 1932, the Nazis became the most popular party in the Reichstag (see p.122). Hitler demanded to be made Chancellor, but Hindenburg didn't trust him and refused his request.

This could have been a dead end for Hitler — Hindenburg was the only one who could legally appoint him Chancellor of Germany.

Hitler became Chancellor with the aid of a Political Deal

1) The Nazis lost 34 seats in the November 1932 election — they seemed to be losing popularity.
2) In December 1932 Hindenburg replaced Papen with one of his advisors, Kurt von Schleicher. Schleicher tried to cause divisions in the Nazi Party by asking another leading Nazi to be Vice-Chancellor — Gregor Strasser. But Hitler stopped Strasser accepting.
3) Papen resented Schleicher because he suspected Schleichler had persuaded Hindenburg to dismiss him. He wanted to get back into government, so he made a deal with Hitler. They agreed that if Papen persuaded Hindenburg to make Hitler Chancellor, Hitler would make Papen Vice-Chancellor.
4) In January 1933, Papen persuaded Hindenburg to replace Schleicher with Hitler — Papen argued that they could control Hitler and use him as a puppet. He was wrong.

'In two months time we will have pushed Hitler so far into a corner, he'll be squeaking.' — Franz von Papen, 1933.

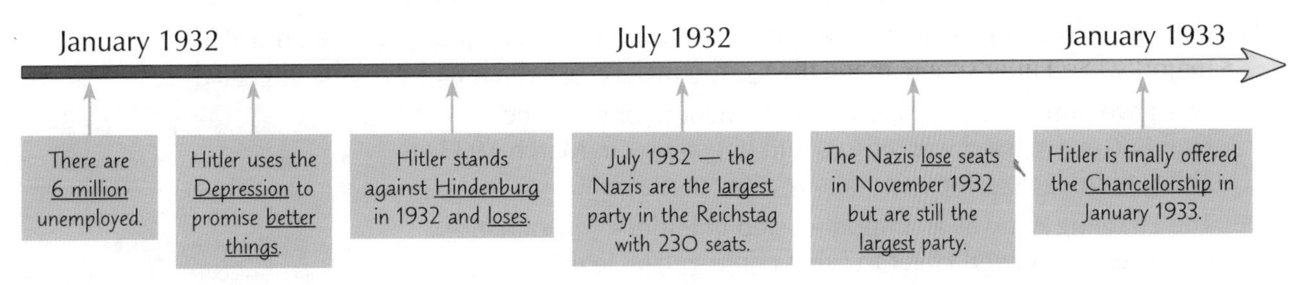

Here are two different interpretations of Hitler's rise to power. There's evidence to support both opinions.

Interpretation 1: 'After the onset of the Great Depression, Germans were willing to support any strong extremist party as an alternative to the democratic Weimar government.'

After the Great Depression, both the Nazi Party and the Communist Party became more popular, and support for moderate parties like Social Democratic Party dropped off.

Interpretation 2: 'There was only one credible party to turn to after the Great Depression hit — the Nazi Party. It was the only party with a charismatic leader who had mass appeal.'

The Nazi Party grew more rapidly than any other party after 1928. Hitler's passion and energy made the Nazis stand out, and support for the KPD simply couldn't keep up.

Papen and Hindenburg misjudged Hitler's strength...

You need to know Hitler's rise to power in full for the exam. Write a summary of events between Schleicher's Chancellorship in December 1932 and Hitler's Chancellorship in January 1933.

Achieving Total Power

After Hitler became Chancellor in January 1933, he took measures to establish a dictatorship.

The Nazis used Dirty Tricks to Win in 1933

Hitler needed to increase the Nazi Party's seats in the Reichstag to get a majority and be able to pass new laws. If they got a two-thirds majority, then the Nazi Party would be able to make changes to the constitution.

This would mean the Nazi Party could change the way the government was structured and give Hitler absolute power.

1) In the elections of March 1933, the Nazis took no chances. Hitler tried to stop other political parties from carrying out effective campaigns. They controlled the news media, and opposition meetings were banned.
2) Hitler used the SA (see p.119) to terrorise opponents. In February 1933, the SA raided the Communist Party headquarters in Berlin and claimed to have found evidence that the communists were planning an uprising against the government.
3) In February 1933, just 6 days before the elections, a fire broke out in the Reichstag. Hitler blamed the Communist Party and used the event to whip up anti-communist feelings.

- Hitler used the fire to claim that communists were a threat to the country. Nazi newspapers used the event as an excuse to publish anti-communist conspiracy theories.
- President Hindenburg issued a decree giving Hitler emergency powers to deal with the supposed communist threat — many basic rights given to the German people under the Weimar constitution, e.g. freedom of speech, were suspended.
- Hitler used these powers to intimidate communist voters. The decree also enabled the SA to round up and imprison nearly 4000 communist members.

Comment and Analysis

The emergency powers granted to Hitler were a turning point — they mark the first step towards making Germany a dictatorship. Hitler justified them by saying that they were necessary to protect the German people. This meant he faced little opposition from the German public.

The Enabling Act helped Hitler to create a Dictatorship

1) In the March 1933 elections, the Nazi Party won 288 seats but didn't have an overall majority. So Hitler simply made the Communist Party (which had 81 seats) illegal.
2) This gave him enough support in parliament to bring in the Enabling Act, passed with threats and bargaining in March 1933. This let him govern for four years without parliament.
3) The Enabling Act was an important step in Hitler's consolidation of power. It allowed Hitler to bring controversial legislation into force to strengthen the Nazi Party's position.

Hitler could now pass laws and amend the constitution without the Reichstag's consent. Other Chancellors in the Weimar government had used Article 48 to bypass parliament (see p.121), so the new Act may not have seemed that extreme to some Germans.

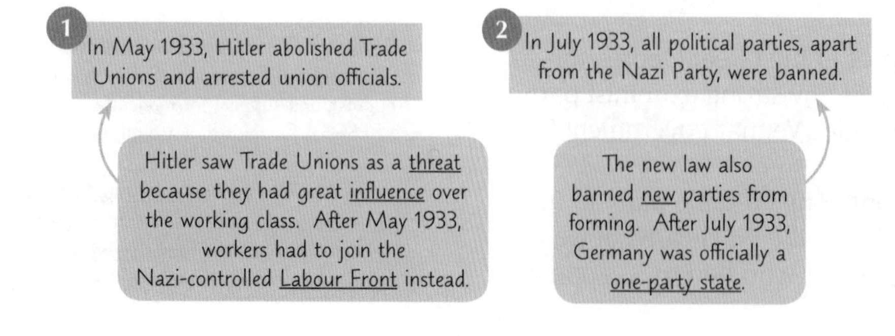

Comment and Analysis

Some Germans thought a one-party state would be an improvement. Parties often couldn't reach an agreement in the Reichstag and Germans were tired of political instability — between March 1930 and March 1933, there were four different Chancellors.

Democracy in Germany had gone up in flames...

In the exam, remember to consider people's circumstances and the limited knowledge they had at the time. Most Germans had no idea what the Nazi Party would grow into after it gained power.

Achieving Total Power

Hitler had power, but he still had enemies.

The SA was a Threat to Hitler

1) The SA (a 'private Nazi Party army' of over 400,000 men — see p.119) had helped Hitler come to power.
2) But Hitler now saw the SA as a threat, because its members were loyal to Ernst Röhm, the SA's leader.
3) The SA was also unpopular with the leaders of the German army and with some ordinary Germans.

The 'Night of the Long Knives' — Hitler removes his enemies

1) Ernst Röhm was the biggest threat to Hitler, but Hitler was also worried about other members of the Nazi Party who disagreed with his views.
2) On the 29th-30th June 1934, Hitler sent men to arrest or kill Röhm and others. Altogether, several hundred people were killed or imprisoned, including Röhm and various other leaders of the SA and senior politicians.
3) Hitler claimed that those who had been killed had been plotting to overthrow the government, so he declared their murders legal.
4) This became known as the 'Night of the Long Knives', and was a triumph for Hitler.
5) It stamped out all potential opposition within the Nazi party and sent a powerful message to the party about Hitler's ruthlessness and brutality. It also showed that Hitler was now free to act above the law.

Comment and Analysis

Most Germans wouldn't have known exactly what had happened on the 'Night of the Long Knives' until a few days later, when Hitler declared the events legal. Even then, there was little outcry. It's likely that some people believed Hitler's claims that the violence was necessary to protect the country. Others were too scared to speak out.

Hitler took full control of National and Local government

1) In August 1934, Hindenburg died. Hitler used the opportunity to combine the posts of Chancellor and President, and also made himself Commander-in-Chief of the army.
2) He called himself Der Führer (the leader) — this was the beginning of the dictatorship.
3) At this point, Hitler reorganised local government — in 1926 he had created branches of the Nazi Party in different areas of Germany called Gau (plural: Gaue). These now became official provinces of Germany, with a Gauleiter (a loyal Nazi) in charge of each (see p.120).
4) Above them were the Reichsleiters, who advised Hitler, e.g. Goebbels who was in charge of propaganda, and Himmler who was chief of the German police.
5) At the top and in absolute control was the Führer — Hitler.
6) Every aspect of life was carefully controlled, and only loyal Nazis could be successful.

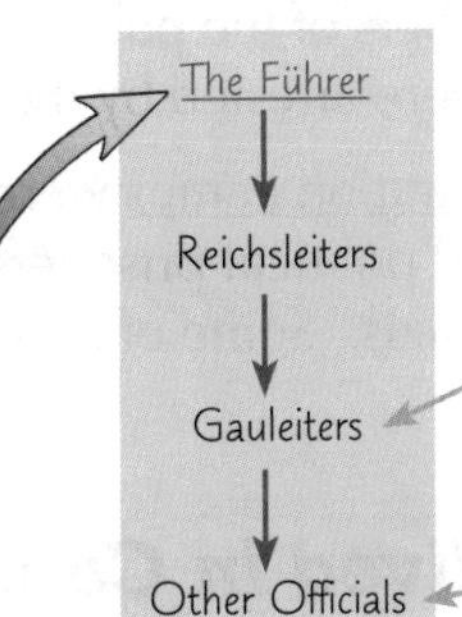

Gauleiters were appointed by Hitler, which ensured he had control over the lower levels of the party.

These included local and district party leaders.

Comment and Analysis

When the Nazis took over, some Germans were glad that someone was at last taking control after the chaos and political weaknesses of the Weimar years.

The army had to swear an oath of allegiance to Hitler, instead of pledging to protect Germany. Some German workers were also forced to take an oath of obedience, promising loyalty to Hitler. Those who refused could lose their jobs.

The Nazis — eliminating opposition...

In your own words, summarise the events of the 'Night of the Long Knives'. Then jot down a couple of sentences explaining why it was a triumph for Hitler.

REVISION TASK

The Machinery of Terror

The Nazis aimed to make Germany a totalitarian state (where the government controls all aspects of life).

Germany became a Police State

1) The Nazis wanted complete control over the machinery of government and people's lives.
2) Hitler's Enabling Act of 1933 (see p.124) allowed the government to read people's mail, listen in on their phone calls, and search their homes without notice.
3) The Law for the Reconstruction of the Reich (1934) gave the Nazis total power over local governments.
4) There were laws to sack civil servants who didn't support the Nazis and accept their rules.
5) The Nazis also made changes to the justice system. Judges didn't have to be 'fair' and unbiased. Instead, they were expected to make rulings that were in line with Nazi Party policy.
6) The Sicherheitsdienst (SD) was the Nazi intelligence service. It was initially run by Reinhard Heydrich — he aimed to bring every German under continual supervision.

The legal system was far from fair...

- In 1933, the Nazis set up special courts where the basic rights of those accused were suspended — they couldn't appeal or question evidence given against them.
- In 1934, Hitler established the People's Court in Berlin, which held trials for important political crimes. Defendants were nearly always found guilty.

People could be Terrorised into Conforming

The government was also prepared to use terror and even violence against the German people.

1) The SS (Schutzstaffel) began as a bodyguard for Hitler. It expanded massively under the leadership of Himmler during the 1930s. Its members were totally loyal to Hitler, and feared for their cruelty.
2) Himmler was also in charge of the secret police — the Gestapo. The Gestapo's job was 'to protect public safety and order', but their methods included harsh interrogations and imprisonment without trial.
3) Local wardens were employed to make sure Germans were loyal to the Nazis. Members of the public were encouraged to report disloyalty. Many were arrested by the Gestapo as a result.
4) After 1933, concentration camps were created across Germany and its territories to hold political prisoners and anybody else considered dangerous to the Nazis. Some of these were later turned into death camps.

Security Police search a car in Berlin on the orders of the Gestapo.

Not everyone lived in Constant Terror

1) Most Germans were prepared to go along with the new regime. Some people accepted the new rules out of fear.
2) Others went along with them because they believed in their aims, even if they didn't approve of the Nazis' brutal methods.

Comment and Analysis

For those that didn't fit in with the Nazi ideals (e.g. Jews), life under the SS and the Gestapo could be terrifying. But Hitler was supported, not feared, by many Germans.

The Nazis exercised control using any means necessary...

'Everybody lived in fear of the Nazis after 1933.' To what extent do you agree with this view? Explain your answer using your own knowledge of the police state. [20]

Propaganda

The Nazis also used propaganda to help them control the German people's lives.

Propaganda aims to Control how people Think

1) Propaganda means spreading information that influences how people think and behave.
2) It gives only certain points of view and often leaves out important facts.
3) The Nazis used powerful propaganda to get the support of the German people. Dr Joseph Goebbels was in overall charge of the Nazis' 'propaganda machine'.

Nazi propaganda took Simple Ideas and Repeated them

1) Nazi propaganda was used to unite the German people and convince them that the Nazis would make Germany strong.
2) Germans were encouraged to hate the countries that signed the Treaty of Versailles. The Nazis said Germany should fight to get back the territory 'stolen' by the treaty.
3) Goebbels created the 'Hitler Myth', which made Hitler seem like a god and the saviour of Germany. This was the 'cult of the Führer'.
4) The Nazis' propaganda also said that Jews and communists were the biggest cause of Germany's problems. One Nazi paper claimed that Jews murdered children for the Passover Feast.
5) The Nazis encouraged a return to traditional German values and a revival of traditional German culture.

A popular slogan was 'One people, one empire, one leader'. Many Germans devoted their lives to Hitler.

The Government had to Approve all Artistic Works

1) Goebbels founded the Ministry of Public Enlightenment and Propaganda in 1933.
2) It had departments for music, theatre, film, literature and radio. All artists, writers, journalists and musicians had to register to get their work approved.

Nazis used the Media as a tool of Propaganda

1) The Nazis wanted to surround people with their propaganda. They used censorship to prevent Germans from seeing or hearing anything that gave a different message.
2) They sold cheap radios and controlled broadcasts. By 1939 approximately 70% of households had a radio, which gave the Nazis a voice in most people's homes.
3) In 1933, only 3% of German daily newspapers were controlled by the Nazis. By 1944, this had risen to 82%. This meant the Nazis could decide what was published in the papers.
4) The Nazis also produced hundreds of films. Many films showed the strengths of the Nazis and Hitler, and the weakness of their opponents. An important German director was Leni Riefenstahl.
5) Another method of spreading propaganda was through posters showing the evil of Germany's enemies and the power of Hitler. Propaganda also let Germans know what was expected of them.

According to Goebbels, radio was a 'weapon of the totalitarian state' — it was another way to control the people.

Nazi propaganda poster, 1935. It says that 'the German student' fights for the Führer and for the German people.

Radio Nazi — broadcasting to you wherever you are...

Cover this page up and then jot down as much as you can remember about what messages the Nazis were trying to put across in their propaganda.

Propaganda

Nazi propaganda was sophisticated and it was everywhere.

Nazi propaganda could involve Spectacular Displays

1) The Nazis used public rallies to spread their propaganda. The annual Nuremberg Rallies focused on speeches by leading Nazis, like Hitler and Goebbels. The 1934 Nuremberg Rally was recorded by Riefenstahl in her film 'Triumph of the Will'.

Hermann Goering at a Nuremberg Rally, as shown in 'Triumph of the Will'.

2) One million people attended the 1936 rally. There were displays of lights and flags to greet the arrival of Hitler. These made him look more powerful.
3) Sporting events like the 1936 Berlin Olympics were used to show off German wealth and power. But the success of non-Aryan athletes like African-American Jesse Owens (who won four gold medals) undermined Hitler's message.
4) Nazi power was also shown through art and architecture, and grand new buildings appeared in Nuremberg and Berlin.

Propaganda was used to change Culture and Society

1) The Nazis promised an empire that would last a thousand years — based on traditional values.
2) Modern art was banned, in favour of realistic paintings that fit with Nazi ideology. Modern art was labelled 'degenerate' and exhibitions were created to show people how 'bad' it was. The Nazis celebrated the works of 'German' composers, such as Wagner, but much modern classical music, works by Jewish composers, and jazz were all attacked.
3) School textbooks were rewritten to make Germans look successful. Children were taught to believe in Nazi doctrines (see p.132).
4) The 'Strength through Joy' programme sought to show ordinary workers that the Nazi regime cared about their standard of living (see p.131).

In the Weimar Republic, artists had started to use ideas that were new and experimental. For more about this, see p.118.

Propaganda was most Effective when Reinforcing Existing Ideas

Surprisingly, it's quite difficult to tell how effective Nazi propaganda was.

1) Some historians say Nazi propaganda was better at reinforcing people's existing attitudes than making them believe something different.
2) Many Germans felt angry and humiliated by the Treaty of Versailles, so Hitler's promises to reverse the treaty and make Germany great again were very popular.
3) After the political weakness of the Weimar Republic, people found the image of Hitler as a strong leader appealing. So the 'Hitler Myth' was very effective and made Hitler an extremely popular leader.
4) Anti-Jewish and anti-communist attitudes already existed in Germany before the Nazis came to power.
5) The Weimar Republic was seen as too liberal by many — they thought standards in Germany had slipped. These people liked the promise of a return to traditional German values.
6) The Depression had left many German people in poverty. This made them easier to persuade, and the Nazis' promises of help extremely popular.

Comment and Analysis

However effective their propaganda was, the Nazis' control of the media made it almost impossible for anyone to publish an alternative point of view.

Nazi spin — sophisticated, but probably not 100% effective...

EXAM QUESTION

'Propaganda was generally ineffective in influencing the German people during the Nazi era.' Do you agree with this statement? Explain why or why not. [20]

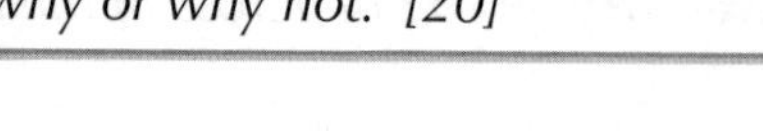

Attitudes Towards Religion

The Nazi Party publicly supported religious freedom, but in reality saw Christianity as a threat.

Hitler wanted to Reduce the Church's Power

1) In the 1930s, most Germans were Christians and the Church was very influential. During the Weimar Republic, the state and the Church had worked closely together and the Church was involved in national matters like education.
2) Some prominent Nazis were anti-Christian and Nazi ideology disagreed with the role the Church had traditionally had in society.
3) Hitler thought religion should comply with the state and wanted churches to promote Nazi ideals. He was also worried that some members of the Church might publicly oppose Nazi policies.
4) The Nazi Party was careful to maintain support from the Catholic and Protestant Churches during its rise to power because they were so popular. However, as Hitler consolidated his totalitarian state, his control over churches increased.

The Catholic Church was Persecuted

1) In July 1933, an agreement called the Concordat was signed between the Pope and the Nazi government. Hitler promised not to interfere with the Catholic Church if the Church agreed to stay out of German politics.
2) The Catholic Church was now banned from speaking out against the Nazi Party, but Hitler soon broke his side of the deal.

Comment and Analysis

The Concordat reassured Christians that Hitler was consolidating ties with the Catholic Church, but he was actually restricting its power.

- The Nazi Party started to restrict the Catholic Church's role in education.
- In 1936 all crucifixes were removed from schools and by 1939 Catholic education had been destroyed.

- The Nazis began arresting priests in 1935 and put them on trial.
- Catholic newspapers were suppressed and the Catholic Youth group was disbanded.

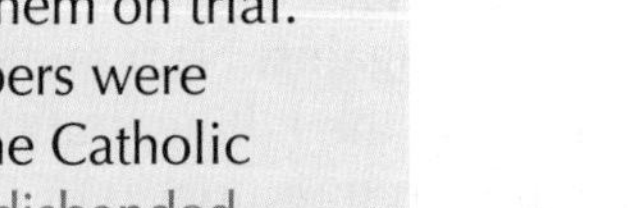

3) In 1937, the Pope spoke out against Hitler in a letter to Catholic Churches in Germany. The stance of the Church had changed, but many German Catholics were too scared to speak out against the Nazi Party.

Catholics tried to protect their religion by avoiding confrontation with the Nazi Party.

The Nazi Party Controlled the Protestant Church

The Protestant Church was reorganised and fell under Nazi control.

1) When Hitler became Chancellor in 1933, there were 28 independent Protestant Churches. These Churches were politically divided — some formed a group known as the 'German Christians'. They supported Hitler and favoured an anti-Semitic version of Christianity.
2) The Nazi Party backed this version of Christianity and believed all Christians should follow its principles. In 1936 all Protestant Churches were merged to form the Reich Church.

The Reich Church 'Nazified' Christianity...

The Reich Church replaced the symbol of a cross with the Nazi Swastika, and the Bible was replaced by 'Mein Kampf' (see p.120). Only Nazis could give sermons and the Church suspended non-Aryan ministers.

3) The Reich Church was an attempt to increase state control over the Protestant Church and make a National Socialist version of Christianity.

Comment and Analysis

Not everyone supported the Reich Church — it was opposed by a Protestant group called the 'Confessing Church' (see p.130).

The Nazis wanted the state to come first...

You might get sources in the exam that give different viewpoints on Nazi religious policies. Don't forget that Catholic and Protestant Christians were treated differently by the Nazis.

Opposition

The Nazis had a tight grip on Germany, but some opposition remained.

The Political Left opposed Hitler, but was Divided and Weak

1) Once in power, the Nazis had banned other political parties, including those on the political left, such as the Communist Party (KPD) and the Social Democratic Party (SPD).
2) But their members formed underground groups to try and organise industrial unrest (e.g. strikes). These networks were often infiltrated by the Gestapo (secret police), and party members could be executed.
3) Their impact was also limited because the different parties of the left were divided and didn't cooperate.

Some members of the Church Opposed the Nazis

There was little opposition to the Nazis in Germany from Christian groups. But a number of Church members did oppose the Nazis, even though they risked being sent to concentration camps:

1) Martin Niemöller was a Protestant pastor, a former U-boat captain, and a one-time Nazi supporter. He objected to Nazi interference in the Church, and was one of the founders of the Confessing Church. He used a sermon in 1937 to protest against the persecution of Church members, and as a result spent several years in concentration camps.
2) Another key member of the Confessing Church was Dietrich Bonhoeffer, a Protestant theologian and pastor who opposed the Nazis from the beginning. He joined the resistance, helped Jews escape from Germany and planned an assassination of Hitler. He was caught and imprisoned, then executed just weeks before the fall of the Nazis.
3) Clemens August von Galen was the Catholic Bishop of Münster, who used his sermons to protest against Nazi racial policies and the 'euthanasia' of the disabled. His protests didn't stop the killing, but they did force the Nazis to keep them secret. Only the need to maintain the support of German Catholics stopped the Nazis from executing him.

The Confessing Church protested against Hitler's attempt to unite the different Protestant Churches into one Reich Church (see p.129).

The Edelweiss Pirates and Swing Kids were Youth Movements

1) The Edelweiss Pirates was the name given to groups of rebellious youths who rejected Nazi values and opposed the Hitler Youth organisation (see p.132).
   - They helped army deserters, forced labourers and escaped concentration camp prisoners.
   - At first the Nazis mostly ignored them, but cracked down after they started distributing anti-Nazi leaflets. Many members were arrested, and several were publicly hanged.
2) The Swing Kids (or Swing Youth) were groups of young people who rebelled against the tight control the Nazis had over culture, acting in ways considered 'degenerate' by the Nazi regime (e.g. listening to American music and drinking alcohol). They were mostly considered a nuisance rather than a threat, but some members were arrested and even sent to concentration camps.

Comment and Analysis

German opposition to the Nazis didn't really threaten their dominance, but it did mean the Gestapo was kept busy tracking down people who had distributed anti-Nazi leaflets, held secret meetings, committed acts of sabotage, etc.

Comment and Analysis

Other Germans expressed their dissatisfaction with the Nazi regime in 'low level' ways — e.g. by grumbling about the government or spreading rumours. Not everyone considers this genuine opposition, but even this was probably risky.

If you weren't with the Nazis, you were against them...

Some people claim the Nazis faced little opposition from within Germany.
To what extent do you think this claim is true? [20]

EXAM QUESTION

Work and Home

The Nazis encouraged women to be homemakers and tried to provide jobs for men.

Women were expected to raise Large Families

1) Nazis didn't want women to have too much freedom. They believed the role of women was to provide children and support their families at home.
2) Women were banned from being lawyers in 1936, and the Nazis did their best to stop them following other professions.
3) The League of German Maidens spread the Nazi idea that it was an honour to produce large families for Germany. Nazis gave awards to women for doing this and encouraged more women to marry by offering financial aid to married couples.
4) Women were expected to dress plainly and were discouraged from wearing make-up and smoking. At school, girls studied subjects like cookery. It was stressed that they should choose 'Aryan' husbands.

A shortage of workers after 1937 meant more women had to go back to work.

Public Works and Rearmament meant Unemployment Fell

1) Hitler started a huge programme of public works, which helped to reduce unemployment — e.g. from 1933 jobs were created as a result of the construction of autobahns (motorways).
2) All men between 18 and 25 could be recruited into the National Labour Service and given jobs.
3) Industrial output increased and unemployment fell.
4) Hitler also brought in military conscription and encouraged German industry to manufacture more ships, aircraft, tanks and weapons for the military. This rearmament meant further falls in unemployment.
5) Trade Unions were banned (see p.124), so workers had to join the Nazis' Labour Front instead. But workers weren't allowed to go on strike or campaign for better conditions, and wages were relatively low.

Comment and Analysis

Although unemployment fell after the Depression, the Nazis fiddled with the statistics to make it look lower than it really was — e.g. they didn't count women or Jewish people without jobs. The official unemployment statistics didn't include this invisible unemployment.

Many groups in society Felt Better Off

1) The Nazis made efforts to maintain the support of German workers. They wanted workers to feel important and believe that they were an essential part of the Volksgemeinschaft.

'Volksgemeinschaft' means a community of people working hard towards the same aims.

- The Nazis introduced the Volkswagen (the 'people's car') as a luxury people could aspire to own.
- They also introduced 'Strength through Joy' — a scheme which provided workers with cheap holidays and leisure activities.
- The 'Beauty of Labour' scheme encouraged factory owners to improve conditions for workers.

© Mary Evans / SZ Photo / Scherl

2) Many members of the middle classes also felt better off — e.g. small-business owners were able to advance more in society than previously.
3) But even though many people felt better off, workers and small-business owners had lost out in some ways.
   - The cost of living rose by about 25% — but wages didn't go up.
   - Workers didn't have the right to strike or resign.
   - Small businesses had to pay high taxes.

Comment and Analysis

During the Depression, one third of all workers had been unemployed. Many Germans had been desperate, so life under the Nazis did feel genuinely better for them.

Hitler reduced unemployment — and gained popularity...

EXAM TIP

It's important to remember that for some Germans life really did get better under the Nazi Party.

Young People

An important key to Nazi success was controlling the minds of German youth.

Youth Movements helped produce Committed Nazis

1) Hitler knew that loyalty from young people was essential if the Nazis were to remain strong.
2) Youth movements were a way of teaching children Nazi ideas — so they would be loyal to the Nazi Party when they grew up.

The Hitler Youth seemed exciting...

- The Hitler Youth was founded in 1926. Boys aged fourteen and over were recruited to the movement. It became all but compulsory in 1936 and lasted until 1945.
- Boys wore military-style uniforms and took part in physical exercise preparing for war. High-achieving boys might be sent to Hitler Schools to be trained as loyal Nazi leaders.
- They also went on camping trips and held sports competitions. Some of those who took part said the organisation was fun, made them feel valued and encouraged a sense of responsibility.

The League of German Maidens was for girls...

- The League of German Maidens was the female branch of the Hitler Youth, aimed at girls aged between fourteen and eighteen.
- Girls were trained in domestic skills like sewing and cooking.
- Sometimes they took part in physical activities like camping and hiking. This gave girls new opportunities that were normally reserved for boys.

Comment and Analysis

After 1936, all other youth organisations were banned and it was almost impossible for children to avoid joining the Hitler Youth. However, towards the end of the 1930s, attendance actually decreased as activities adopted an increasingly military focus.

Education across Germany was 'Nazified'

1) Education in schools meant learning Nazi propaganda. Most teachers joined the Nazi Teachers' Association and were trained in Nazi methods. Children had to report teachers who did not use them.
2) Subjects were rewritten to fit in with Nazi ideas. Children were taught to be anti-Semitic (i.e. prejudiced against Jews) — for example, Biology courses stated that Jews were biologically inferior to 'Aryans'. History courses explained that the First World War was lost because of Jews and communists.
3) Physical education became more important for boys to prepare them for joining the army. They sometimes even played games with live ammunition.
4) In universities, students burned anti-Nazi and Jewish books, and Jewish lecturers were sacked. Jewish teachers were also dismissed from public schools.

German children were always being bombarded with Nazi propaganda. Erika Mann, a German who opposed the Nazis, described Nazi education in Germany. 'Every child says 'Heil Hitler!' from 50 to 150 times a day...[it] is required by law; if you meet a friend on the way to school, you say it; study periods are opened and closed with [it]... [The Nazis'] supremacy over the German child...is complete.'

German Youth eventually became involved in Fighting the War

1) During the Second World War, members of the Hitler Youth contributed to the war effort — for example, helping with air defence work, farm work and collecting donations for Nazi charities.
2) Towards the end of the war, many Hitler Youth members ended up fighting alongside adults. They were known for being fierce and fanatical fighters.

Comment and Analysis

The Nazis' attempts to impose their ideology on children weren't always effective. See p.130 for more about how unofficial youth movements resisted Hitler and the Nazis.

The Hitler Youth — not everyone's favourite youth group...

EXAM QUESTION

'Germans joined the Hitler Youth because it looked like fun'. To what extent is this true? [20]

Nazi Discrimination

The Nazi belief in the idea of a 'master race' caused a huge amount of harm.

Hitler wanted to 'Cleanse' Germany of 'Inferior' groups

1) Most Nazis believed that Germans were members of a superior ancient race called the 'Aryans'. Hitler thought people who were not pure Aryans (e.g. Jews) did not belong in Germany, and had no part to play in the new German Empire.
2) He wanted to 'cleanse' the German people by removing any groups he thought 'inferior'. Jews were especially targeted, but action was also taken against other groups.

Hitler always claimed the Jews were responsible for many of Germany's problems.

- Many Romani (gypsies) and Slavs (an ethnic group from central and eastern Europe) were sent to concentration camps. The Nazis believed that they were racially inferior.
- The Nazis practised eugenics policies — they wanted to create a strong race by removing all genetic 'defects' from its gene pool. Many people with mental and physical disabilities were murdered or sterilised. Many people of mixed race were also sterilised against their will.
- Homosexual people were sent to concentration camps in their thousands. In 1936 Himmler, Head of the SS, began the Central Office for the Combating of Homosexuality and Abortion.

Nazis Changed the Law to Discriminate against Jews

1) In 1933, the SA organised a national boycott of Jewish businesses, which resulted in Nazi-led violence against Jews. The violence wasn't popular with the German people, so the Nazis decided to use the legal system to persecute Jews instead.
2) Over time, the number of jobs that Jews were banned from gradually increased.
3) The Nuremberg Laws of 1935 were based on the idea that Jews and Germans were biologically different. They removed many legal rights from Jews and encouraged 'Aryan' Germans to see them as inferior.

- The Nuremberg Laws stopped Jews being German citizens.
- They banned marriage between Jews and non-Jews in Germany.
- They also banned sexual relationships between Jews and non-Jews.

Some Jews were given passports enabling them to leave Germany but preventing them from returning.

4) Jews were later forced to close or sell their businesses, and they were banned from all employment.
5) By 1938, all Jewish children had been banned from attending German schools and jews were no longer allowed in many public places, including theatres and exhibitions.

Comment and Analysis

The Nazis' racial policies aimed to isolate Jews from the rest of society. 'Aryan' Germans were even encouraged to break off friendships with Jews and avoid any contact with Jewish people.

Kristallnacht 1938 — the 'Night of the Broken Glass'

1) In November 1938, a German diplomat was murdered in Paris by a Jew.
2) There was anti-Jewish rioting throughout Germany — thousands of Jewish shops were smashed and almost every synagogue in Germany was burnt down. In the days that followed, thousands of Jews were arrested and sent to concentration camps.
3) The Nazis claimed that the events of Kristallnacht were a spontaneous reaction by the German people to the Paris murder. In fact, they had been planned and organised by the Nazi government. Few ordinary Germans had participated.

Comment and Analysis

Kristallnacht was a turning point in the Nazi persecution of Jews — it was the first widespread act of anti-Jewish violence in Nazi Germany. After Kristallnacht, conditions for German Jews got even worse.

Nazi Germany — a climate of cruelty and fear...

Make a timeline showing how conditions in Germany became gradually worse for Jews between 1933 and 1939. Show all the important turning points.

Revision Summary

Now you've had your fill of Weimar and Nazi Germany, test your knowledge with a revision summary.

- Try these questions and tick off each one when you get it right.
- When you've done all the questions for a topic and are completely happy with it, tick off the topic.

The Weimar Republic, 1918-29 (p.113-118)

1) Describe the events of the German Revolution in 1918.
2) Name the three separate bodies of the Weimar government and describe what each one did.
3) Give two weaknesses of the Weimar constitution.
4) Give five terms from the Treaty of Versailles and explain why they were unpopular in Germany.
5) Why did Germany feel 'stabbed in the back' by the Weimar government?
6) What was the Kapp Putsch?
7) How did Gustav Stresemann try to build better international relationships?
8) How did life improve for the working classes and women under the Weimar Republic?

Hitler's Rise to Power, 1919-33 (p.119-123)

9) What was the Twenty-Five Point Programme?
10) Describe the events of the 1923 Munich Putsch.
11) How did Hitler reorganise the Nazi Party between 1924 and 1928?
12) How did the Weimar government deal with the Depression?
13) Which party rivalled the Nazi Party's popularity during the Depression?
14) Describe how Hitler rose to the position of Chancellor.

Nazi Control and Dictatorship, 1933-39 (p.124-128)

15) What was the Enabling Act? When was it introduced?
16) What happened on the 'Night of the Long Knives'?
17) Describe three powers the Nazis had that suggested Germany had become a police state by 1934.
18) What were the aims of Nazi propaganda?
19) What was the 'Hitler Myth'?

Life in Nazi Germany, 1933-39 (p.129-133)

20) What was the Concordat? When was it signed?
21) Why was the Reich Church created?
22) Name two members of the Church who opposed the Nazis.
23) Who were the Swing Youth?
24) What expectations did the Nazi Party have of women?
25) Describe one measure the Nazis used to reduce German unemployment.
26) How was education in Germany affected while the Nazis were in power?
27) What were the Nuremberg Laws? Why were they important?
28) Describe the events of Kristallnacht.

Exam Hints and Tips

These pages will show you how to use your knowledge to get those all-important marks.

You will take 3 Papers altogether

1) Paper 1 is 1 hour 15 minutes long. It's worth 52 marks — 30% of your GCSE. This paper will be divided into 2 sections:
   - Section A: Historic Environment (see p.33-43 for more information).
   - Section B: Thematic Study (see p.3-4) for more information).

The Thematic Study covered in this book is Medicine in Britain, c.1250-present (see p.5-32).

2) Paper 2 is 1 hour 45 minutes long. It's worth 64 marks — 40% of your GCSE. This paper will be divided into 2 sections:
   - Section A: Period Study (see p.44-45 for more information).
   - Section B: British Depth Study (see p.86 for more information).

The Period Studies covered in this book are The American West, c1835-c1895 (see p.46-66), Superpower relations and the Cold War, 1941–91 (see p.67-85) and Early Elizabethan England, 1558–88 (see p.90-112).

3) Paper 3 is 1 hour 20 minutes long. It's worth 52 marks — 30% of your GCSE. This paper will be divided into 2 sections, both about a Modern Depth Study (see p.87-89 for more information).
   - Section A: 2 questions on a source, testing knowledge and understanding.
   - Section B: A four-part question based on 2 sources and 2 interpretations.

The Modern Depth Study covered in this book is Weimar and Nazi Germany, 1918–39 (see p.113-134).

Make sure you know which Thematic Study, Period Study and Depth Studies you're studying. It might not be the ones we've covered in this book. And remember... some of your exam papers will contain questions on topics you haven't studied — IGNORE THOSE. Only answer questions on the topics you've studied.

Remember these Four Tips for Answering Questions

1. Don't spend Too Long on Short Questions

1) Learn the rule — the more marks a question is worth, the longer your answer should be.
2) Don't get carried away writing loads for a question that's only worth 4 marks — you need to leave time for the higher mark questions.

2. Plan your Essay Answers, but not the others

1) You don't need to plan answers to the shorter questions in the exam. That will waste time.
2) For longer essay questions, it's very important to make a quick plan before you start writing.
3) Think about what the key words are in the question. Scribble a quick plan of your main points — cross through this neatly at the end, so it's obvious it shouldn't be marked.

3. Stay Focused on the Question

1) Make sure that you directly answer the question. Back up your points with relevant facts. Don't just chuck in everything you know about the period.
2) You've got to be relevant and accurate — e.g. if you're writing about the rise of the Nazi Party, don't include stories about a London camel called George who moved rubble during the Blitz.
3) It might help to try to write the first sentence of every paragraph in a way that addresses the question, e.g. "Another way in which Chamberlain was an important cause of World War Two is..."

4. Use a Clear Writing Style

1) Essay answers should start with a brief introduction and end with a conclusion.
2) Remember to start a new paragraph for each new point you want to discuss.
3) Try to use clear handwriting — and pay attention to spelling, grammar and punctuation (see next page).

Exam Hints and Tips

In Paper 1 and Paper 3, the examiner will be marking you partly on your spelling, punctuation and grammar (SPaG). SPaG is worth nearly 5% of your overall mark, so don't forget to write nicely (as my mum would say).

Remember to Check your Spellings

1) You should leave about five minutes at the end of the exam to check your work.
2) Check as many questions as you can, but make sure you read over the questions which award SPaG marks especially carefully. (Marks are shown very clearly at the end of each question.)
3) There won't be time to check everything thoroughly, so look for obvious spelling mistakes...

where / wear / were

your / you're

though / thought / through / thorough

there / their / they're

to / too / two

of / off

silent letters, e.g. know, science, could

effect / affect

double letters, e.g. aggression, success

don't confuse 'past' with 'passed'

If you're not confident with any of these things, learn them now.

4) Make sure you haven't repeated words like 'and', 'but' and 'because':

Cholera became an epidemic in 1832 and it killed thousands of people and it eventually declined.

Using 'and' both times sounds really boring.

Cholera became an epidemic in 1832 and it killed thousands of people, but it eventually declined.

This doesn't sound so repetitive.

5) Don't worry if you find a mistake when you check your work. As long as you make your corrections clearly, the examiner won't mark you down.
6) If the mistake is just one word or a short phrase, cross it out neatly and write the correct word above it.

believed
Many settlers ~~beleived~~ that Native Americans were lazy and savage.

Spell Technical Words correctly

1) There are a lot of technical words in history. You need to be able to spell them correctly. Learn these examples to start you off. The underlined letters are the tricky bits to watch out for.

alliance · argument · biased · controversial · consequences · defence · democracy

fascism · foreign · government · interpretation · parliament · source · successful

2) You'll also have to learn how to spell names and technical terms from the topics you're studying. Go back through them and make a list of tricky names and words. Here are some to look out for:

Names of historical figures: Gorbachev · Hippocrates · Khrushchev · Pasteur

Names of places: Afghanistan · Czechoslovakia · Roanoke · Ypres

Technical terms: anaesthetics · détente · putsch · vaccination

Learn this page and make spelling errors history...

Mnemonics can help you remember how to spell tricky words. For example, you can remember 'biased' with the phrase 'Bleary Insomniacs Avoid Sleep Every Day'. Or something similar...

Exam Hints and Tips

How do you spell 'penicillin'? That's no problem for you. You've got all the tricky words down — now you just need to make sure your ideas are presented well by using correct punctuation and grammar.

You need to Punctuate Properly...

1) Always use a capital letter at the start of a sentence.
   Use capital letters for names of particular people, places and things. For example:

   All sentences start with capital letters. → *In 1933 Hitler was made Chancellor of Germany.*

   The name of a person. A title. The name of a country.

2) Full stops go at the end of sentences, e.g. 'General Custer was killed in June 1876.'
   Question marks go at the end of questions, e.g. 'How successful was the Nazi propaganda?'
3) Use commas when you use more than one adjective to describe something, or to separate items in a list:

   Elizabeth I was intelligent, confident and powerful.

4) Commas can also join two points into one sentence with a joining word (such as 'and', 'or', 'so' or 'but'):

   The work of Galen was central to medieval medical teachings, so doctors found it difficult to disagree with him.

5) Commas can also be used to separate extra information in a sentence:

   Gorbachev, who became General Secretary of the Communist Party in 1985, was more open to the West than previous leaders.

...and use Grammar Correctly

1) Make sure your writing isn't too chatty and doesn't use slang words. It should be formal.

   Edward Jenner's smallpox vaccine was well successful. — This language is too informal for an exam.

   Edward Jenner's smallpox vaccine was very successful. — This is more appropriate.

2) Don't change tenses in your writing by mistake:

   The mountain men explored the West first — they hunted animals for their skins.

   Both verbs are in the past tense — which is correct. Writing 'hunt' instead of 'hunted' would be wrong.

3) Write your longer answers in paragraphs.
   - A paragraph is a group of sentences which talk about the same thing or follow on from each other.
   - You need to start a new paragraph when you start making a new point.

   You show a new paragraph by starting a new line and leaving a gap (an indent) before you start writing:

   From 1933, Hitler started a programme of public works, such as the building of huge new motorways. This gave jobs to thousands of people.
   Even though there was increased employment, the Nazis altered the statistics so that things looked better than they were. Wages were also poor.

   If you've forgotten to start a new paragraph, use a double strike (like this //) to show where the new paragraph should begin.

4) Remember — 'it's' (with an apostrophe) is short for 'it is' or 'it has'.
   'Its' (without an apostrophe) means 'belonging to it'.
5) It's always 'should have', not 'should of' (and also 'could have' and 'would have' too).
6) If you know that you often confuse two words, like 'it's' and 'its', watch out for them when you're checking your work in the exam.

That's that, then — all that's left to do now is to sit the exams...

Good SPaG is a great way to get marks in the exam. So make sure you've learnt all the stuff on this page, and also everything about anything that's ever happened in all of history, and you should be okay.

Index

Index

Index